W9-ATH-342

Vision, Tradition, Interpretation

Religion and Reason 35

Method and Theory
in the Study and Interpretation of Religion

GENERAL EDITOR
Jacques Waardenburg, *University of Lausanne*

BOARD OF ADVISERS
Th. P. van Baaren, *Groningen*
R. N. Bellah, *Berkeley*
U. Bianchi, *Rome*
H. J. W. Drijvers, *Groningen*
S. N. Eisenstadt, *Jerusalem*
C. Geertz, *Princeton*
K. Goldammer, *Marburg*
P. Ricœur, *Paris* and *Chicago*
M. Rodinson, *Paris*
K. Rudolph, *Marburg*
N. Smart, *Lancaster* and *Santa Barbara, Calif.*
G. Widengren, *Stockholm*

Mouton de Gruyter
Berlin · New York · Amsterdam

ST. JOSEPH'S UNIVERSITY

3 9353 00232 2624

Vision, Tradition, Interpretation

Theology, Religion, and the Study of Religion

Eric J. Lott

BL
41
.L68
1987

Mouton de Gruyter
Berlin · New York · Amsterdam   1988

Mouton de Gruyter (formerly Mouton, The Hague)
is a Division of Walter de Gruyter & Co., Berlin.

Library of Congress Cataloging in Publication Data

Lott, Eric J.
  Vision, tradition, interpretation.
  (Religion and reason ; 35)
  Bibliography: p.
  Includes index.
  1. Religion — Study and teaching. 2. Theology — Methodo-
logy. I. Title. II. Series.
BL41.L68   1987   291'.01   87-7321
ISBN 0-89925-347-4 (alk. paper)

CIP-Titelaufnahme der Deutschen Bibliothek

Lott, Eric J.:
Vision, tradition, interpretation : theology, religion, and the study
of religion / Eric J. Lott. — Berlin ; New York ; Amsterdam :
Mouton de Gruyter, 1987
  (Religion and reason ; 35)
  ISBN 3-11-009761-3
NE: GT

Printed on acid free paper.

© Copyright 1987 by Walter de Gruyter & Co., Berlin. All rights reserved, including
those of translation into foreign languages. No part of this book may be reproduced in
any form — by photoprint, microfilm, or any other means — nor transmitted, nor
translated into a machine language without written permission from Mouton de Gruyter,
a Division of Walter de Gruyter & Co., Berlin.
Typesetting: Asian Research Service, Hongkong. — Printing: Ratzlow-Druck, Berlin. —
Binding: Dieter Mikolai, Berlin. Printed in Germany.

To Cara, Dave and Debs

Preface

This book serves a dual function. It is intended in the first place as a 'textbook' for students in religious studies, especially those who wish to examine in a more sustained way than is usually the case how theology and religious studies relate to each other. This has naturally meant a rather close look both at the theological process within any religious tradition and the various other systematic studies of religion(s) that have emerged in the past century or so. As an attempt to discuss the interdependence, as well as the distinctive roles, of Theology and the Science of Religion, what I have written is also an essay in self-understanding. In moments of introspection I am a trifle baffled to find myself playing out two roles that some scholars would obviously like to see as quite disjunct, and which others would see as indistinguishably one. Neither extreme seems to me entirely plausible. Though I would plead for much greater interaction than is usually the case between these two approaches to religious traditions, as a 'religionist' I accept, in the appropriate place, the 'neutralising' rules required if one's account of religious traditions is to be fair to the tradition(s) concerned. To be 'neutral' at the proper time is not to be for ever theologically neutered, as it were; as a theologian I have some fairly clear convictions about how things are in this universe of ours. Yet this does not, I believe, entail a disjunctive schizophrenia, two worlds that coexist but never converge or creatively interact.

Nor do their points of interplay necessarily diminish their distinctiveness. Theology and 'Religion' *can* engage in a dialectical interaction which enhances the validity and authenticity of each; but if schizophrenic disjunction is to be avoided, we need to allow these two 'disciplines' to bed down together to the extent of enjoying conjugal consummation from time to time. This does not mean that the offspring which might result from such times of union will necessarily be a new integral 'theological science of religion', though this is perhaps what a growing number of scholars seem to envisage; and if such is a felt necessity of our times there is no point in the champions of methodological rigour on either side of the marital bed saying this must not be. My own position is that while we have to move beyond either polarised antagonism or tolerant co-existence, the greater interdependence desired will in fact more fully authenticate the distinctiveness of the two approaches. But in view of the intrinsic interdependence, to delineate any precise methodological autonomy for each will call for great subtlety, or the distinctiveness will be overstated and oversimplified.

Our understanding of either approach, and certainly of their interrelationship, must hinge largely on our analysis and interpretation of the intrinsic character of religion (and here we have to affirm the incongruity of setting 'faith' over against 'religion', even if in perhaps all religions there are core points of experience that seem to transcend the tradition). In particular it is in the interdependent, perhaps dialectical, relationship between the primal *vision*, the diverse forms manifest in the *tradition*, and the *interpretive* process (in further interaction with contextual life) that provides the key for understanding how theology is to relate to religion and thus to religious studies. The early chapters, therefore, attempt to delineate what I find to be typical features of religious traditions and of the 'theological' process in these traditions, looked at phenomenologically. For confirmatory material I have referred most frequently to the religions of India, with occasional reference to traditions such as Islam and Christianity (also 'religions of India' of course). In particular, and without apology, I have drawn considerably on the diverse types of Vedantic theology as illustrative, perhaps even paradigmatic, of ways in which theology can be seen to relate to its religious grounding. Then, more explicitly 'methodological' discussion, with reference to numerous kinds of approach to the investigation of religions, is taken up in later chapters. Naturally, I have had to be selective throughout; I trust that the selection is of sufficiently representative types, even if some writings of great importance may have been missed.

There are many people to whom I am indebted in the writing of this book. Professors Ninian Smart, Nicholas Lash and John Hick, Dr. Timothy Mark and Revd Kenneth Cracknell offered very helpful comments on an earlier and brief draft of this work. I have also benefitted greatly from frequent discussion with Dr. Christopher Duraisingh, until recently a colleague here at U.T.C. Professor Jacques Waardenburg, the General Editor of this series, has been very patient and encouraging. And my indebtedness to my wife and children is immense; it is they who, in recent years, have most shaped my own vision and interpretation of life.

United Theological College,
Bangalore, S. India

Contents

Introduction: Relating Theology & Religious Studies

In the wide-ranging field of studies often referred to comprehensively as 'religious studies', understanding just what is *theology's* place within this field is a crucial current problem (Whaling 1985: 177-210). How do the diverse theologies in our religious traditions relate to (or differ from) the various other kinds of studies attempted in religion? Or rather, how *should* the theological process in any religious tradition interact with such wide-ranging studies — i.e. with history of religions or comparative religion, with sociology of religion, psychology of religion and so on? Is there perhaps a single systematic 'science of religion' emerging — some would call it a comparative science of religion — which integrates the findings of the other perspectival studies, and with which theology can interact in a more neatly delineable way? While such a homogeneous 'science of religion' has not yet developed very clearly (Wiebe 1985: 33-60) it may well do in the future; if it does, how will it differ from an inclusive theology of religion? Can theology itself legitimately be called a 'science' as, for example, Karl Barth affirmed, primarily on the basis of 'its conformity with its object or its appropriate treatment of it' (Barth 1936: 2). In reply, however, it can be argued that such 'appropriateness' in systematic theology can only be scientifically established by 'formal criteria of scientific validity' from which theology cannot be independent if it is to be a 'science' (Pannenberg 1972: 269). Here, no doubt, it all depends on what we mean by 'science'. In general, though, we have to acknowledge that while there are certainly analogous characteristics found in the systematic investigation/reflection within a religious tradition and the investigative procedures pursued in any 'science', most scholars in religions tend to see a *basic divergence* between the theological and the scientific or the comparative approaches to religion (Pummer 1972: 99-102; Smart 1973a; 1973b).

This puts the matter in very general terms; and indeed many scholars concerned with methodological issues in religious studies do seem content merely to assert the crucial difference between these two approaches, and leave the gap as wide as possible. Methodological bridge-building is indulged in by very few, and some of these attempts we shall look at later. Still only a small number are prepared even to affirm a 'positive co-existence', as H.-W. Gensichen does (1970), in which religionists drop any crypto-theological stance, and theologians accept the findings of both the historical and the phenomenological approaches to religion if there is to be fruitful dialogue.

Frank Whaling, in a 120-page survey of 'Comparative Approaches' (Whaling 1985(I)), has made a more substantial effort to discuss this problem of 'Comparative Religion and Theology' (177-210). There is, he asserts, greater convergence than is often recognised. With considerable optimism Whaling argues that in view of the overlap of subject-matter in these two disciplines, it is 'unthinkable that the scholar of religion would not wish to use the critically researched data provided by the theological disciplines' (180). Nor need we assume that theology must always function as the 'conceptual vehicle of a particular religious tradition, often Christianity' (181). For it is possible to erect 'universal theological categories' (e.g. as attempted by W.C. Smith) that are 'relevant to all the world's religions. This can be a global theology in which no one tradition's value judgements are determinative. If this is, or can be, the case, then naturally the relationship of theology to comparative religion is changed.

Whaling then goes on to note that while by 'theology' it is usually *Christian* theology that is meant, yet more inclusive theological reflection (such as that by R.C. Zaehner and R. Panikkar) is possible. In any case, all this theologising, particularist or not, provides 'raw material' proper to the scientific investigator. It is unfortunate that often such input from theology is held to be suspect by certain kinds of investigation. We also have to recognise, Whaling affirms, that in the call for global dialogue and intercultural awareness there is a convergence of attitude between at least some representatives from each side. Nor is the concern about particular 'faith' and 'commitment' a straightforward matter, as there are very different kinds of commitment. He sees it as an unresolved question as to whether at least in some cases personal commitment can be an aid to understanding; naturally, theological value judgements derived from one's own faith will probably be a hindrance to understanding.

Whaling then introduces two ways in which theology differs from the comparative study of religion. Theology, he says (*ibid.*: 206) is concerned primarily with 'knowledge (or science) of God'. Though religious studies of all kinds should accept that religious phenomena 'point beyond themselves' to a transcendent Object of faith, this 'is not the direct concern of religious studies'. On this score theology is usually normative and particular, whereas religious studies are not. Even when theology becomes non-normative, it still concentrates on Ultimate Reality, in a way that religious studies will not, even though such theological attitudes are an essential part of 'impartial comparison'.

Then, religious studies is concerned with 'the religious phenomena of man, and man in his religious dimension . . . not directly with transcendence, but with man's response to transcendence'. Comparative religion thus ranges much more widely than theology. 'However, there is an implied complementarity' here, an 'integral connection' between the two, though many scholars of religion will not be able to agree with the kind of 'integral connection' proposed by, for example, W.C. Smith and G. Schmid. One of the problems of this position, Whaling notes, is that as soon as any theological content is given to the general category 'transcendence', it is 'usually couched in the terminology of a particular religion' (*ibid.*: 207). Thus comparative religion strives to be 'inherently pluralist and impartial; theology tends to be particularist and partial'. How is it possible for the two to be 'integral'?

Whaling concludes that a possible solution could be 'to apply comparative religious categories to the notion of transcendence', thus accepting that 'transcendence is ineffable' and that any religion's attempt to conceptualise transcendence necessarily qualifies it, i.e. is less than the unqualified Reality. Thus, again we can see the possibility of 'overlap' between the two disciplines. Whaling does not take us any further in trying to work out the implications of such convergence, but points to the work of F. Streng along these lines.

Whaling, then, clearly sees the need for new directions in the relations between theology and religious studies, and has usefully outlined some of the problems and some possible ways forward. There are, naturally, some points he makes and examples he gives of possible ways of rapprochement, that raise further questions. Can we, for example, usefully envisage the emergence of 'universal theological categories' other than in terms of general typologies, phenomenologically grounded? The alternative seems to be but a disguised, perhaps modified, theology from one or other tradition. Whaling is right to point out that theological reflection *can* incorporate reflective responses to traditions other than that of the concerned theologian (cf. the final chapter below) and that this *may* help in comparative understanding. Such inclusive reflection, however, is still primarily theological, however dynamic has been the process of interaction with other traditions.

On the other hand, to limit theology to 'knowledge of God' is questionable, *unless* this involves a reflective 'science' that is far more inclusive than what would often be understood by 'knowledge of God' (at this point religious study helps theology to become more broad-ranging); that is, unless the 'knowledge of God' embraces those diverse religious phenomena of any tradition through which 'God' becomes known and with which experience of

'God' is concomitant. In other words, can a 'science of religion' distinguish as sharply as Whaling does 'God' and 'religion', 'transcendence' and 'responses to transcendence'?

So, then, the methodological questions arising from the ways in which theology and religious studies interact are far from resolved, even if this appeared to be the case a decade or two ago (Pummer 1972: 99). Merely to assert incompatibility of goal and procedure (from either side of the divide), though partially true, is no longer possible; even to urge respectful co-existence does not adequately recognise the extent and the organic nature of interaction that is inevitable, possible and proper. Crucial questions, of very great importance to both sides, indeed concerned with essential content of subject-matter as well with methodological awareness, remain unresolved, even if in some cases already debated at great length.

There is, for example, the issue of faith's relationship to history as a critical discipline (Harvey 1967), or the questions raised by the empirical approach to religious life. Is scientific detachment and empirical analysis at all appropriate to the study of religion? (Dudley 1977; 21-42, 119-152; King, in Whaling 1985 (I): 127-37). And this raises the question of the essential character of religion, of what constitutes the 'religiousness' of religion; does the 'peculiar character, the very nature, of religious facts as such give them the right to form a special science . . . the science of religion'? (Pettazzoni 1954: 215). And this may well involve questions of and attempts at definition; there is, too, the question of whether or not a *cognitive dimension* and its doctrinal or *conceptual* articulation are of the essence of religion; and is a search for some kind of coherence fitting in the search for what is typically religious? What, then, is the essential task of theologies; what is involved in the process of interpreting and communicating the tradition's meaning? How far is this theological process dependent on the 'matrix' of religious life, its myth/ritual/symbolism? How important is a *trans*-conceptual or an intuitive dimension in understanding a religion's life and meaning? Do we need somehow to incoporate this trans-empirical perceptual matrix of a tradition into any approach to the study of religion if methodology is to be at all commensurable with the essential character of the subject-matter?

There is, thus, the question still pressed from both sides of the divide: What is the role of religious commitment in the study of religion, whether of a single tradition, or a more wide-ranging comparative study? Is faith essential to authentic understanding? Or has all faith-commitment to be suspended in a properly systematic approach to religions?

There is, too, the question of how one religion, with its own theological commitment, is to relate to others in the pluralistic religious situation which religious studies themselves make increasingly explicit? Are we, for example, to think of an underlying unity of religious perception? Or should we look more for multiple points of perceptual convergence, especially by means of dialogical interaction? And what is the role of the scientific study of religion in such a dialogical process?

A number of other issues too are no doubt involved in the general question of how theology relates to the study of religions. In attempting at least to begin a response to this problem, we can agree emphatically with the many from within the two disciplines who hold that the systematic study of religions must in various ways be *distinguished* from theology. Each has certain distinct aims, a distinct task, distinct methodological criteria. What is not adequately recognised on either side, however, is the extent to which there must also be *convergence* if each is to function in ways most appropriate to its own interest. Too few scholars seem aware of the complexity of interrelationship between the two. And it is the insufficiently recognised convergence that much of this book will attempt to draw out more clearly.

The problem in essence is that *theology* begins as reflection on and formulation of perceived meaning *from the perspective of grounding in a particular religious tradition and in the kind of faith-commitment expected of participants in this tradition.* A theology's meaning-concern, therefore, is also a truth-concern; in fact, the affirmation of what are perceived as the *ultimate truths* of human existence will probably be a theology's *primary* concern. There may, of course, be considerable tensions even within a tradition's theology regarding just what these truths mean, i.e. in what ways a particular faith-affirmation may either be further explained (or elaborated), or be shown to be significant for human life. Indeed, when the theologians of a tradition accept the need for faith to incorporate some of the perspectives of scientific approaches – as has increasingly been the case, especially in the Christian tradition in the West – then already within the theological discipline we find in some ways the same kind of problem as that between theology and the 'sciences of religion'. For example, the acceptance by many Christian theologians of the legitimacy of the historical critical approach has led to considerable tensions (as well as great fruitfulness no doubt) within theology. It has led to new ways of looking at sacred tradition and to revision of modes of meaning-formulation, though without abandoning certain basic faith-commitments. Compatibility between faith and critical study has long been *assumed* by many such scholars, though the resulting tensions often remain unresolved. The point to note, however, is that there has been a deliberate modifying of the theological task from *within* a theological tradition. There has in general *not* been the same attempt to correlate theology (here specifically Christian) with the scientific or systematic study of other religious traditions. Perhaps, where other very distinct kinds of faiths and belief-systems are involved, such 'correlation' is seen as a greater threat.

At this point we might define more clearly what is meant by 'theology' and 'theologian' (Whaling: 1981); there is not much to be gained by tracing the history of these terms (Pannenberg 1972: 7-8). Used in a strictly literal sense we can only refer to those who systematise belief-systems in theistic traditions; 'theology' *can* be equated with 'knowledge of God', which will tend to sharpen the distinction of its concerns from the broader concerns of religious studies (Whaling 1985: 306). However, the term 'theologian' can also be a simple analogous term to use in referring to one who, in *any* religious tradition, reflects on the meaning of the tradition and who articulates its meaning in various ways. In the chapters which follow, though, I often use synonyms or periphrastic terms other than 'theology/theologian', if only because these tend to be used as typically Christian terms. In the sciences of religions 'theology' is also often used to indicate any mode of approach to religious phenomena that is thought to be determined *a priori* by some particular or esoteric presupposition of what religion is. This may well then become a presupposition of what religion is in general. For example, if a theist defines religion in terms of faith in God (or assumes that every reference in Theravada Buddhism to a transcendent reality must somehow be a reference to 'God'), we have a case of general presupposition arising from a particular religious background.

It is, however, not only this obtrusion of personal religious commitment that we find as the ground for accusing scholars of being 'theological'. Any kind of *normative* as against the purely descriptive approach intended by some sciences of religion is sometimes called a 'theological' approach. We need not at this stage attempt a further analysis of these categories; we can at least note the serious questions various recent philosophers of science would raise when any scientific discipline claims to be purely descriptive, and certainly if strictly 'objective' and 'value-free' description is what is intended (Kuhn 1970; Lakatos and Musgrave 1970; Barbour 1974; Whaling 1985: 375-90). In every human scholarly discipline, we find all manner of values and assumptions built into our study. There is, we might hope, the constant interaction of objective with subjective dimensions in our humanness; normative and descriptive cannot be divorced in any absolute sense. A completely value-free or theory-free scholarly approach to religious traditions and their phenomena is just not possible if it is to be a systematic account.

Yet scholarly accounts of religion have often not recognised the *theoretical framework* within which they describe and account for religion (Wiebe 1983). Some scholars argue that it is precisely because there has been no clear, consciously adopted and generally accepted theory in religious studies providing the categories by which to account for religious phenomena, that no 'science' has yet emerged (Penner and Yonan 1972). To try to avoid explaining religious phenomena in any terms other than religious categories, or those used within the concerned religious tradition, is perhaps rightly seen by those who espouse a more rigorous study of religion as precluding any kind of scientifically systematic account of this dimension of life.

Theory, then, is inevitable and is necessary in the systematic study of religion; but not all theories are as *appropriate* as others, and appropriateness undoubtedly is (as Barth contended) a key characteristic of any cognitive discipline that is to be truly 'scientific', however difficult it may be to establish precise criteria for what comprises appropriateness. To be 'scientific', however, our theories accounting for religion and providing a framework of meaning for religious phenomena, certainly need not be merely a result of inductive inference; there will also be the 'creative imagination' (Wiebe 1983: 297) at work in drawing empirical data together into some coherent, integrated and thus systematic pattern.

This brief digression into one aspect of the problem indicates something of the significance of the general problem of theology's relationship to scientific study in religions. Clearly, this whole question of theory-framework for such a study is but one of the problems in analysing theology's status and role in all this.

There is a peculiar *irony* in this deep-seated tension in the relationship of theology to religious studies. The initial intention to engage in 'scientific' investigation of religion emerged in the last decades of the 19th century as a deliberate attempt to *disengage* from the restraints of theological commitment and to develop a discipline that would be quite distinct from theology (Pummer 1972; Waardenburg 1973; Sharpe 1975: 136-7; Rudolph 1981: 97, 104). Much was written then, and still continues to be written, from the perspective of a 'science' of religion (or more generally 'the history of religions') implicitly or explicitly aiming to distinguish and more decisively eliminate theological commitment in such study. This process echoes the similar· and much earlier process of disengagement on the part of other sciences in their refusal to continue to recognize theology as the 'queen of sciences'.

Strangely, very few theologians, or even philosophers of religion, have attempted to describe how theology relates to the systematic study of religions. Systematic theologians such as Tillich, Rahner, Pannenberg, Schlette, Tracy and others have in their various ways attempted to show, usually in very general terms, that Christian theology must respond to the fact of other religious traditions. Generally they have advocated some form of *theology of religions*. Even fewer systematic theologians have recognised that the systematic study of religion is essential to the systematic task of the theologian. Hendrick Kraemer, deeply influenced by neo-Orthodox Protestant theology, undoubtedly took such systematic study of religions as a serious part of the missionary task of the Christian Church. He was, of course, able to see *cultural* values in the 'non-Christian World'. But his radically dialectical view of the Christ-revelation meant that, in terms of *revelatory* and *salvific* value, he was able to respond only in a deeply ambivalent, often explicitly negative way (1938: passim). The response of Catholic theologians such as Karl Rahner and H.R. Schlette at least attempts to develop a more *positive* theology of religions. Paul Tillich's theological method of 'correlation' too lent itself to ways of more positive interaction in which some form of dialogical theology is called for; and in his later years Tillich was increasingly drawn to the phenomenological reality of Eastern religious thought and experience and recognised the 'Significance of the History of Religions for the Systematic Theologian' (Brauer 1966). Then Process Theology, as expounded for example by John Cobb, clearly can also provide a positive theological frame-work for accepting the historical and religious reality of other religious traditions (1975: 31-43). And a similarly anticipatory theology of religions, though worked out within an Hegelian rather than Whiteheadian framework, has been impressively elaborated in Pannenberg's writings which we look at in some detail later.

There can be no questioning the seriousness with which a theologian like David Tracy also takes cultural pluralism in trying to do justice to the Christian theological task today (1981: 447ff). To date, however, Tracy's theological inclusiveness has not been able to make any substantial response to the theological content of other religious faiths, even if he has attempted to incorporate insights from both phenomenological and anthropological studies regarding the basic structuring of religion and thus regarding the role of theology within a religious tradition. The writings of Raimundo Panikkar, though methodologically 'diffuse', clearly need to be taken seriously as a strikingly original form of dialogical hermeneutics (cf. Whaling 1985; 199-204).

Then there have been just a few other recent attempts to push theological response to religious pluralism further, as with Panikkar, to point the way to a dialogical or hermeneutical engagement through which a transcendent 'theology beyond theologies' will emerge (Davis 1974-5; Raschke 1981). In such a constructive dialogical or 'religiological' (Pummer 1972) theology it is intended that no *one* traditional doctrinal system or the ontological commitments of any one tradition should provide the framework for the emergent theology of religions; it is envisaged that a new theological framework will develop. We will need to look at this kind of approach more closely, noting also the attempts of George Rupp along these lines.

That there is a striking convergence between this approach to what is seen as the theological task and what scholars in religions such as Mircea Eliade see as the hermeneutical task of a science of religion does not necessarily mean that this is the most appropriate kind of rapprochement. Yet *intrinsic to the methodological self-understanding of each discipline* are good grounds for seeking *greater interaction*, a more 'positive co-existence' (Gensichen 1970). Both, in general, see any methodological merging with the other as the most serious threat to the authenticity and purity of their own methodology. And both have now long been in search of such methodological autonomy from the other, as each strives for recognition as an authentic science. The *irony* of this is not just that such a divorce has been so agreeable to both parties, but the fact that *no complete divorce methodologically is possible or even desirable*. Few – even theologians – would deny that the dominance of religious studies by theology could not continue as before the initial 19th century attempt to develop a science of religion. Theology was then still regarded as 'queen' of all *religious* sciences, even if she had already lost her position as sovereign over *all* scholarly disciplines. That many theologians and scholars in religions today regard each other with such uneasy suspicion, and would perhaps like the other to be something of a minor consort in their own court, often amounts to a refusal to recognise the rightful validity of the other.

More important, though, is the widespread inability to recognise the necessary inter-dependence of these two approaches, a position that results in a distorting self-understanding in each case. For reasons that will be elaborated later, if theology (I refer here specifically to *Christian* theology) is to function effectively and authentically as *theology*, theologians need a far more thorough understanding of religions and religious structures than is generally the case. Probably the most pressing issue in theology today concerns the grounding of theological articulation in that creative cultic matrix of myth/symbol/ritual in interaction with its broader contextual life (Wainwright 1980: 1-4). In other words, theology is essentially contextual reflection on the basis of its own religious grounding. A second issue of great current importance is how any distinct theology is to be articulated in relation to the plurality of religious traditions and theological systems in the midst of which it exists (Pannenberg 1972). Religion (and the study of religion) thus poses a number of critical questions for any theology that it will be self-destructive for theologians to continue to ignore.

Then, any science of religion is similarly confronted by questions regarding the essential nature of religion and the process by which religion both functions and is understood, questions that in various ways call for greater *theological* sensitivity. And here, as usually in the following pages, the term 'theological' is used in the broad sense of the diverse kinds of reflection and articulation of meaning called for in religious traditions. Thus, even within any one tradition there are various levels of meaning experienced, and expressed, often verbally, in greater or less systematic form. Formal systematic meaning-expression *may* be highly conceptual and sophisticated. Other forms of meaning-expression may appear to be without systematic doctrinal pattern. *Any*, certainly verbal, expression of religious meaning, however, will always include *some cognitive content* (Santoni 1968: section III; Wiebe 1981: 123-51); but we discuss the diverse levels of theological articulation later.

For the moment we merely note that if we are to understand a religious tradition, or a number of religions, then whether our primary intention be to understand a religion's historical development, or its social or psychological or ethical dimension, the ways in which people of that tradition have expressed *their* understanding of the meaning of their religion is essential in the process by which we arrive at any systematic understanding. For such perceptions are in various ways in *interaction with the primal matrix of meaning of the concerned tradition.* Thus the theological dimension, functioning at its various levels, is crucial to the science of religion. Unless we are blatantly reductionist, we cannot account for or understand, let us say, the social structuring of a tradition without taking into serious account the belief-structures in that tradition. Max Weber's sociological theory of a systemic linking of belief-structure and social structure may be in need of revision, but it still has some validity (1946: 267-287; = Robertson (ed.) 1969: esp. 41). The doctrinal systems intended to express a tradition's faith cannot be seen in a simplistic way as the direct basis for that tradition's socially structured life. The relationship is far more complex; but those belief-systems and the theologies related to them are *systemically related* to the tradition's matrix of meaning that is the centre and basis of that tradition's social and cultural life. Thus the professed conceptual systems of any tradition, even when proven to be the official formulations of a minority elitist group, must be taken into account if there is to be a comprehensive systematic understanding of that tradition.

Perhaps the primary task of any theology is the *communication of meaning* to those within the tradition (who will have, of course, already experienced *some* 'meaning' as they participate in the life of their tradition). But the tradition's meaning is also to be communicated to those still uninitiated into such participant status. And although we do as humans, just as do other biological forms, communicate at levels of life other than the verbal and conceptual — for we are still biotic as well as noetic beings — our humanness and religiousness are now so closely bound up with these noetic/verbal powers of communication that our religiousness and the conceptualising process are inextricably linked for us. Anthropological studies of primal societies have greatly helped us to value more primal forms of perception and communication (Van Baal 1971). Yet those who suggest that all conceptualising, and thus theologising, necessarily distorts, perhaps even destroys, primal cultural experience and communication are in effect saying that post-primal humans can only be truly participant in their culture or religion by a radical stripping off of many features characterising a way of being normally human. This is just what transcendentalists such as J. Krishnamurti may say; and of course it is typical of almost all religious traditions that they expect we relearn how to be essentially human by a process of radical repentance, renunciation, initiation, regeneration, reperception; a change in our 'vision' of things is required in many religious traditions as the way to integral experience of that tradition's transcendent vision and inner life; we are to become 'as little children' in some sense. But does this mean we are to give up as false and distorting of reality all sophistication of adult humanness like thinking, reflecting, talking, systematising? Even, for example, in Japanese Zen Buddhism, in which an ultimately authentic way of perceiving things involves a recovery of pre-verbal perception, it is clearly presupposed at least that the *path to* this ultimate experience is richly enabled by highly sophisticated words and concepts (Suzuki 1958).

In any case this somewhat artificial dichotomy of true religious experience and verbal conceptualising of meaning can hardly be allowed in any *science* of religion in which every attempt to communicate meaning within the tradition will be seen as an essential part of the data.

Some might argue that the above discussion misses the point. The real problem is not how important the tradition's expressions of its self-understanding are for a scientific understanding, but whether or not theological commitment, the *particular faith-perspective found within the tradition, is a necessity* for any person seeking understanding of that tradition. This question may seem easily disposed of. We can say there is no valid reason why a tradition cannot be studied, and an authentic account of that tradition provided, by a scholar who is not personally committed to the tradition's ontological affirmations, i.e. who is not a committed theologian of the concerned religion (Pummer 1974: 166:-8). Surely, we might reply, while a certain kind of understanding is dependent on faith, as a long line of theologians in many traditions (as well as Augustine and Anselm) have contended, faith is equally dependent upon some degree of cognitive understanding even by the participants in the faith community.

Here, however, we are concerned with the question of a non-participant, a non-believer, attempting to give an account of and provide understanding of a religious tradition. Just as there are different meaning levels and ways of meaning-expression, so 'understanding' occurs at many different levels and from many different perspectives, as is usually recognised within religious traditions themselves. We might, perhaps, think of the non-believing account from the perspective of a particular discipline as continuous with this graded perception of the inner reality of a religion. However, the scholar labouring to contribute to a particular scientific understanding of religion will not feel over-grateful for being placed on the bottom rung of such a ladder of understanding.

We might prefer to respond, as a number of scholars in religions have done, by arguing that while 'methodological atheism' (or positive denial, whether subtle or overt, of the ontological truth of the concerned religion) is undesirable and probably results in a distorted picture of the concerned religions, *methodological agnosticism* is fully desirable and necessary for a true science of religion (Smart 1973b: 578, 74ff). But even the term 'agnosticism' seems inappropriate here. What is intended, no doubt, is to allow room for a science of religion (from whatever particular perspective) to develop a systematic account of religious phenomena without needing to affirm — as a theologian in the end would — that these phenomena not only express a certain *perception* of ultimate reality, but truly *are* such. In other words, a science of religion needs to maintain a certain ontological neutrality. We may also note here in passing that sometimes theology too, in some forms of articulation may be expressed with some 'distancing' from faith affirmation. This may be more in the form of theological exploration — investigating 'God' as a 'problem', for example — (Kaufman 1972), or raising questions in relation to traditional forms of faith, even if ultimately it is religious commitment that underlies such reflection and its questioning.

With a scientific approach to religion, we might say, it will be the reverse: while attempting to understand and describe a religion from the perspective of the believer, any 'science of religion' will not be ultimately committed to the believer's position, but will need to go on to incorporate this position into the systematic conceptual framework of a discipline, and thus to look at it from a perspective that does not directly result from faith. It will involve a different kind of perception. If we are concerned *only* for an internal theological perspective surely we might as well leave the whole thing to the theologian!

And this raises again that central methodological problem in scientific approaches to the study of religions, viz. *reductionism*. 'Explanation' of many kinds may become reductionist (Pummer 1975: 168-71; Dudley 1977: 139-35; Wiebe 1981: 61-81). We will assume that a 'reductionist' account in religion is one which attempts to explain religious phenomena not only in terms of *one* perspective (this often happens within a tradition's own theology, when e.g. the tradition's essential meaning is explicated from one key concept, or perhaps one type of normative experience is given ultimacy) or from a perspective which is not found explicitly in the tradition itself; to this extent *all* accounts other than strictly theological accounts will be reductionist. By 'reductionism' we will assume, however imprecise this may seem, an account which attempts to explain the religious phenomena in terms that are intrinsically *not compatible* with the meaning expressed by the tradition's theologians. Such 'intrinsic' incompatibility will always be arguable; there will always be *some* believers who will fail to see compatibility between their faith and *any* attempt to give an account of that faith that is not in explicitly traditional categories. To avoid an unacceptable kind of reductionism, therefore, a scientific account of religion, to be still recognisable as 'religion', needs to incorporate with sufficient prominence that perspective of believers and theologians which gives inclusive coherence and thus ultimate meaning to the diversity of phenomena (perhaps to the outsider a bewildering diversity) in any tradition. The many details of a tradition can be described in such a way that no one will thereby see the point of it all. Or one particular segment of tradition could be isolated and analysed similarly without relating to that which gives inclusive meaning to such particulars in it. Again in the end a scientific study of religion needs to give due prominence to the inclusive vision of the tradition's meaning-articulators.

These, then, are some of the questions that arise when we reflect on the nature of religion, on the role of the theological process within religious traditions, and on the ways in which theology is to relate either to the systematic study of religious life, or to particular scientific forms of investigation of religious traditions. Clearly there are many different kinds of interaction possible between Theology and Religions. In the following chapters we shall attempt to examine this interaction in more detail.

1

Religion: A Preliminary Analysis

Any attempt at an anatomy of essential structures of religious life immediately faces the vexed question of a *definition* of religion. The field of religious studies is bestrewn with the decaying corpses of rejected definitions, found to be either too vague to be of any functional value, or too specific to include types of religion that are found at the other end of the spectrum; or perhaps too cumbersome to be anything other than a summary description of typical features found in traditions which by general consent are part of the comparative field of religious studies. We will look again at this question of definition when we come to more explicitly methodological discussion in chapter eight. For now, we merely note that the *assumptions* underlying the analysis of religion in this and subsequent chapters will very quickly surface.

One of the assumptions we should certainly begin with is that religious life in its empirical manifestations (if not in the perception of its participants, whose integral comprehension of their tradition may well lead them to see all its phenomena as a simple whole) is immensely complex. There is a vast range of phenomena to be found even within one tradition, with its beliefs and life-practices, its rituals and ethical attitudes, its esoteric inner life as well as its outward forms, its intense and its casual participants, its priests and its prophets, its classical scriptures and its continuing process of interpretation – and so one could continue with a much longer list of diverse ways of being religious. No wonder many have despaired of ever formulating a definition of religion that would be neither so vaguely essentialist or so cumbersomely descriptive as to be of little or no methodological value.

Clearly, another assumption of this 'anatomy' is that a wide range of religious traditions has to be taken into account, i.e. investigated comparatively, if we are to arrive at anything like an inclusive analysis of what are essential features of religion generally. Avoiding a formal definition, then, we shall look at a number of basic and typical *dimensions* of religious traditions, thus to some extent following the approach of Ninian Smart (1969: 16-17; 1973a:

42-4).[1] Such an enumeration, with some illustrative elucidation in each case, of what are found to be features of 'inner structure' as well as outer manifestation, should help to lead us towards a formal summary description of religion. From the outset, however, we need to note how each common dimension is found in usually quite *distinctive* form in each religious tradition. While my illustrative material is taken largely from the numerous 'great' traditions found practised in the Indian sub-continent (including Christianity and Islam), from time to time I will also refer to more 'primal' traditions; for the dimensions listed are essentially characteristic of primal religious life too, even if some dimensions are much less prominent than others.

1. There is a *ritual* dimension in religion – repeated cultic acts by which the tradition is transmitted and continually re-established, and by which that tradition's adherents participate in its life. Comparative studies make it fairly clear that there are a number of distinct types of ritual to be found in common even between what appear to be very disparate religious traditions. Sacrifice, initiation, reciting sacred words, observing sacred times, celebrating sacred festivals, congregating at sacred places, bearing sacred marks – these are but a few typical ritual acts. However, without relating such rituals to other dimensions within any given tradition, it could be quite misleading merely to assume that any such typical ritual must have the same significance in all religions. The question of each tradition's goals, the total *intention* within which that act is performed, is of crucial importance in determining its particular meaning for the concerned tradition.

Sacred action is frequently related closely to sacred word. In the Indian Vedic tradition, for example, what is done by way of sacrifice is invariably accompanied and made effective by the recitation (and singing) of the sacred *mantra*; and this is equally true of priestly *pūja* (more Agamic than Vedic) in Hindu temples today. There is, indeed, no religion with a more elaborate ritual dimension than that of Brahmanic Hinduism in its orthodox form. Yet, even in those movements in Indian religious history when there has been strongly felt antipathy towards the Brahmanic ritual structuring of the sacred – the

---

1 M. Pye, *Comparative Religion* (1972), proposes only four basic and invariable elements in religious life: religious action, religious groups, religious states of mind, and religious concepts, which are further divided into 30 sub-themes, and followed by 11 other comparative features.

numerous *bhakti* devotional movements, frequently, for example – not only do we find the emergence of new patterns of common community practice, and therefore 'ritual', which becomes accepted as essential sacred tradition; frequently, too, we find that the ancient sacred places and symbols still carried life-shaping potency, and even the new ritual may well be patterned on the old. Thus, for example, many ecstatic poets (Vaishṇava Āḻvārs, Śaiva Nāyanārs, etc.) of the *bhakti* movements, while frequently bemoaning the deadness of traditional rituals as formally enacted, at the same time in almost every verse sing lovingly and with deep veneration of the sacred shrines, the 'fields of auspiciousness' (*puṇya-kshetras*) by which the greatness and glory of the Lord had been manifest in the cultic tradition (Kingsbury and Phillips 1971; Ayyangar 1981). Admittedly their references are mostly mythological; but the mythic stories were integrally rooted in the ritual and iconographic structuring, the image-embodiment being the focal point of such mythically undergirded cultic ritual. In the broad sweep of Indian religious history, of course, there was not only the change from Vedic ritual to the perhaps more indigenous sacred traditions of the Vaishṇavas, Śaivas, etc. The ritual transition also involved a change in intention and goal, which is of crucial importance in analysing the role of ritual, as we noted above.

Those who interpret rituals as essentially and invariably *functional* in character are at least partly correct. Sacred acts usually are in some way life-enabling; whether consciously or not, they refer in some way to human well-being, except with certain kinds of 'black magic', which we may take to be aberrative and atypical religious ritual. It is doubtful, however, if 'functionalism' should be taken as the *primary* orientation of religious rituals, though there are many types of ritual in which life-enhancement of some kind is very prominent. A number of rituals in primal religious communities did develop especially as a means of coping with *crisis* points of human experience, as the human psyche felt threatened by the life-transition, the new orientation, required in moving into some new phase of life, or perhaps into some unknown territory with its alien environment and strange new Powers. Such rituals thus relate to both time and space, and to coping with new encounters in each dimension. Thus the term 'rites of passage' and the elaboration by Arnold van Gennep (1960) of themes related to such rites. In such primal enabling rituals there may not be any explicit calling upon a clearly focussed sacred Power. But there will be the sense of being drawn, by means of the ritual, into a larger life-dimension, of being attuned to a larger 'world'. And in many cases such 'attuning' will be explicitly related to some clearly named sacred Power (cf. Turner 1969).

Other crisis-type rituals are very explicitly 'environmental' (Hultkrantz, in Honko 1979; Harris 1979). Their aim is to achieve harmony with some aspect of the human environment that is potentially threatening: there may be the felt need for the regular renewal of cosmic life, perhaps through micro-cosmically enacted sacrificial ritual, or there may be ritual action to ensure the fertility of the earth, crops, cattle, humankind, or aimed at some other forms of life-enhancement. Other ritual actions aim at appeasing sacred earth-Powers whose animosity may have been aroused because of human intrusion into earth's life (perhaps by impounding of water, or the building of a house, or the cutting down of a tree; in each case the sacred Power of the water, earth, or tree calling for appeasement).

Other rituals may be aimed at attaining some form of earth-transcending status, i.e. a technique intended to induce a sense of rising above the limitations of time, space, matter. Along with this and perhaps as of primary importance, there may well be the aim of achieving union with the sacred Power, probably through whom the transcendence is realised.

There may well be, then, some ambiguity regarding just how 'functional' (in the sense of merely furthering specific human goals) all these rituals are (cf. Jackson, in Whaling 1985(II): 179-230). That they frequently also include a sacred dimension that draws the participant beyond such a manipulative approach is abundantly clear. Indeed, some very 'primal' rituals can be seen to refer only to the 'enhancement' of the sacred Power of Presence. This may perhaps be by way of doing obeisance to, even making an offering to, some strangely formed rock in which a mysterious Presence is perceived. *Incidentally*, such worship may lead to an expectation of life-enhancement, but this is not the primary aim. Indeed, we might affirm as a general rule that the Sacred is as such never thought to be entirely manipulable, however regularly ritualised and however direct the aim to receive some mundane blessing as a result of the ritual. As the *bhakti* tradition in India puts it: all devotion to the Sacred Power, whether by means of a regular ritual or not, must in the final analysis be 'End-devotion', meaning it is to be for the sake of the Sacred Power itself, not for the sake of the benefits available through that Power.

Rites of 'initiation' do not *only* relate to the transitional stages in the natural process of human growth, such as puberty, with its peculiar emotional challenges. Initiatory rites also include cultic acts enabling the 'passage' into a new state of 'enlightenment', and thus enabling entry into a community 'consecrated' to a specified sacred way of life. Such is the case with Jainas, Buddhists, Vaishṇavas, Śaivas, Tāntrikas and other such types of religion in which a sacred vow (*dīksha*) marks the moment of initiation for the novice. As an essential part of the process, preceding and usually continuing after the initiation, a regular religious discipline, as a kind of personalised, interiorising ritual, will be expected. This is the 'means' (*sādhana*) by which the 'goal' of this particular consecrated way of life is to be attained. In Indian religion generally, we might call this type of spiritual discipline a transposed form of earlier ritual. The primary orientation here is an inclusive renunciation of all, in order that the one supreme Goal may be served; life-enhancement, in the sense of the satisfaction of life-expectation, or the expansion of the personal or social ego, is not what is looked for.

In most religious traditions, however, it is usual for both kinds of initiation to be performed within a tradition, making for distinct levels of participation within the tradition. In some cases the initiation into the higher 'enlighten-ment' may coincide with entry into adulthood, or the attainment of puberty. This is the case with the sacred thread ritual for the 'twice-born' in Hinduism. In a number of Christian communities, also, the initiation rite (baptism/con-firmation/entry into sacramental participation) includes both these aspects, though the explicit aim may well be focussed on entry into the sacramental life of the community.

All the orthodox Hindu life-sacraments (*saṃskāras*) relating to marriage, conception, birth, first rice-eating, first hair-cutting, putting on the sacred thread, death, etc. are clearly akin to rites of passage. They are connected mainly with natural solar seasons, whereas many Hindu *festivals* are held on a lunar basis. It is the *saṃskāras* that became the most important focal points of life-transition in the orthodox family of the 'twice-born' communities; and this is despite the fact that in the earlier Vedic tradition the most prominent priestly ritual acts were the great sacrifices (*yajñas*) offered to the deities upon whom life's seasons and blessings were so dependent. Such sacrifices were offered, then, primarily to glorify the concerned deity, to 'enhance' that deity's sacred being and greatness. However essential to human and cosmic life were the blessings of the deities, each perceived in relation to cosmic powers, such expectation seems decidedly secondary in that Vedic consciousness. Yet in course of time, at least for some schools of priests, the great deities were seen as merely nominal; the significant reality was the sacred ritual itself, for it was thought to possess its own power to fulfill the desires of those who sacrificed.

Perhaps inevitably, Vedic sacrifices were eventually displaced by the tradi-tion of temple worship-service (Agamic *pūja sēvā*), and by the offerings made to the image-embodied deities of the sacred places. And the function of the key-rituals changed accordingly. Now the primary aim is to gain *darśana*, or 'vision', of the sacred Being on earth, and along with this, whatever auspicious blessings he/she was peculiarly able to bestow, or whatever was the perceived need of the devotee/pilgrim/supplicant. In this way the ritual dimension, so closely linked with worship of the sacred Focus, if anything grew in importance in the development of Hinduism at various levels of its life; for other changes took place too, the details of which we cannot go into here.

At least some mention should be made of the felt-need within many traditions for purification, though variously understood, and the widespread sense of danger from diverse kinds of pollution (Dumont 1970; Lannoy 1971: 143-56). Taboos, many unconsciously held, are prevalent in human societies generally, markedly so in Indian society. Much of the complex inter-relationships expected of the caste system and its hierarchy is based on attempts to control, divert, remove the evil effects of pollution. Travel, eating, drinking, physical relations of any kind, sex in particular, thus contact with women, and many other activities in life are seen as potentially polluting, and call for counter rituals, either to avert or to remove such contamination. Even those with a deep sense of their dependent relationship with an all-powerful deity may well also have a constant fear of debilitating pollution; thus, again, we find distinct levels of religious perception operating at the same time and within the same tradition, even within the same participant.

Rituals of many kinds and functioning at different levels, in other words, are typically a central feature of religious life, though the particular intention with which any ritual is done, even if not explicit and conscious, is essential to understanding the meaning of ritual and how rituals relate to other structures of religious life.

2. Then there is the *mythic* dimension, though again we need to note the great variation in extent and style of mythic articulation within different traditions (Maranda 1972; Bolle, in Whaling 1985(I): 297-349). Myth is normally found closely interrelated with ritual, often providing, through the narration of sacred drama, that overarching sacred cosmos within which ritual is experienced as meaningful, as is very clear for example in early Vedic India. Thus ritual's microcosmic action usually intends to relate the participants to the myth's macrocosmic drama. But the *purpose* of mythic forms is varied too, even if there are certain repeated patterns and structures to be found trans-culturally.

In that myth in many cases provides the meaning for religious *action* (whether in a formal ritual context or in a broader life-context), the mythic dimension can be seen as a kind of *primal theology*, and therefore overlaps to some extent with the doctrinal dimension which follows below. As with other symbolic religious forms, however, it is clear in the history of any religious tradition that the same mythic story, perhaps in modified form, may be used in different stages of the development of the tradition to communicate very different meanings. Indeed, even in a religion's 'classical' period, myths may lose their primal meaning; or are perhaps narrated with a moralistic, exhortatory intent, as for example the story of Rama and Sita has been used in recent times in India; a more truly 'mythic' dimension may also be experienced at some deeper existential level in the telling of the story. Nor is it impossible, in the interaction of cultures, for one tradition's myth to be narrated in another tradition, perhaps with a very different intent: thus the myths of creation, the flood, and so on, are taken over by the Hebrew tradition. The question then arises, which we will not discuss now, to what extent do levels of symbolic meaning deeper than our conscious intentionality still make their impact. Is there necessarily a shared world of significance for the deepest levels of human consciousness deriving from common myths and symbols? (Eliade 1959; Campbell 1959-68). It obviously oversimplifies the functioning of human consciousness to assume that there will always be some single and determinable primal meaning in any given myth and in the authentic mythic consciousness.

We take up the functioning of myth again in Chapter six; here we note merely that myths are often stories about religious heroes, gods, demons and suchlike divine and semi-divine cultic figures. By reciting the events of their sacred lives — lived out in a sacred history with trans-historical dimensions — the myth-telling community seeks to share in their victories in the sense of repeating, on the more limited scale of their own lives, that archetypal experience. This means the believer is to see his/her universe as structured similarly to the sacred world of the mythic story. Myth-telling thus usually involves a certain world-view, and a certain world-view usually involves mythic counterparts.

That this kind, or some similar, mythic structuring is typical of religious traditions is suggested by, for example, the way we find new religious movements setting their new ontic and ethical affirmations within a world-view, a religiously described universe with clearly mythic dimensions quite often taken over from the mythology of the tradition they may in many other ways have rejected. Thus we think of such disparate reform movements as Buddhism, Jainism, Śaiva Liṅgāyatism; or Israel working out its distinctive position vis-a-vis

Canaan, Babylon and Persia, yet still incorporating some mythic features from these traditions. The modified form and placing, thus the new intention, of the old myths must be allowed their full weight. For the restructuring may well mean that a distinctively new world-view has been born. That it is still a mythically perceived world is the point at issue here, and that this mythic dimension is so unavoidable that when necessary even dangerously misleading myths of the rejected religious world-view may have to be taken over. Even when a kind of early demythologising is attempted (for example, the Buddha's rejection of the Brahmanic world of gods, priests, sacrifices, etc. as soteriologically of no value) the result is invariably a *re*mythologised view of things.

Despite the impressive work of Max Müller, the 'father of comparative religion', on the Vedic texts, his notion that the early Vedic deities were mythically perceived only as the result of a cosmically distorting 'disease of language', now appears almost comically wide of the mark. His theory that an earlier intuitive and authentic sense of the Infinite in and through the diverse phenomena of nature was transposed to the erroneous personification of each natural power in mythic form – myth thus being a distortion of true religion – to a large extent reflects the then quite widely-held western view that myth, as the Greeks had taught long before, can only be a distorted form of truth. It now seems clear that in the Vedic vision of things myth was always intrinsic not only to the being of the gods but to the Aryan perception of reality and its infinite dimensions.

There has recently been a suggestion (Whaling 1985(I): 271) that *scripture* should be included along with the mythic dimension. Scripture plays such a prominent role in literate religious traditions, or in most of them, as to carry a kind of 'dimensional' character of its own within the general structuring of such traditions. To some extent, also, the role of myth in pre-literate traditions is analogous to the role of scripture in literate communities; and the mythic dimension in the literate tradition will typically make up a substantial part of scripture, along with other material expressing the ritual, doctrinal, ethical and perhaps other dimensions. In any case, scripture will typically function as the early repository of the creative matrix of mythic and symbolic imagery of the concerned tradition. When scripture is seen as divinely revealed, or as incorporating such divine revelation, as in varying degrees in Judaism, Christianity, Islam, Sikhism, and in some theistic groups in Hinduism, the books of scripture themselves are likely to be venerated as sacred, or as sacred vehicles of the divine revelation. In Indian traditions generally, though, it is not that which is written and read that is thus venerated, but that which is *heard* (i.e.

śruti, 'that which is heard', or *śabda*, 'sound', 'voice', being common terms for authoritative scripture); it is heard by the great seers of old as an authentic part of the eternal Sound or Word, and it is heard in the 'listening' (*śravana*) of true seekers as Gurus in every generation transmit its liberating truth. In the ritual context, however, it is not the Guru but the *mantra*-chanting Priest who transmits the 'sound'. In much Indian religion, then, it is *oral* transmission of the sacred word that is the dominant model, though in the case of sacred books like the Bhagavad Gita, the *reading* of the text has become a sacred duty, indeed one of the daily 'sacrifices' in this transposed personalised form of the ancient ritual practice.

3. A *doctrinal* dimension, even if in minimally articulated form, will be found as part of every religious tradition, becoming more prominent when attempts are made to give more clear conceptual and propositional form to the tradition's basic word-view and its undergirding perceptions. There will inevitably be, however, some cognitive dimension even to the performing of ritual and the telling of myth, for these will necessarily convey some kind of life-enhancing, liberating *meaning* to that tradition's participants. Even where there is a very strong imperatival sense that the ritual *must be done* (as for example in the later Vedic school of Ritualism, which denied that ritual is to be done for the sake of God, but that it carried its own legitimacy), this priority of ritual duty will always be linked with belief in the effects of such ritual acts, and thereby with a perception of the nature of the world and its structuring within which ritual is seen to be effective. Ritual acts therefore presume some kind of cognitive meaning, and typically this will be expressed in the form of some doctrinal schema.

Again it should be stressed how greatly varied will be the extent of the schematising of a tradition's doctrines. Such systematic doctrine may remain minimal, as in most primal religion, or in very early Vedic religion. Or it may become highly schematised, perhaps even highly sophisticated in form, as in the six *darśanas*, or philosophical schools of Hinduism, in the various schools of Buddhism, and in the theologies of Christianity and Islam. So metaphysically sophisticated have the *darśanas* (or 'viewpoints', 'visions') of India become that their religious grounding is today often quite overlooked and they are seen as 'pure philosophies' (Radhakrishnan 1931(II): 445). In reality they are based on and shaped by very definite religious doctrinal positions, and to forget this rootage is to diminish the significance of these systems as integrally related to religious communities and their vision of life; and both potency and coherence are weakened by being reduced to systems of speculative metaphysics. At the other end of the scale of sophistication we may note again that even mythic expressions of a religious position can be seen as primal attempts at the articulation of meaning; on the other hand no systematic doctrine will be without its mythic dimension. Thus myth and doctrine shade imperceptibly into each other.

The affirmation and elucidation of the key doctrines on which any tradition is grounded and by which it conceptually coheres is of crucial importance in that religion's attempt to understand and interpret the meaning it perceives in its tradition. As the tradition responds to its changing environment — social, cultural, political — this 'elucidation' will necessarily entail some degree of re-interpretation. Thus 'tradition', the process of 'handing on', includes not only the conserving of the accumulated life of the past, but also its 're-visioning'. However, as these and related themes will be discussed at considerable length in later chapters concerning the theological process, let us not spend further time now on the numerous issues involved.

4. A *social* dimension, and some form of institutionalised community life, is also typical of religious traditions. Any view of religion as in essence 'the alone with the Alone' has either to ignore as insignificant this communal aspect of religious traditions, or assume that all such institutions, often presenting us with something of a problematic history, are lower-order non-essentials in the religious life. At the other extreme some sociologists of religion have seen *every* aspect of religious life as convincingly explicable in terms of the fulfilling of needs that are basically social needs.

There are two principal aspects of this social dimension in religion: First we find the formation of a religious community with its own inner structuring; then there is that dimension of its life that relates to society at large, to the human community generally. In some situations, perhaps now increasingly rare, there may be only the former: an integrated community with its common religious life of ritual action, mythic imagery, doctrinally expressed faith, ethical commitment — in toto the sharing of common life-perceptions and common life-patterns. In our world of increased cultural interaction this experience of relating only to a single community will now be true only of a few tribal groups, very strict monastic communities, and the like.

The sense of being a sacred body of people has been typical of a large number of religious communities. There was Israel's sense of being a holy people of divine convenant, with its parallel in the early Christian belief that they were the 'saints', 'called out' (*ekklesia*) into a 'new covenant'. There is the

Muslims' sense of belonging to the one community (*ummah*) of those who submit themselves ('Islām') to the sovereignty of Allah as revealed in the Quran
and worked out in the Islamic code for life (*sharī 'at*); this finds even stronger
form in the Sikh community's sense of its sacred togetherness as people of the
Panth (way), or the Khalsa (meaning either 'holy', or 'belonging to'), for 'the
Khalsa is the Guru, and the Guru is the Khalsa'. The saying most oft-repeated
by Sikhs meeting together will probably be; 'Waheguru ji ka Khalsa' (The
holy Khalsa belongs God). Nor is this sense of sacredly constituted togetherness absent from Hindu religious groups. The Śaiva Lingāyats, for example,
strongly emphasise commitment to the 'company of holy bhaktas'. Many
religious communities, then, inspire this sense of fierce and utter loyalty to
the life of the community. Frequently, of course, such ardent loyalty will be
related rather to a sub-sect within a larger religious community, the group in
fact to which participants have the more immediate sense of belonging. Thus
the Lingāyatas and other such sub-sects within 'Hinduism' in course of time
have become distinctly identifiable and separate communities.

It has often been assumed that in traditions such as Jainism, Buddhism, and
various forms of Hinduism in which ultimate value is given to the individual's
transcendental release from his bondage to the empirical world, with its social
ties, there can be no serious social dimension. This is far from the case, though
we will need to note later that certain forms of these traditions can lead to
considerable ambiguity towards one's social existence. Here we can note the
great significance of the Indian concept of *dharma* (O'Flaherty 1978); though
variously interpreted, it has cosmic pervasiveness and is especially significant in
establishing an ontic/ethical basis for society. For the Hindu in particular this
undergirding *dharma* implies the cosmic ultimacy of the community into which
one is born, and this means a particular community within a hierarchically
ranged caste system, as traditionally taught. In Jainism and Buddhism the
sacred *sangha*, or the community of monks, bikkus, arhats, etc. is the primary
'community'. Yet for lay-people too there are the usual close social groupings
that, religiously sanctioned, form the context in which they are to work out
their upward path. Obviously, giving alms to those already on the way to the
higher state is one way by which they may attain the more sacred *sangha* life.
Indeed, their life-style in that lower social grouping is to correspond in a less
rigorous form to the exalted rule of the *sangha*, which is equally true of the
Jaina's way. But here we touch on the ethical dimension. Thus, for both monk
and lay-person the sacred *sangha*-life is essential in differing ways.

We can even broaden this and include Indian religious life generally; there is initiation into both the sacred community in a general sense (i.e. the sacrament of investing the sacred thread by the three upper castes) and into some more specialised status of enlightenment and liberation (i.e. the 'vow' taken through a Guru). Here again we see two levels of social structuring, which is made more complex though by the many more social levels we find in the caste system. The way caste functions, however, confirms the thesis of a necessary inter-action of religion and society. Not only is there a strong sense of community within each caste group; the distinctions and inequalities seen between the different groupings is explained, traditionally, in terms of the outworking of the law of *karma* (the previous *action* of an individual determines present conditions; present action will determine future conditions) and *karma* relates closely to the theory of *dharma*. Thus religious doctrine provides the con-ceptual grounding for India's pluralist society.

In general, then, we see typically in religious traditions the concern to function at the two levels of a social dimension noted above. Few have such a rigorously exclusive and separatist attitude as to withdraw totally from the wider human community, though this has not been and is not now unknown. More generally traditions are structured to accommodate both aspects; there is the community as the sacred society with its concern to preserve its own inner life, and there is this community's interaction with the wider human com-munity, part of which may already be seen as the 'people' or 'laity' that stands between the sacred world and the profane world. There are no doubt other religious movements (early apostolic Christian and Islamic for example) that would see no distinction in sacredness between a common laity and a special group comprising as it were the essential heart of the movement. Thus Apostles write of the common laity as the 'holy saints'; but this was soon to change.

5. There is an *ethical* dimension in religion. It has sometimes been assumed that in tribal communities this ethical dimension will take the form mainly of negative taboos; though even where a positive code of life-behaviour may not have been worked out explicitly, it is very clear that modes of relationship with other people, as well as with the natural world, have always been im-mediately implicit in any primal vision of life. Indeed such implications have worked themselves out effectively in the most simple form of primal society. Taboo regarding the feared power of either sacred or profane objects is only one aspect of the way people order their lives within such a primal vision.

It is, as we saw, possible to see the whole range of human cultural behaviour, including and perhaps especially primal culture, as responses to the task of relating to environment, natural and human, by way of adaptation, or attunement, or transcending, or transforming. Hence, some anthropologists (Harris 1979; Hultkrantz in Honko 1979) find 'cultural ecology' to be the most significant way of understanding human cultural behaviour. While this interpretation undoubtedly draws out a very important 'functionalist' aspect of culture, the danger is that it may ignore the equally, perhaps even more important 'transcendent' signification of culture (cf. Sahlins 1976) and especially of religion as closely intermeshed with culture. Religion is not merely adaptation to the material environment.

Nor should the ethical dimension in religion be seen primarily as rules developed for the regulating of a religious community in order that its life together function smoothly and amicably. No doubt a large part of religious ethics is in fact concerned with the relationships of the community's members one with another, as well as with people and situations outside the sacred community. Much of the Brahmanic *dharma-śāstras*, the Buddhist *vinaya* rules, and the Jaina monk's discipline, as well as much Jewish, Christian and Muslim ethical life, does relate to such relationships, as often also do primal taboos. What we need to note, though, is that the religious ethical dimension invariably has a crucial reference to the tradition's *transcendent* dimension, or at least to its religious doctrines. Interpersonal relationships are not dealt with in any merely pragmatic way. Ethical life is patterned according to a peculiar vision of the universe, so that doing things in a particular way will be, as it were, structurally required. It will involve the sacred Focus of the tradition, or relationship with a level of being that the believer sees as going beyond empirically explicable relationships. Explanations in terms of 'legitimation' are just not always appropriate.

Very diverse types of religious tradition exemplify this general observation. The true Muslim is expected, for example, to give alms regularly and generously to the needy of the community because of the implicit Islamic faith in Allah's attributes, the greatest of which are to be beneficient and merciful; the character of those who 'submit' themselves to Allah is to be appropriately commensurate with his character. In any case the duties (*dīn*) required of the Muslim conform in a general way with the *imān* or faith-doctrines that are to be confessed. But the specific case of the divine character being the motivating factor in generous treatment of the needy is similarly found in Judaism and Christianity, which are replete with texts urging a merciful attitude because God (or Christ) has been merciful, forgiving, helpful, etc. towards us, his people. That a righteous life is required because God is righteous (and therefore presumably the universe is ultimately structured according to his righteousness) is an even more emphatic biblical stance. And this is equally, perhaps more, true of those religions in which divine *grace* is seen as the final means of salvation, i.e. that a certain kind of life-stance will be expected that reflects this grace-dependence. It is rather rare to find a tradition where the sense of abandonment to divine grace is so extreme that there is no concern at all for any kind of appropriately patterned life-style. Sheer antinomian grace-cults are not common.

In a number of Indian religions, i.e. those which are not strongly theistic, or not grace-based, the doctrinal motivation can be very different, though there is an analogous role for the ethical dimension. *Dharma* in Brahmanism and Buddhism has a richly varied meaning, but essentially refers to the proper cosmic ordering of things, hence their 'rightness', even their 'righteousness'. The social order, into which the individual is to fit by virtue of his essential inner nature, corresponds to the cosmic order, and in turn the cosmic process is worked out in all its detailed ramifications through the dynamism of *karma*, each individual chain of karmic actions contributing to the destiny of the whole process. For the theist this can all be seen as the expression of the continually active will of God. Thus again we find ethics holding an intrinsic place in relation both to the Transcendent and so to the tradition's perception of the cosmic pattern.

In some religious schema, however, e.g. a strictly non-dualist position, it must be admitted that the ethical dimension, while still empirically important, and even helping to prepare the mind for the ultimate realisation of oneness, is not seen as *directly* related to this ultimate reality; and this is so even within the ostensive acceptance of the *karma*-theory (in the end the Advaitin says that our *karma*-bondage is only lack of true insight into reality). While this *karma*-doctrine, and the sense of need for freedom from the consequent cycle of rebirths and re-embodiments, provides an equally prominent undergirding for Jainism and Theravada-Buddhism, the ethical outworking of their liberation schema is very different, and is much more directly part of the process of attaining the supreme goal. Various prescribed acts of compassion, of self-discipline, and especially of the practice of non-injury to all life-forms (particularly in the case of Jainism) are seen as essential to the path that ends in the transcendent state of ultimate tranquillity. We see clearly that qualities required in the ethical/spiritual discipline seem eminently commensurate with outstanding qualities used to describe the 'ineffable' ultimate destiny, e.g. stillness, desirelessness, bliss, insight, purity.

6. The above point seems to introduce us rather appropriately to an aspect of religious life underlying everything else we have so far delineated, and that is the *experiential* dimension. Both in terms of its psychological features and its spiritual authenticity within the concerned religion's own norms, experience will necessarily be greatly varied; for people differ by temperament as well as to the extent they participate authentically in their tradition. Here 'authenticity' can be determined by a number of different norms: the degree of personal faith, commitment, intensity of devotion, understanding, etc. In any case, there is in most religions the assumption that the true authenticity of religious experience cannot be measured by outward forms, which is one reason why within most traditions there are those exponents of the faith who have little patience with any strictly behavioural approach to their religious life. They would stress, rather, the inner 'sacral sentiments', which will include mental attitude, emotional feeling, values, expectations, motivations, insight, volitional sincerity, as well as such more specifically 'religious' categories as faith, spiritual joy, love and peace, commitment to the way of truth, sense of wonder, communion with the divine reality, inner maturity, attainment of life's ultimate goal, and so on.

In every religion, above all some normative value will be given, in the matter of authenticity of religious experience, to *participant relationship to the sacred Focus* of the tradition. Most traditions, at least in their secondary literature, refer reverently and perhaps in hyperbolic or legendary style to those blessed and heroic souls who have been seen as having made outstanding progress towards the perceived goal of life and evinced a high degree of the spiritual qualities expected of the 'saintly' in the tradition. Or they will perhaps be revered as outstandingly adept at the esoteric skills or the secret wisdom of the tradition. In other words it is experience in the *inner life* of the tradition that is given high priority in a religious tradition's evaluation of its own history. Most interpreters from within will find the culmination of all the other dimensions of the tradition's life – rituals, myths, doctrines, ethics, etc. – in this experiential dimension, though this will no doubt depend on the particular viewpoint of the interpreter concerned. Generally, though, participation in the outward life of the tradition is seen as perfected in a sense of awareness of the tradition's inner dimensions.

As for the *character* of religious experience, which a number of well-known definitions of religion (including those of Schleiermacher and Otto) have taken as the essential and definitive core of religion as such, we have to take seriously the distinctive character of each tradition, even though it is possible to enumerate certain predominant types of religious experience. To propose a particular kind of experience as definitive of all religious experience contradicts the empirical reality of the variety of religious life. Diversity must surely be taken as typical of religion at every level of participation in actual traditions. Despite the significant and historically valuable contributions of, for example, Friedrich Schleiermacher and Rudolf Otto to our understanding of religious life – both in their different ways giving emphasis to the *sui generis* character of religious *experience* – by reducing religious experience to one particular type, distinct in each case, they misrepresent the possible range of such experience. Schleiermacher's 'feeling of absolute dependence' and Otto's 'sense of the numinous that is both tremendous and fascinating' both depict one important type of religious experience. And although both have been criticised for taking their interpretation of the Judeo-Christian religion as normative for all authentic religious experience, the types that they describe can also be found beyond the Judeo-Christian traditions. The numinous transcendentalism of Otto's type has close affinity to the monotheistic experience of Islam for example; and Schleiermacher's dependence-type, with a special quality of religious *feeling* as essential, clearly has close affinity with the *bhakti*-stream of Indian theism with its sense of God-dependence as decisive. But what of those numerous contemplative religious types, with their fully developed traditions, in which it is pre-eminently a sense of absolute *in*dependence that is sought as the *summum bonum*, and in which there will be an accompanying sense of inner tranquillity rather than the awful sense of the numinous?

At this point we will leave the question of the character of religious experience, as in the next chapter we attempt to elucidate features that are generally typical of this visionary core of religious traditions; it will in effect, then, be a continuation of this discussion of the 'experiential dimension'. We now move on to aspects of religious life that do not perhaps have quite the same kind of 'dimensional' character as the six discussed above, yet need to be brought out as clearly as possible in any analysis of the broad features of religion.

7. It has already become quite clear from the way that a number of the other 'dimensions' of religion had to be referred to in the above discussion that each religious tradition is, as it were, *organically structured*, with each of its component parts being *interdependent* upon other parts within the tradition as a whole. In the analysis of any particular dimension of a religion we have continually to bear in mind its interconnection and interaction with other

aspects of the total structure. No phenomenon in a tradition can properly be understood in isolation from other phenomena, for each functions in inter-action with the others, thus forming an integrated whole. Clearly this aspect of religion is not only of significance in understanding a single tradition, but also in attempting to understand religion in general, whether as a broad-ranging comparative view of religions, or as a study focussed on some typical religious phenomenon as it occurs in diverse religious settings. But we should not conclude from this that *no* comparing is possible, as scholars like Hendrik Kraemer have argued on the very basis of this organic (he called it 'totalitarian') character of religious traditions. It does mean, however, that a legitimate comparative approach will need to recognise the intra-relatedness of phenomena within a tradition, and will therefore need to be that much more cautious and subtle in attempting analysis.

8. Another feature of religious traditions that may not have been brought out by listing the six 'dimensions' above is the way each functions as a *dynamic process*; whatever significant continuities there may be in each tradition as it appropriates its past heritage, there are also continual changes, transitions, one might even speak of 'mutations'. In general this mutable, processive character of a religion's ongoing life has tended to be overlooked by comparative religionists almost as much as it will probably be denied by the devotees of a tradition. Will not the majority of those committed to the trustworthiness of a given tradition tend to regard it as in its essentials immutable? Orthodox Hinduism has regarded its heritage as the *sanātana-dharma,* the 'everlasting righteous way' unchanging in essential form from early Vedic times to the present; a number of modern apologists, however, have had little difficulty with the notion of perpetual change, reflecting the continual cultural and social changes of the ages. And Buddhists, with their fundamental doctrine of all cosmic existence in perpetual flux, have had little problem with a more dynamic view of history, and of the history of the tradition. It is a fact of course that a tradition with an extremely conservative view of its history will tend not to allow the tradition to change as rapidly as those who see their own history in more dynamic terms. Within parts of orthodox Islam (and not merely the *sunnis*) the fact that rigorous attempts are made by some leaders to prevent social and cultural change itself reflects the view that the immutable law of God has been revealed in its perfection in the Quran and the Hadith, and our duty is merely to submit more fully to this law. A more dynamic view of the process of history need not lead us to see every change in our tradition

as a necessary or desirable change, or to believe in the inevitability of progress. That for better or worse, even in matters of religious tradition, change of some kind is historically inevitable is the point being made here. We may question, for example, whether even the most militantly conservative Imam can prevent people's *perception* of things from undergoing change. For in any religious tradition, the same form of prayer or of ritual as that performed for genera-tions may well have, to a greater or lesser extent, different *meaning* for each generation. And when perceived significance changes, the honest interpreters of the tradition, its theologians, will need to re-view their interpretations. The historical process, especially the processes of religious history, is necessarily a hermeneutical process, and the different ways in which people interpret their history, i.e. their subjective impact on it, itself has consequences for that history's development.

9. Then we need to note the inherently *symbolist* character of religion (cf. Chap. 6 below). Here we are concerned primarily with the structural mani-festations of religious traditions; symbolism is invariably characteristic of these traditions. In their ritual and mythic forms of expression the symbolism is clear enough – icons, archetypal images, symbolic gestures, dramatic actions, imaginative narrative, and so on. Even periods of violent iconoclasm and the puritanical fervour that would try to 'cleanse' a movement of all symbolic imagery invariably ends with some symbolic corporate forms of communica-tion. We might think of the Quaker meeting sitting in a silent circle awaiting the Spirit's prompting; the silent circle itself is a quite potent symbolic image. The Prophet cleansed Mecca of all defiling images of the gods of pre-Islamic Arabia; yet the black unshaped Kaaba-stone there remains a potent focal symbol for the millions of Muslims each year making their Hajj.

Similarly, we find that invariably a tradition incorporates certain key-symbols; it may be one core-symbol, or a cluster of inter-related symbols (Whaling 1985: 371). These stand out or are high-lighted by the tradition as of peculiar significance, and from them other symbols, as it were, take their cue. Thus, in Theravada Buddhism we find the *bodhi*-tree, as the place of enlightenment or of attaining 'buddha-hood', occupying the central place, accompanied by the footprints of the Buddha, and the wheel of Dharma (the 'right' teaching of the Buddha), and probably the ancient round pot which is the 'fulness' of nirvanic joy. What is of great significance, though, is that these early Buddhist symbols, along with the *stūpa* or burial mound containing the holy relics of Buddha or his outstanding followers, were also pre-Buddhist symbols. The tree, for example, is a relatively common primal symbol, as is the pot, both signifying fulness of life, fertility and plenty in the primal context; no doubt they may also have signified the 'spirit' of the tree and the pot. In a later chapter we see what happens when such a symbol is transposed through the life-transforming experience of the Buddha. And yet, there is a sense in which the spirit of the primal tree was still preserved, in the transposed sense of 'great compassion' for all creatures, for all life. So perhaps the old symbol was not *entirely* turned upside down; the new interpretation proves more inclusive than at first appears. The symbols, too, become central for Buddhist doctrine and ethics, not merely ritual and myth, and are thus bound up integrally with the process of the interpretation of life and its realities.

To speak of all religious traditions as 'symbol-systems' (e.g. Geertz 1973: 90-125) can imply something rather more than this, however. To say that a religion is a culturally structured symbol-system does not, of course, *necessarily* mean that such a symbol-system is not real, though it will probably sound like this to conservative adherents of some religions, and even seems implied by the way some scholars speak of religions as 'symbol-systems'. But we return to this issue later.

Assuming, then, that symbols are intrinsic to religious life in all its diversity, it is clear that the precise role of any given symbol in communicating meaning to participants in a religion is rather complex. No single or simple meaning can be assumed of any one symbol (cf. Eliade, Chap. 6 below). Some from time to time seem to lose their signifying potency, perhaps because social and cultural changes render them obsolete in so far as they belonged to a culture or cultural set of values no longer acceptable. Within Indian traditional symbols, we find, for example, that much explicitly sexual imagery is now unacceptable to many interpreters of the tradition. Then we find sometimes that symbols in a tradition change their order of priority in the dynamic process of the tradition's history. The fortunes of the female deities of Hinduism associated with central male deities as consorts in many cults have varied over the course of the years; certainly the sacred symbols the deities (male and female) carry in their hands, or around their necks, etc., have been ascribed differing degrees of importance. And this largely depends upon how effectively these symbols can be interpreted and incorporated into the emerging central religious perception of reality in that tradition. We can think of the skulls and the *liṅga*, originally phallic, of Śiva. The skulls are still included, but now do not carry the same meaning-potency for many Śaivas; with the *liṅga* the case is very different, as for most Śaivas today, indeed for some centuries, the phallic connotation of the *liṅga* of Śiva has been virtually ignored (even denied categorically by some apologists, despite the obvious phallic shape of *some* liṅgas) and its significance as creative or generative power, or its aniconic representative power of the mystic presence of Śiva with the soul, will be brought out, and with outstanding success (Nandimath 1979: 68-74).

We note, then, that for successful transposition in the process of a religious tradition's history, its central symbol, to remain central, may need to be radically re-interpreted. If the central symbol itself is changed for some other symbol, we may presume that the tradition itself is either 'lost', or is incorporated into another tradition, by taking now a lower-order position in its symbolic and perceptual priorities. Thus, in medieval Christianity and in various phases of the development of Hinduism, a variety of primal symbol-systems have been incoporated by one means or another. In Hinduism, for example, numerous primal 'symbois' were introduced into the great Brahmanic tradition either as vehicles, or as consorts, or merely as secondary symbols, to the major deities of the incorporating tradition, or group of traditions. To what extent these primal symbols necessarily remain embedded deep in corporate human consciousness, or in the unconscious, erupting in times of stress, in dreams and suchlike, is another matter. Whether in fact no primal symbol is ever 'lost' or not, it does seem necessary to stress that it is not possible to conceive of these symbols as possessing some *wholly* objective reality (W.C. Smith 1981: 85-7); even in their most primal functioning in human life they have been meaning-communicators, and the perceptions of reality that people in primal and various other traditions have discovered from interaction with these symbols, i.e. their *interpretation* of symbols, is crucial to our understanding of and appropriation of any of these potent signs from our past. The symbol itself never stands bare and uninterpreted, even though, as with the Christian cross, this means reckoning with layer after layer of interpretation of its meaning for our life and our liberation. However unarticulated and unsophisticated the extent to which the symbol's perceived significance is drawn out, that significance, that is the symbol's meaning for the participating community at any given time, is intrinsic and essential to its existence as a 'symbol'. At the same time, in drawing out this significance, and in articulating patterns of meaning for our time, no conceptual scheme can totally 'rise above' its symbolic undergirding. Thus, there remains a continuing interaction between the given symbols of our heritage, that 'matrix' of hidden worlds of meaning, and the changes of a dynamic historical process in which the interpreter himself is a potent contributor.

10. A further aspect of the cultural forms of religious life, and closely related to religion's symbolic character, is the *aesthetic* — its various forms of art, poetry, music, gesture, drama, dance, etc. — much of which is often ignored in accounts of religious traditions (Whaling 1985: 271). Even this reference will be inappropriately brief. Some may regard this aspect of religion as peripheral embellishment, merely a way of pleasant ornamentation that may even serve to distract the eye or ear from what is more seriously central to essential religious life. This is no doubt one reason for some puritan traditions' rejection of an aesthetic form of communicating religion; aesthetics is seen as frivolous. And there is a more theologically solemn reason, in Judaism and Islam especially: the beyondness of the One, the Creator of all, can be conveyed through finite artistic form only at the dreadful risk of blasphemy by trying to compare the Incomparable to some finite creature. In Islam this is the unforgiveable sin of *shirk*. At the opposite end of this transcendental spectrum, we find that the fully realised soul in the non-dualist form of Hinduism, having earlier been spiritually elevated by contemplation of a variety of aesthetic and symbolic forms, once the transcendent state is attained is no longer thought to need any further crutches of this kind. It is interesting to note, however, that in the history of Islam it was through the Sufi mystics that at least certain aesthetic forms (music, certain types of poetry) were most developed.

This aesthetic dimension of religious culture serves to remind us that we should not take our concern for 'meaning' and 'significance' in any crudely cerebral way, but they should remain as *intrinsic* to the form of expression as possible. For aesthetic forms of expression, in religion as elsewhere, do not necessarily carry some 'meaning' that is not implicit in the form itself; it may be an expression of sheer creativity, or of joy in the beautiful, experienced as intrinsic to the essential reality of things. For is not the Creator an eternal dancer, the Hindu may ask, for example? Or is not his nature and his eternal form one of essential beauty? Do we not share the eternal bliss of the Ultimate by experiencing the joy of any kind of aesthetic life? In other words, not all artists will be greatly concerned about expressing meaning *beyond* whatever form they work in.

For others this will clearly not be the case. The *mudras*, or gestures, used in Indian dance, with its essentially religious grounding, are each meant to signify some aspect of life seen as lived in relationship with God. Then other aesthetic forms of expression in religion will be more spontaneously enacted, being seen as the fitting way to express some deeply felt religious experience; yet in this very process of artistic expression they point to a faith-experience that is meaningful beyond the aesthetic form itself. Much religious poetry is of this kind, as too is religious art generally. The ecstatic poets of South India some fourteen hundred years ago, poured out their sense of wonder, joy, despair, shame, and a vast range of other inner experience (Ramanujan 1973). Yet their poetry is not merely emotionally and aesthetically expressive; they also point to the Lord, and to the world of meaning patterned around this sacred Focus, as the One because of whom their emotional life is 'significant'. And presumably neither the sacred Lord nor the sacred experience related to him could be adequately expressed in mere prose; the passion, the mystery, the depth of meaning in it all called for poetic form (cf. pp. 49ff. below).

11. Thus, the *central role of some sacred object*, or *sacred Focus*, in every religious tradition needs to be recognized. If there is any central and integrating point to the immense and complex range of phenomena found in any one tradition, or certainly in many of them, it is this central sacred Object to which the tradition's adherents seek to relate. To be a participant in the tradition is, in the end, to be a participant in this sacred Focus. We have to say 'in the end', because it is undoubtedly true that in any tradition there are many who see such participation as a rather distant, though maybe ultimately necessary, goal. Their preoccupations may, for the time, be with what the tradition evaluates as lesser and more proximate goals of life – eventually to lead to the ultimately desirable goal. This, no doubt, implies a kind of perceptual elitism within each tradition, as indeed most traditions themselves also assume. It is assumed that there will be various levels of participation and experience, though the degree of reality, legitimacy or religious significance attached to 'lower' levels of experience will vary from tradition to tradition. 'Bhakti', for example, as a category of experience (literally meaning 'sharing in', thus 'devotion to', then 'trust, love, etc.') makes room for a remarkably wide range of devotional levels, from sheer trust in someone to help in giving some desired blessing, to love solely for the sake of the beloved. 'Faith', in Christianity and other religions, or 'Islam', in the sense of 'submission' or 'resignation to', can also carry varied levels of religious experience, all of which can be accepted within the concerned tradition as quite authentic, even if not fully mature. This still leaves room for each of these religions to presume a kind of charismatic elitism, even though the elitism of a special priestly or other birth-determined functionary with special powers, would be denied. In many traditions, however, the degree of visionary maturity will be closely related to progress in the tradition's regular spiritual discipline; others may well stress the unearned gift of divine

grace as the cause of the saint's special insight, powers, etc. In any case, religious traditions typically assume that some participants are more authentically related to the sacred Focus of the tradition's life than are others.

This sacred Focus is in one sense the 'objective' aspect of the experiential dimension described above. In describing any religion, then, to be descriptively objective, it is not enough to refer to rituals and social ordering, to analyse myths and doctrines, or even mystical states, without giving appropriate prominence to that sacred Object towards which often participants perceive all these other things to be oriented.

In many traditions we may find not just one identifiable Focus, but a cluster of sacred foci, probably integrally interlinked. In any case no single form of sacred Object emerges as common to all traditions, though it is possible to identify a number of general types, thus forming a typology of the Sacred. While 'patterns' of the sacred have been found by a number of scholars – Tiele, Van der Leeuw, Eliade, etc.) it is doubtful if any fully satisfactory morphology has yet been proposed. What we shall attempt in the next chapter is neither to identify a single essential type of sacred Focus, nor to list a number of types, but suggest a number of basic common characteristics of the ways in which participants in a wide range of religious traditions have perceived and shared in the life of their sacred Focus. In what ways have they experienced this as an integrating focus to life, as a visionary centre to their religion and to their perception of the universe?

2

The Visionary Centre of Religious Life

Though it has been argued in the previous chapter that the various dimensions of religion all share an organic interdependence of structure, is it not necessary, in order to account for the strange fecundity of religious life, to find some creative source that might be regarded as more 'primal' than other dimensions, by which they are nurtured and on which they are ultimately dependent? Perhaps not, in that every dimension of religion is to some extent dependent upon all other dimensions. Yet, I have already referred to the ritual/mythic imagery in which religious traditions are grounded, and in which our doctrinal and ethical articulation is deeply embedded, as such a 'primal matrix of meaning'. Without some more integrating centre, some more inclusively creative focal point, however, can we think of the phenomena found in myth/ ritual/symbolism as in themselves providing this primal role?

The search for the primal dimension in religion, especially in the sense of a chronologically prior element in religion, though mostly fruitless in the past, has not been abandoned altogether (La Barre 1972). The search has been for that in religious life about which we can say, 'this was in the beginning', 'this is the primal source of it all'. Thus, theories about the essential character of religion, at least in the half-century subsequent to the emergence of Darwin's evolutionary principles, usually reflect ideas about its origin (Waardenburg 1973; Sharpe 1975). If we can say how religion originated, it was thought, we can then plot the course of religion's history from this seminal beginning; knowledge of origins, indeed, not only ensure knowledge of essence, but a reliable method of study too. An early such theory of origins, as we saw, was Max Müller's 'disease of language' idea. 'In the beginning', he said in effect, was the inner sense of the Infinite evoked in the experience of natural phenomena, nature-powers that in diverse ways conveyed infinitude to humans. But in the mythical personifying of these separate powers, by which mere *nomina* were changed to *numina*, the 'disease of language' crept in.

Understandably few other scholars found this source-key to be the one that fitted the door to the religious world they were intent on exploring. Thus, others looked to the animistic principle (Tylor), or the discovery of *mana-power* (Marett), or the sense of *taboo*, or totemic sacrifice (Durkheim), or the belief in spirits and the veneration of ancestors (Spencer), or the failure of magical practice (Frazer), or the innate myth-making structure of the primal mind (Levy-Bruhl), or some specific, deep-rooted psychological need (Radin), or internal family relationships, or even the high gods (Schmidt). The history of these varied theories, and the search for some primal principle to simplify the later complex developments of religious traditions, and identify an under-lying pattern, or series of patterns, has been sufficiently recounted elsewhere (esp. Waardenburg 1973). Perhaps most enduring have been those theories (eg. Durkheim, Mauss) which have asserted: 'In the beginning was socialised humanity – religious perceptions are determined by the structures and needs of social existence'.

Whatever truth there may be in some of these diverse accounts of the essential structures of religion, are we not in the end thrown back to the irreducibility of the fact that the human being is *homo religiosus*, that there is a primal and inexplicable fact that humans have experienced their universe and their own life within it in a religious way? 'In the beginning', perhaps we may say, 'was the religious vision of life'. This is not quite the same as saying that there is an innate religious faculty, a 'sensus numinus', or that the primal mind is structured in a certain vision-seeing way. This locates sacredness rather too much in the psyche. It is rather that within religious traditions we find, typically, there is 'envisioned', in diverse ways, a sacred Focus that provides the integrating centre to all other dimensions of religious life. We may there-fore, assume this basic 'visionary' grounding for all religion. The key factor is this visionary character of being religious, the *what* of religiousness, not so much the *how*, though the visioning process *is* important, as well as the Object of religious vision. For this does draw us immediately into the complex con-comitant world of religious traditions, as well as the psychic states of partici-pants in such traditions. But people tell myths, sacrifice, relate to sacred totem life-forms, and so on and so on, because of this deep and ultimately inexplic-able compulsion to be religious; none of the ways of being religious in itself is the key to this religiousness.

Without attempting to reduce religious ways of perceiving to any *one* essential vision, as some have done, surely mistakenly, we can try to delineate this religious 'visioning' in a number of ways. Many would no doubt want to leave such visioning as part of the *ineffable* area of human experience. Indeed, do not many religious traditions refer to the core of their experience as 'inexpressible', 'indefinable', even 'unknowable'? And the *via negativa* in theological as well as mystical descriptions of God are well known in Christian and Muslim writings as well as in certain Hindu forms of theology. We can presume that such expressions do tell us something essential about the character of this central vision of religion, but we can also presume that such expressions are not meant literally in the sense that *nothing* can be said and *nothing* known. It is surely the more-than-ness of such visioning that is intended; it cannot all be told. In Indian traditions the theistic systems have usually taken this position.

I will attempt to draw out twelve features that seem invariably to typify religious visioning in its diverse contexts.

1. Beginning where the previous chapter left off, we find that in essential religious visioning there is typically an orientation to, or integration around, some *transcendent Focus*. A dimension of experience, and of the ground-structures of experience, is perceived that is more than, or that goes beyond, what is empirically observable. This is the sacred object of religious life, which though in various ways 'inseparably related to' (to use a Vaishnava expression), yet is distinct from mundane life. Without implying that there is no real cognitive content to religious perceptions, there is a sense in which religion is essentially a matter of 'experiencing-as' (Hick 1973), that is, experiencing the same world as the non-believer, but perceiving it in this extra-ordinary way, finding this trans-empirical dimension within it and beyond it. We refer to this transcendent Focus of religious visioning as a sacred *Object* in the sense that all religious activity, ultimately, is oriented to this focal point, whether seen as personal or impersonal. Thus it is the *goal* of all religious activity, no doubt seen by the participant as the end-referent of all existence, even of all words in our human discourse.

In the Indian religious tradition generally, great emphasis is given to 'vision', often meaning 'direct experience' or 'immediate perception'. And 'vision' is the term normally used of one's ontological commitment; so we speak of Śaṅkara-*darśana* Rāmānuja-*darśana*, etc. The former, pioneer spokesman in the early 9th century for a 'vision' having very great impact on Indian religious attitudes, saw as the focal point of true religious experience a transcendence of pure Consciousness (Lott 1980: 30-1, 39-46); the truly transcendent is that which is experienced in the sheer freedom of unrelated selfhood, free from any limiting interaction with finite objects, the identity of the pure Subject. In view of the differentiated experience of the empirical world in which the individual self exists, this vision of transcendence also posits two dialectically poised levels of existence, the everyday world of empirical life, and the realm of absolute reality. Relational existence, then, in this monistic transcendentalism is inevitably a distorted world of unreality in comparison with the level of experience of the transcendent subject that is at the centre for this non-dualist vision. Indeed, Śaṅkara asserts at the outset of his most important work (Brahma-Sūtra Commentary) that to confuse subjective with objective existence is to confuse light with darkness.

Śaṅkara's 'highest Self', the ultimate Brahman, the 'Great One', is essentially impersonal Consciousness, beyond all qualification and all distinct attributes in its ultimate being. It is amazing that within the same general tradition, *Vedānta* (the most highly sophisticated of the theologies grounded in the Hindu religious traditions) there are perceptions of the one Transcendent that are so strikingly different. Rāmānuja, in the 11th century, was equally concerned for the transcendence of the supreme Self and for that great Being's distinct otherness (*paratva*). For Rāmānuja, however, essential to such sacred transcendence are the 'countless glorious attributes', eminently personal in character, that are ascribed to the supreme Being by his theistic tradition (Lott 1980: 32-4, 46-56, 130-41). Equally striking is his insistence, in direct contrast to his fellow-Vedantin, Śaṅkara, that authentic knowledge or experience of that supreme Self, and authentic existence in the world, just like the character of the supreme Being, is essentially *relational*. Thus, for this theistic Vedantin the divine 'accessibility', divine love, is of equal significance in visioning the sacred Focus, if we are to understand the true nature of its transcendence (Carman 1974: esp. 77-87). Even the 'immediacy' of the vision of the Transcendent is mediated through the loving devotion of his subjects. A fellow-theistic Vedantin, Madhva (13th century), also grounded in much of the same Vaishṇava religious tradition as Rāmānuja, saw the *self-determining sovereignty* of God as the mark of his true transcendence, and as the only valid criterion for interpreting the sources (Lott 1979: 27; 1980: 34-7, 56-65). In this and in other ways the theologians of Vedānta, some grounded in very similar ritual/ mythic/scriptural traditions, others having variant resources, provide diverse ways of looking at the sacred Focus of their traditions. Yet all have a common concern to do justice both to the supreme Being's otherness, and to his experienced relatedness in a way that will enhance the richness of the transcendent dimension. For Śaṅkara, of course, relatedness was lower-order experience; the transcendence of pure Consciousness, pure Being, pure Subjectness was primary.

The criterion of divine sovereignty in the interpretive style of the so-called 'dualist' Madhva, reminds us in some ways of other monotheistic visions of the sacred One. In Islam, along with the decisive vision of Allah's transcendent oneness, with his majestic sovereignty of character, there is his transcendent *will* by which all things are as they are, and to which all creatures are to submit (*'islam'*) if they are to know their summum bonum. Interestingly the Hindu theologian Madhva too, in depicting the divine character lays great stress on his 'fulness of qualities', in type akin to the ninety-nine beautiful attributes of Allah, and also finds decisive the all-determining *will* of this supreme Lord as that which makes the decisive ontological difference between the Lord and all else. He is the 'all-determiner' (*sarva-svatantra*); all other beings, thus the whole universe, are 'other-determined' (*paratantra*) i.e. controlled and directed by his all-powerful will. There is a striking convergence of theistic type here, which has parallels in other traditions too, such as Judaism and Christianity. But then, we can also find convergence of type, in the Judeo-Christian-Muslim understanding of the nature of the transcendence of the central sacred Focus, with the other two Vedantic visions described above.

There are, however, types of sacred Focus that seem very different from the theistic and trans-theistic types so far taken as illustrative of the transcendent dimension in religious visioning. We shall therefore refer briefly to the transcendence of the state of Nirvāṇa in Buddhism, the state of Kaivalya isolation in Yoga, Jaina's goal of purified tranquillity of the soul, and the tribal vision of powerful Spirits and sacred Ancestors. Can the great goal of life envisioned by the Buddha be described at all as 'transcendent' or as concerned with 'religion' (Ling 1979)? Is it essentially no more than a heightened awareness of dimensions of human consciousness that have no reference beyond this world, though a world that is radically revisioned in the experience of Nirvāṇa? We return to this question in the next chapter; here we briefly note the following point.

In that virtually every religious tradition *can* be re-interpreted similarly, thus eliminating trans-empirical reference, a general comment seems called for. Because any religious vision is one which perceives the same world as that of the non-religious viewpoint, but sees it in a distinctively religious way (e.g. as against the atheistic way, the theist sees a God-structured world, or a world seen as essentially based on and related to a Being who is yet beyond the world), it does not mean that the religious way of seeing can be interpreted in categories which are basically the same as a secular, non-transcendental perspective; i.e. that it is merely a matter of different disposition, with the 'transcendent' language merely being a heightened account of similar realities. Because it is 'this world' that is the raw material for religious ways of seeing, it does not mean that such a vision does not take us beyond 'this world'. Even on the premiss, then, that Nirvāṇa is a way of experiencing life within the limits of the empirical world — and so much in the tradition suggests a breaking of these limits — the attempt to provide a 'secular', 'non-religious' interpretation of Nirvāṇa seems mistaken (Ling 1979: 3-88). A tradition such as Theravāda Buddhism may not use the imagery of another 'world' so often as do other traditions. Yet there are frequent indications of a realm of being that is not limited to, that is beyond, the finite or ordinary and all that empirically is found, according to the Buddha, to be characteristic of such a plane of existence.

So, then, the Nirvāṇa for which the Buddhist longs and to which life is directed is first and foremost beyond all *duh-kha*, literally meaning the 'dis-stress' or 'dis-ease' of an ill-fitting axle in its wheel hub, but usually translated 'suffering'. And *duhkha* is said to be a ubiquitous characteristic of life in this world. Life is thus at every point 'distressed' because it is prompted by *desire* and linked with that *dependent* mode of being typical of karma-determined life. The Nirvanic level of experience, then, is blissfully beyond desire, dependence and all those egoistic passions that both cause and are symptomatic of our pervasive distress. Nirvāṇa is manifestly 'transcendent' in its range, leading beyond the limitations of what is normally to be expected of life in this world.

To give some more clear flavour of the way the Theravāda Buddhist perceives Nirvāṇa, a quotation from the 'questions of King Menander' will suffice (De Bary 1972: 32):

Whoever wishes to be free from age and death . . . set free from passion, hatred, dullness, from pride and from false views, he crosses the ocean of rebirth, dams the torrent of his cravings, is washed clean of the three-fold stain, and destroys all evil within him. So he enters the glorious city of Nirvana, stainless and undefiled, pure and white, unaging, deathless, serene and calm and happy, and his mind is emancipated as a perfected being.

We should not, of course take too literally phrases like 'entering the glorious city of Nirvāṇa', though this is quite a striking example of the way a vision of transcendence is so naturally, in religious language, expressed in terms of known space/time experience. But this passage does raise another question for us. Having identified Nirvāṇa as the transcendent Focus in Theravāda Buddhist experience, we now have to admit that the picture at the centre of Buddhist vision may not be quite so simple. For at every point in the pursuit of this transcendent goal which clearly *is* central, Nirvāṇa is closely and inextricably linked with the *way* by which this transcendent level of existence is attained, i.e. the *Dhamma* (in Sanskrit *dharma*) of the Buddha's teaching of ethical purity and compassion, and the meditative discipline in which this culminates. And this way of *dhamma* is, in turn, closely linked with the source of such a 'noble way', the Buddha's own person. We might even add here the community of followers of the way, i.e. the *sangha* of sacred *bhikkus*, for the early three-jewelled 'creed' of the Buddhist movement was: 'I go for refuge (i.e. as my life-hope) to the Buddha; I go for refuge to the Dhamma; I go for refuge to the Sangha'. The 'sacred Focus' here, then, is not an uncomplicated single point of transcendence. Yet it can be reiterated that it is the Nirvanic goal which is the most significant focal point, and that while the other elements linked so closely with the Buddhist vision are essential as assistants on the way to Nirvāṇa, and thus also carry trans-empirical features, in themselves they are not the ultimate End, not *the* transcendent Focus.

Perhaps a further word is needed about the *Buddha's* role here. It would seem that gradually in very early Buddhism the tranquil image of the one who had opened the way to Nirvāṇa, no doubt his memory reinforced by a variety of mythic imagery, became a potent focal point for Buddhist meditation. At first presumably the Enlightened One was not taken by his followers as a living personal presence, but more as a life-paradigm, a guiding point for the ethical endeavour and meditational attainment so important in the way the Buddha had taught. Did not the 'last instructions' he gave make it clear that the life of the Buddhist community did *not* depend upon his presence; 'You must be your own lamps, be your own refuges, taking refuge in nothing but yourselves' (De Bary 1972: 29). Yet certainly at some point, early or late, we see the Buddha's own potent presence, his person, as the embodiment of the Way and the exalted end of Buddhahood to which all his followers, indeed in some sense all creatures, aspire. In this 'new' vision of the Buddha he is seen as triple-bodied, as encompassing a cosmic Body of Essence (*dharma-kāya*), a heavenly Body of Bliss (*sambhoga-kāya*), and a recurrently earth-descending Body of Transformation (*nirmāṇa-kāya*) (*Ibid.*: 94-5). And so it is now the Buddha himself who fills the vision with its transcendence of cosmic proportions, and what we earlier called a non-theistic type is in its new conceptual range more akin to a theistic visionary type.

While we cannot discuss the transcendent foci of other traditions in such detail, we can at least note a few general features of the Jaina (Jaini 1979) and Yoga traditions and see how they converge with the Buddhist vision. The goal in these two traditions is the 'isolation' (*kaivalya*) of the soul in its essential purity, tranquillity, consciousness, bliss, infinitude and freedom. Indeed the purification of this transcendent inner life, its release from all karmic and finite fetters, and thus its emergence into a state of omniscient, blissful tranquillity, is what is aimed for in a discipline either of rigorous ethical and ascetic practice, or of yogic meditation and posturing (or rather an integration of ethical, ascetic, yogic and meditational discipline with different emphases). Thus, while differences in the ways these traditions structure their life-disciplines are important, it is probably the affinity that is more significant; ethical purity (with such concerns as chastity, compassion for all creatures, total truthfulness of life, detachment from possession, etc. being prominent), and contemplation of some transcendent focal goal, with the two in various ways integrally linked.

For the Theravāda Buddhist, however, there is no eternal soul whose essential attributes are the basis of this contemplation, as is the case in Jainism and Yoga. One object of Buddhist meditation is indeed the very opposite: the fleeting and insubstantial character of all things is to be reflected on. Again, though, for all three traditions, integral to the vision of the transcendent state to be realised is the focal 'image' (esp. Jaini 1979: 191-202), the paradigmatic persons of the Buddha, the Jina (or Jinas, i.e. those who have 'overcome', which is the root meaning of 'Jaina'), and the 'Lord', the latter seen in Yoga as the ideal liberated and perfected Soul, rather as a *Primus inter pares* who can help other souls on their way to liberation and perfection. This is a transcendent Focus that seems to stand mid-way between typical theism and a contemplative type.

When we turn to at least some aspects of primal religious experience and the types of sacred foci they manifest, we find both continuity and discontinuity with what we have outlined above. For example, though the goals of tribal religious life may be very different from those we have identified above, and there may not be the single transcendent Focus that we saw in some of these 'great' traditions, that there are analogous transcendent Foci at least in some 'little' traditions is undeniable; powerful Spirits, heroic Ancestors who still strengthen and guide the life of the community, and numerous focal points of life-potency without which the mundane affairs of the community cannot function. Generally, then, we have here clusters of sacred Foci together serving to provide cohesion to the primal vision. But what is significant is that we also have the same type of enabling sacred persons, or it may be in some cases disabling sacred persons, such as an angered female 'Power' or 'Spirit' of rural tribal religious vision in South India. In that these Powers are often associated with various powers of the natural world — trees, streams, the ground, and so on, we find also a generally *diffused* sense of the sacred, as indeed in almost all forms of Hinduism too. And it is often when there are human acts of vigorous interference with nature, such as building a dam, constructing a house, digging a well, that the Power of that place needs to be pacified. In orthodox Hinduism, forgiveness is asked of the Earth even for treading on her. There are, of course, a number of other ways in which these focal points of transcendent Power in primal traditions function in relation to human life. As we noted, that they are also *enablers* to human endeavour is also evident, in some ways akin to the enabling function of the Jinas, the Buddha and the 'Lord' of the yogic path. That other sacred Foci, with equally transcendent dimensions, are not of this 'personal' type, and that in many traditions it is just this impersonal focal point that is the ultimate goal to which all is in the end oriented, is also very clear.

2. Secondly, when we speak of religious 'visioning', we need to give equal weight to *both its 'subjective' and its 'objective' aspects*, as has been implied in numerous ways in the discussion above. The term 'vision' is intended to express this, as it were, bi-focal character, that is the fact or process of visioning and the transcendent Object of vision.

If we might refer again to the Śaṅkara vision of unrelated subjectivity as the model of transcendence, we should recognize that even in this type of sacred Focus there is also a necessary sense of this reality as *Object*. Certainly it will be characteristic of the experience of the sacred Focus in the pre-enlightenment stage, and during the process in which the seeker has still not reached the point of identity-realisation. At this point the Transcendent confronts the seeker in its distinctiveness, its otherness. Brahman, says the non-dualist, is 'an approachable, obtainable, cognisable entity' (e.g. *pratipanna-vastu*, Śaṅkara's Brahma-Sūtra Bhāṣya I. 1.1), and to this Being a rich range of glorious qualities can be attributed (Lott 1980: 121-9). Later, of course, it becomes necessary to assert that these are not really distinct attributes of the One, though they remain essentially definitive. (Thus Brahman *is* knowledge, infinite, bliss, etc. and does not *possess* such qualities as though they were distinct from his essence). Throughout, too, the non-dualist exponent has to be true to the religious resources and scriptures that provide the grounding for his interpretation of the Transcendent, or should do so ostensibly. To do this, a kind of bridging dialectic is required, with two modes of approach moving between the distinctiveness and the unrelatedness, between the sense of Brahman as sacred Object and as ineffable Subject and so on.

There is little doubt that many believers in traditions widely disparate from Śaṅkara's non-dualism would also feel that it is more fitting to their experience of the sacred Focus to speak of it as the sacred *Subject* rather than *Object* (e.g. Brown 1955: 140-66). In delineating our primal religious 'vision', however, it seems inevitable, and indeed appropriate, to refer equally to the subjective *and* objective aspects involved, for both are integral to such visionary experience in religion. And in two senses from the point of view of the 'visionary', the Focus is that to which the whole of life and effort is to be oriented, i.e. it becomes a life-goal to be attained, that to which we move. Thus it is the *Object*. It is also the ground of all we do, that which shapes and compels, which draws the visionary on, which is somehow seen as the foundation of all life. Thus it is the *Subject* too. Moreover, the Object experienced is as essential to the vision as the experience of visioning such an Object. Human subjectivity is no doubt crucial here, but we distort its inner nature if we attempt to reduce the religious vision, experienced in community participation, to the wholly subjective, or to anything other than a complex *interaction* of subjective consciousness in relation to objects of experience; i.e. both the process of visionary perception and the sacred Object of religious perceiving comprise the 'vision'.

The question of the truth-status or ontological reality of the 'Object' is a different matter (Wiebe 1981); at least its objectivity within the visionary experience of religious people must be assumed. There is, religiously speaking, an experience, a perception, a consciousness, and there is a transcendent Object, the focal point of this subjectivity, which is experienced, perceived and of which the religious visionary is conscious. Naturally this subject/object issue is of considerable importance both in the process of 'objectively' studying religious traditions, and in the process of 'objectifying' the vision in the reflection and conceptual articulation of the 'theologian'. It is interesting that while Rudolf Otto's 'Holy One' in its numinosity certainly expresses great concern on Otto's part for the 'sacred Object' in his delineation of what is essential to religious experience, we are left at the end wondering if his greater concern was not for the *'sensus numinus'*, that is for what he saw as that inbuilt religious faculty in the human psyche, a tendency that has re-appeared in the work of a number of phenomenologists. Concern for 'what appears to the religious mind' can become concern only for the religious mind's subjectivity as a psychological phenomenon, and the subject/object dialectic is lost.

If we further analyse the character of the sacred Focus and its visioning, we find that in many traditions, though in greatly varied forms, there are also microcosmic/macrocosmic dimensions which further complicate the subject/ object issue. This may often result in an essentially triangular structure in which transcendent Object, inner self and outer universe are held together in a vision involving a continuity of their being. Such a triadic perception is common to a wide range of traditions – the 'three-body' vision of Buddhism, the three-*liṅga* forms in the Hero-Śaiva sect, the God-man-world structure of much theism, and especially the 'three ultimate entities' (supreme Lord, sentient beings, insentient matter) of Vaishṇava and Śaiva theism. Some perceive a more simple *dualism*, as sometimes in radical monotheism, as in Zarathustrianism, in the Sāṃkhya system, and in Jainism, though the last two also imply an essential triadism of karmic matter, bound souls and the liberated experience.

Whether central religious perception is in terms of an essential dualism or triadism, their inter-relationship will be differently understood. In other words the vision includes a distinct perception of each part making up the whole, with the transcendent Object determining the perception of the other inter-related entities, whether souls and world or whatever.

3. Thirdly, while religious focal perceptions are experienced as being in con-junction with all manner of empirical objects and situations, there is always *a sense of perceptual immediacy*: the transcendent Object is not seen as ultimately *dependent* upon accompanying empirical factors, even when these contingent features are so much part of the vision that the visionary speaks of a 'mediated immediacy' of knowing (Baillie 1939: 178-96). On reflection the theistic believer, for example, may say 'I believe in God because there is a purpose to be seen in the creative process', or 'because God's saints (or his acts of salvation) are great.' In the initial moment of faith, however, there is an unconditioned 'I believe', 'I know', 'I love', 'I worship'. This does not necessarily preclude doubt at the same time: 'I believe; help my unbelief' (Mark 9.24).

In other words, religious visioning is not based on an inferential process. Perhaps it was for this reason that the Vedantic theologians – with their usually very close links with Hindu religious tradition – so adamantly rejected inference as a means of authentic or reliable knowledge of God; whereas the Hindu Logicians, with a somewhat weaker connection with cultic religious life, gave inferential proof a very prominent role in their system of God-knowledge (Lott 1976: 128-37).

In iconic traditions in which image-devotion is central to the ritual, there will be a close but dialectically subtle relationship between seeing the divine image and inner visionary perception. We shall explore this more fully in Chapter seven, where it will be seen that the cosmic vision of the image-oriented Vaishnavite, in its conceptual outworking, shows an intrinsic correspondence with the image-devotion so central to Vaishṇava ritual. This is an instructive illustration of how religious imagery generally provides the creative grounding for the patterns of meaning seen in cosmic life and for ways of articulating these patterns. The point being made here, though, is somewhat different. Even though a Vaishṇava theologian (say, Piḷḷai Lokācārya of the 'Southern' school) might state that God in his image-form, has made himself vulnerable to the vicissitudes of life in the world, and has become dependent upon the devout care of the faithful (cf. p. 95 below), he would not want to say that our God-vision is in reality derived from and dependent upon the mediation of the image. For one thing the point he is really making is that God is unbelievably gracious. And his basic position (and that of the 'southern', Vaishṇava sect generally, called followers of the 'cat-method' of divine sovereign grace) is that the saving work of God is according to his sovereign will; it is not to be controlled or mediated by ritual practice. Thus the vision of God too is unmediated and direct, the result of his free grace. Perceptual immediacy, then, is presupposed and asserted even when such great importance is given to the process of mediation, and when the potency of the mediating image-tradition is so apparent.

By contrast and taking a somewhat different logical tack, we might look briefly at the Sikh tradition. It is of historical interest that one of the major streams (with the Muslim Sufis, a Yoga sect and the theistic Sant movement generally) flowing into this vehemently anti-iconic 16th century Sikh movement was a Vaishṇava cult, more precisely a Rama-cult that itself was strikingly restrained in ethical attitudes and in ritual practice (McLeod 1968). We can do no better than begin where the Sikh scripture begins, with the Japjī's opening words, the keystone of Sikh worship and faith (Singh, Fraser 1960: 28):

There is one God,
Eternal Truth is iiis Name;
Maker of all things . . . Timeless is his image;
Not begotten, being of his own Being;
By the grace of the Guru, made known to men.
It is not through thought that He is to be comprehended,
Though we strive to grasp Him . . .
How then shall we know the Truth?
How shall we rend the veils of untruth away?

Abide by His Will, and make thine own
His will . . . written in thy heart.

A few verses later (35) comes a section of verses exulting in the divine Name which is always to be at the centre of devotion:

Of him who truly believes in the Name,
Words cannot express the condition; he himself will later repent
Should he ever try to describe it . . .
Such is the power of his stainless Name,
He who really believes it, knows it.

This last couplet is repeated 7 times as a refrain, following such lines (35-6) as:

Through belief in the Name
The mind soars high into enlightenment.
The whole universe stands self-revealed . . .
The spirit of those imbued with faith
Is wedded to realisation of Truth.

Basic themes, then, are the oneness of God, the form-less (the *Nirankār*), his incomparable greatness, his utter independence, the impossibility of describing this God; yet he makes his will known and this is to become the basis of the believer's life. Moreover, it is only through meditating on his Name (that which by his grace he has revealed of himself) that there can be inner certitude, i.e. the knowledge of 'inner faith'. Mediation of the divine presence through images is ruled out. Yet this incomparable God does mediate his will, his presence, his power and the inner vision of his true being through his self-manifest Name.

Ultimately, then, the divine vision is immediate in character; in this tradition as in a number of other theistic traditions, such immediacy is expressed in the faith that only God can reveal his own inner being to the soul. Or as a later verse puts it: 'Out of the unmanifest, unmovable ground of his Being, to us and in us, he made himself manifest' (105); or again (130):

O mine eyes, it was the Lord who gave you light; look on none but him . . .
When by the grace of the Guru
I was granted understanding, I saw there is .... none beside God.
These eyes of mine were blind,
But when I met the true Guru,
They were graced with divine light.

4. Thus, fourthly, as a corollary to the immediacy of religious perception is the way in which such experience is seen as *self-authenticating*, for its validity *will not be considered dependent upon some other source of knowledge more*

reliable than the certitude derived from the vision itself. However irritating such a claim may appear to some philosophers of religion, and however much even theologians may search for other validating means to religious knowledge, the believer in the end bases life upon the certitude of faith, or the self-authenticating force with which religious vision presents itself. Admittedly, revelationists, theists mostly, will often argue that their vision is a reliable reality because it is so declared in scripture and scripture must be reliable because it is inspired by the supreme Being. Use of such a circular argument has been ridiculed in the Indian traditions both by non-theists and by those who feel their vision does not require any confirmatory buttress.

The being of God, the ultimacy of the Ritual, the desirability of Nirvāṇa — these are to their adherents in themselves quite independent of subordinate authorities, however useful such confirmatory evidences may be in their lower-order capacity. Theologians may sometimes have attempted, in an apologetic role, to base the validity of their tradition's faith on its social and psychological benefits, or upon its rationality; but this will hardly be the basis of faith as the believer perceives it. I am not for a moment suggesting that the attempt to be coherent in articulating faith is theologically improper, as Chapter five below should make clear. Yet, in the end reasoned proofs of any kind will be inferential in form, and thus dependent upon some non-visionary factor. To the believer, therefore, such argumentation will not carry much weight; some will say it is as good as denying the vision's own validity. On this issue it is instructive to follow the course of Islamic theology (Watt 1962), as well as Indian theological history.

In Indian religions generally, as we noted earlier, *anubhava* or some synonym meaning 'experience', the sense of immediacy of perception, is given central import. Despite elaborate systematising of the formally accepted 'criteria of valid knowledge' (*pramāṇas*), such as testimony, observation, inference and analogy, in the end the Vedantic theologians fall back on the validating competence either of revelation or of inner experience. Admittedly, both could be said to be implicit in 'testimony' (i.e. the testimony of scripture), or 'observation' (i.e. as the immediacy of inner perception). Those expounding a strictly theistic position stressed the revelation of scripture; non-dualistic trans-theists stressed the ultimacy of direct inner perception (Murthy 1974). In fact these two positions may not be so far apart, because Vedic scripture is 'that which is heard' (*śruti*) and many interpreters see this as a reference to the inner hearing of primal seers, their immediate knowledge of reality; thus scripture is grounded in experience and is in turn to lead the seeker who truly 'listens' to its inner meaning and to experience of the same ultimate Reality. While all this has a certain scholastic, schematised ring in its style of expression, perhaps it does in essence typify an important aspect of what we have been referring to as religious visioning. It is a quality of inner perception that will almost certainly draw into its orbit a wide range of concomitant phenomena that may be seen as confirming the truth of, perhaps as cohering with the inner meaning of, the central perception. Thus the whole universe can be seen to tie in with the centre point, as the spokes of a wheel (the *dharma-cakra* of Indian imagery) tie in with and revolve around its hub, perhaps smoothly, perhaps at times wobbling uneasily with ontological anomalies. For many good reasons, reasons that might be seen as intrinsic to the inner vision itself (e.g. 'God is love' etc., or , 'Nirvāṇa is the only truly desirable goal of life') it can be argued, and will be argued later, that an authentic religious vision needs to show as coherently and inclusively as possible that it is valid for human life. In the end, however, people convinced of the reality of a religion will be thus convinced only because of the compulsion of an inner perception and its self-authenticating power. Vedantins and many other traditions in Hinduism, mystics of many faiths and evangelical Christians all seem to be agreed that some form of inner 'experience' is the ultimate 'reason' for faith. Even the Ritualist school (Dasgupta 1975: 367-403) with little concern for inner realisation of experience, posited the self-validating power (*svatah-prāmāṇya*) of Vedic revelation as the mark of its sacredness (i.e. that its authority is not given from any other source, not even by God) and to this the Vedantic theologians also agreed.

5. Fifthly, the experience of the transcendent object *evokes a sense of wonder*, though this may range from the awe-ful fascination of Otto's *Numinus* to the quiet contemplation of the wondrous bliss of Nirvāṇa for which the Buddhist strives; or there may be the tribal's ambivalent relationship — including fear, awe, fascination, dependence, affection, perhaps even resentment — with the spirits and powers of the tribal's environment and of the ancestral past; or the Jaina's strenuous engagement in the soul's purifying pilgrimage to the perfection of isolated omniscience; or there may be the theist who dwells, perhaps with erotic imagery, on the unaccountable love of the Lord. All involve experience of unaccountableness that evokes some sense of wonder.

Perhaps the Bhagavad Gītā's 'vision of the universe in the form of the Lord' illustrates the sense of visionary wonder most dramatically (Zaehner 1969). But the Gita also draws together strands of experience first described in the older Upanishads (as well as strands of Yogic and Buddhistic experience).

Thus in the Upanishads also the great Being is said to be 'wonderfully perceived, wonderfully spoken of, wonderfully heard' (Cf. Mukhopadhyaya 1960: 2-3). But it is in the *theistic* vision that this sense of wonder is most explicit and most forcefully expressed, particularly in describing the great and glorious attributes of God. There are Islam's ninety-nine glorious attributes of Allah, depicting varied distinct aspects of his character, all of which are expected to evoke awe in the believer. The Vaishṇava faith too repeats again and again the six special attributes of 'Bhagavān' (Carman 1974: 163), as well as a wealth of other 'gloriously auspicious qualities'. Each divine attribute stands out as wonderfully greater than analogous qualities in human life. Traditions with an inward-oriented vision will less often attempt such explicitly wonder-evoking descriptions. Present though the wonder may be, its tone is more subdued.

6. Sixthly, religious vision reveals that *reality by which all else is evaluated*, or a mode of existence which *determines the meaning of all existence*. As we noted in the previous chapter, Schleiermacher's attempt to define the essence of religion as the consciouness of being absolutely dependent does correspond to an important strand (i.e. the theistic) of religious experience, emphasising its subjective side. It unfortunately ignores those religions with just the opposite goal. For the Theravāda Buddhist, the Jaina, Sāṃkhya, the non-dualist Vedantin all see the experience of absolute *in*dependence as the essence of their tradition. A more accurate way of including this sense of a central Reality that determines the meaning of all other realities would be to say that in the light of the central vision, human life is revalued, is usually found wanting in its present condition, and is given an absolute point of reference for redirecting it. The result will normally be a critical evaluation of the way human and even cosmic life is now found. It is described as sinful, or fallen, or in bondage, or corrupt, or polluted, or deluded, or unenlightened, or weakened, or flawed, or simply in need of the transcendent power the vision reveals, or perhaps in need of re-orientation to that visionary object. In any case the vision usually provides also the means of setting right this wrong condition, as we see in the next two points.

Then there will frequently, though not always, be a similar variety of speculation in conceptualising the vision, often mythologically expressed, concerning the *cause* of this flawed condition of things, and inner tension in a religion's perception of reality can result from this. There is God and Satan in Judaism, Christianity and Islam, with attempts being made to resolve the ambiguity by greater emphasis either on the absolute sovereignty of God, or on the effect of misused human freewill. A similar difficulty sometimes arises in Indian systems which include God and the intractable law of *karma*. Either *karma* must be made subject to the divine will, or it becomes an independent cosmic power to which even God is subject, as the Buddha assumed was the case in theism and hence rejected it. Few religions are prepared to allow an eternal struggle between opposing realities as part of the essential faith, as the Zarathustrian texts do.

7. A seventh invariable feature of religious visioning is its *soteriological concern*. The social anthropologist, Melford Spiro, and others posit this concern for salvation as one of the definitive aspects of religion, along with some sense of transcendence and human limitation. Spiro (1968: 96) goes on to describe the transcendental aspect in terms of 'culturally postulated superhuman beings', though we have already seen that there are types of transcendence that posit 'superhuman beings' only as lower-order beings. The concern in religion for 'salvation' is, however, manifestly central, and this motif is clearly linked with the transcendence of the sacred Focus on the one hand and the felt limitation of the human condition on the other. To be convinced that the human condition can be set right from whatever fundamental predicament (sin, evil powers, lack of insight, profanity, pride, desire, etc.) it is felt to be flawed with, some state of being not itself subject to the same flawed condition would seem to be called for. Thus, for a soteriology to emerge, we might expect to find the assumption both of limitation and of transcendence over that limitation (i.e. appropriate to the way this limitation is perceived). And some such three-cornered structure is typical of religion, within which there is invariably a central soteriological concern.

We might look first at a tradition which superficially seems to give least weight to such a concern — Islam. In Islam the central vision is of the sovereign will of Allah to which all creatures are to submit themselves. The cosmic process is seen as already controlled by that all-powerful, all-wise divine will. Thus there is little of the passionate concern, say, for forgiveness of sins, or doubts about the status of one's soul, that we find in various periods of Christian history. Except for just a few Sufi expressions (Cragg 1976), there is little sense of the agonising separation from the Beloved that is found in some forms of *bhakti*-religion, in which inseparable union with the Beloved is the desired goal. There is little of the unrelenting search for transcendent insight into the mystery of that ultimate Reality by which liberation from all the limitations of finitude is assured. The human race, rather, is to understand that Allah in his great mercy, has revealed his beneficient will in all clarity, and there remains just one simple duty; to resign oneself to this will in all its concretely revealed forms. Believe the doctrines; fulfill the duties.

Yet, it is precisely in this emphatic call to faith and obedience as the only possible mode of 'Islam', of submission, that we see a pervasive soteriological assumption underlying this religious vision. It is not merely that the joys of paradise are held out as life's hope for those who faithfully obey, or the pains of hell for those who do not and who therefore fall from the ladder of crossing. Rather it is a fundamental recognition that 'Islam' is the crucial need of humanity; its condition is fatally flawed and its future bleak as long as the human race remains in the darkness of its non-Islamic state, i.e. as long as there is no conscious submission to the Quranic revelation with its clearly stated law of life. There are, of course, other kinds of more explicit soteriological concern in addition to this basic but more implicit Muslim stance. The festivals of Islam for example in several cases have a general soteriological intent. Thus Bakrid, the 'cow festival' has atoning intent, the 'festival of breaking (the fast)' will probably include prayer for remission of sins, increase of rains, abundance of crops, preservation from misfortune etc. Muharram, feast of the 'sacred', includes the Shiites' fervently expressed concern, especially in the corporate procession of self-mortification and mourning, to share in the salvific merits of the martyrdom of Ali and his sons.

The soteriological direction of Indian traditions generally is explicit and unambiguous; even sophisticated metaphysical systems are clearly, if not always explicitly, motivated by a concern for 'release' (*mukti, moksha*). The Vedantin sets out upon the metaphysically arduous path of *Brahma-jijñāsa* or 'Enquiry into ultimate Reality' (Brahma-Sūtra I.1.1), only if he is a *mumukshu*, one who is compelled by desire for transcendent liberation. The Buddha's soteriological path took a different direction: metaphysical questions seemed to have little interest, to the extent that modern interpreters even refer to the Buddha's 'pragmatic' approach to religious questions. Certainly he was not willing to waste time on what he saw as merely speculative matters with unnecessary notional complications, and was committed to propounding a way of salvation that could be seen to be effective in leading seekers to their desired peace and bliss. To describe the Buddha as a 'pragmatist' with *no* interest in the doctrinal aspects of the process, however, is undoubtedly to exaggerate his end-oriented approach. Doctrinal undergirding is inescapable at each stage in the Buddha's account of the soteriological process. Even so, speculation in general is subordinate to soteriological effectiveness.

The Buddha's image of the human condition was that of a man dying from a poisoned arrow (Rahula 1967: 14). It is irrelevant to ask 'from where', 'why', and so on, especially as in the meantime the danger to the poisoned man's life increases. The only appropriate response is to remove the arrow and apply an antidote to its poison. And so there will be the healing of the Nirvanic state the seeker hopes for. The Buddha's teaching is eminently salvific in its scope.

While there may be very different perceptions of the human condition, of what is to be done and what hoped for in the *primal* religious vision – in its diverse forms – or indeed in the literate traditions as more 'popularly' practised, a soteriological intent of some kind will typically be central. Most often this is seen as an intention to remove some perceived evil threatening human, and perhaps cosmic, existence. Indeed, if one had to select a single prayer to represent the most pervasive *popular* concern in all religious life, it could well be the petition from the 'Lord's Prayer', 'Deliver us from evil', however diversely either 'evil' or the desired deliverance from it may be understood. We have to stress that it is a 'popular' concern, for in the vision perceived as the most ultimate in many traditions, it will be assumed that the participant is to move beyond concern for salvation *from* any particular predicament and move on to delight in the summum bonum for its own sake. We see this, for example, in much 'mystical' reflection in the Christian tradition. In a number of Indian traditions too, concern for salvation from a particular life-problem is to be superseded by desire for ultimate release; then concern for release (from the bondage of karma, the cycle of rebirths and all attendant evils) loses its centrality, as delight in the final goal itself now becomes ultimately desirable. For the theist, in Indian and many other traditions, rather than praying to God for a particular blessing, or for help in the problems of life, or for the salvation of one's soul (even in the sense of ultimate release from bondage), the most desirable goal, as understood by key interpreters within these traditions, is rather loving God because of the divine glory, beauty, love – because God is God.

At the other extreme from such an altruistic vision of the summum bonum is another soteriological attitude pervading many of the religious traditions of India, and found analogously elsewhere; that is, the *Tāntrika* type (Bharati 1965; Bhattacharya 1982). The literal meaning of *tantra* ranges from 'loom', 'framework', 'type', 'contrivance', 'system', 'schema', etc. to its more religious sense of a potent means or technique of attaining one's religious goal, an approach that has frequently been described as 'magical'. Now this probably carries a value-judgement that is unwarranted in relation to many features of the *tāntrika* approach. For example, a central feature is the sacred circle (*maṇḍala*) or 'wheel' (*cakra*).

In *tāntrika* cultic practice this circular form is taken as the intrinsic symbol of the wholeness or perfection of reality, and accompanied by appropriate reflective exercises enables participation in that reality. Historically this circular symbol relates to sexual imagery, which does not necessarily entail antinomian sexual rituals, though in fact at various stages in *tāntrika*'s history, and especially in its 'left-handed' manifestations, esoteric sexual practices have been prominent as a means of goal-attainment. The 'left-handed' practitioners are those who see potency in the abnormal; what is the means of spiritual destruction for the general populace becomes the means of salvation for enlightened 'hero-souls'. Linked with this esoteric soteriology, even in the sexually restrained traditions, is the conviction that cultic Power lies in the female aspect of symbolised reality. Thus, for example, the consorts of the great Gods Śiva and Vishṇu, i.e. Śakti ('Power') and Śrī ('Auspiciousness'), are often seen as necessary to their 'lords' for their creative and saving activities. This is especially so at the mythic level of faith-expression; but even in 'classical' theological writings, where the independent sovereignty of these Gods is often stressed, the creative and boon-granting role of the female consorts is often explicit.

Even in the *Buddhist* movements in India, Nepal and Tibet, in spite of the great ethical stress in the Buddha's teachings, *tāntrika* ideas and practices made a powerful impact, especially as worked out in the third type of Buddhism, the *Vajrayāna*, or 'Thunderbolt Vehicle', whose name implies the direct and drastic potency of its technique (Tucci 1980). Historically the process may have been the other way around in the more northern areas. That is, the Buddha's way was perhaps incorporated into the *tantra*-grounded religious tradition already in practice. Either way, the Buddha's 'noble path' underwent great change, with a loss of its unambiguous emphasis on the path of ethical-meditation, and this loss may well have been an important factor in the decline of Buddhism in India, if only because it undermined the ordered *saṅgha*-life that was its basis.

In the *tāntrika* religious type, then, soteriology is central and is often linked with a view of the transcendent goal as a level of extraordinary independence and of the means of its attainment as a technique of extraordinary potency. Thus there is the tendency to see the soteriological path (rather than the sacred Focus) as all-important. However, very early in the development of India's religious traditions, the *tantra*-path raised questions concerning the soteriological process that were of continuing importance. Linked as was this *tantra-way* with *yoga* and with liberating insight of inner *jñāna*, it challenged the attitude of ritual-for-ritual's sake and compelled greater interiorisation and reflection, along with a creative perception of the microcosmic/macrocosmic dimensions of religious vision. Taken full circule, however, these very insights moved back to the magical attitude inherent in the bare ritualism they challenged earlier.

8. Religious vision then provides not only *the supreme goal for the believer*, but in many cases the *perceived means for attaining that goal also*. Sometimes the identity of these two is quite explicit, as in Vedānta and the Christian faith: Brahman and Christ/God are the summum bonum of life and the way by which this goal is attainable. Even when these two aspects of the religious life are distinguished, as in Jainism and Buddhism, goal and means have to manifest some kind of commensurability that seems credible to the believer, even if not to the non-believer. An instance of non-credibility might be the practice of 'left-handed' Tantra noted above, in which five taboo substances are taken as the means of liberation – meat, fish, sex, alcohol, and an esoteric use of rice.

We might also note that there are cosmological and eschatological, as well as soteriological, dimensions to the goals of many religious faiths. The realisation of cosmic, communal and personal goals often requires the operation of some creative and saving *power* transcendent to the believer's own being. This is an aspect of religion to which Gerardus Van der Leeuw (1938) especially has drawn attention. In many traditions goal-attainment results primarily from personal effort towards the stilling and subduing of all cosmic powers. We have seen that the Buddhist tradition illustrates both extremes here: the Elders' (Theravāda) way sees individual quietening endeavour as central, while the Thunderbolt way turns to the dramatically transforming power of Tantric techniques. In other Indian religions a more complex synthesis of these diverse methods is achieved, and in Chapter Four we look at how the Bhagavad Gītā works out such a synthesis.

9. Ninthly, religious vision also carries with it *a sense of ultimate obligation* for the believer. To experience the Object of the vision is to sense the inescapably binding character of that vision on the believer. There is a sense of need to enter into some new relationship with the Object, to attain that Object, or to be attuned to it. In relationship to a personal God, obviously the sense of obligation will be peculiarly intense, but it is also present even when the sacred

Object is quite impersonal. When the Upanishad declares that 'Brahman is to be known (or attained)', the non-dualist Vedantin who interprets this in an impersonal sense still feels the force of the implied imperative.

The sense of obligation may or may not be expressed in *ethical* terms, or by way of taboos, specific actions to be performed, a process of enlightenment to be entered upon, an initiation to be passed through, renunciatory practices to be embraced. There is such a wide range of ways in which the vision's binding character is accepted. In his 'moral imperative', Kant indicated that the most essential feature of religion was, for him, this ethical obligatory aspect; undoubtedly it has been central in various periods of the Jewish, Christian and Muslim faiths. Though it is true that a specified way of ethical life is characteristic of any religious tradition, it is this dimension that is most susceptible to change with changing cultural and political circumstances, even when the central vision might appear to remain constant. Thus the Christian's 'obligation' has been expressed in a striking variety of ways in different eras. The ethical implications of the Cross for example, will be seen very differently by Christian slaves (or slave-owners) at Corinth in the first century from the desert fathers of the second century; different again the interpretation of the later 'rules' of the Benedictines and Franciscans, or of Constantine (with his vision of the Cross in the sky by which he was to conquer the Roman world), or the Coptic ascetics with their literal cross-bearing discipline, or popular Latin Catholicism, or a 20th century liberation theologian – and so we could go on. This diversity of interpretation arising from a common symbol within a tradition does, of course, raise further questions. Not least is the question of whether there are not even contradictory *core*-perceptions emerging from and in some sense evoked by a common mythic/symbolic matrix undergirding an ongoing tradition. For example, are there not disparate perceptions of the Cross? Yes, there are, but the 'core-perception' surely, is that in some way yet to be articulated the Cross reveals the heart of ultimate reality, and thus is of ultimate value to, or lays an ultimate obligation on, the Christian.

10. Tenthly, religious visioning also has an *inclusive character*. This may be cosmically perceived, as in a vision of God who creates all, or who contains all within his being, or who is causally determining of all that exists and all that happens. In many cases there is a kind of epistemic inclusiveness, in which everything is perceived as in some sense tinged with the light of the Transcendent lying behind it. Some Buddhist accounts of the enlightenment of the Buddha, for example, portray the whole of creation as at least momentarily

transformed and expressing joy at the new hope of final release that had arisen in the world. Or the inclusiveness may be more existential, with the whole of one's existence dominated by the experience of this one real Existent, or this one ultimate Goal.

In this latter sense, then, a religious vision also has an *exclusive* character, in that it is the focal point to which all other existents must be referred for grasping their value and meaning. We might question, though, whether there are not some traditions which have formulated the *inclusiveness* of their vision in ways of such extreme paradox that introduces tension eventually making for unresolvable contradictions. Tension does not *always* prove creative, nor does it always comprise the 'dialectic' necessary to any transcendental vision. However, we take up this point again later. If there is intrinsic inclusiveness in the primal vision, surely this should not be lost in the systematising process.

11. A rather different form of visionary inclusiveness is its *participatory* character. The sociological emphasis on the social dimension of a religious perception clearly has to be taken very seriously. The forms in which the vision is expressed — whether ritual, doctrinal, ethical or communal — will inevitably be shaped by sociological factors. And even if we cannot accept that a religious perception is *created* by social structures and needs, certainly a religious *tradition* emerges from a shared community vision (cf. Shinn 1977). Thus a religion is grounded in a vision of transcendence that is capable of being shared by others. One of the few objective tests we can apply to ascertain a vision's authenticity as *religion* is to ask if it is shared by a community and if a continuing tradition has emerged. Faiths are corporately held and traditions are community experiences, whatever the impact of individuals in the process of creating and transmitting the tradition. In the practising of the same, at least the participants will *intend* to share the same focal experience. Whatever psychological disparities or differing levels of experience may be recognised between one believer and another, as all share in their tradition's symbols, rituals, festivals, myths and in other socially structured acts, there will be a sense of corporate participation. The central vision is both discovered and further created by sharing in the life of the community.

12. Finally, there is the *conceptual seminality* or the *hermeneutical impulse* of religious visioning. The core perceptions of religious communities are never wholly void of cognitive content, which in many traditions is experienced in a rich diversity of conceptual forms that undergo varying degrees of modifica-

tion as the process of interpretation continues. The extent of conceptual changes depends largely upon the degree of change found in the social/cultural context; but these are issues we will need to discuss at some length in some of the following chapters.

3

The Theological Process in Religious Traditions

In this chapter the attempt will be made to identify certain common features in the ways in which religious traditions, especially literate traditions, articulate the meaning-patterns perceived in their traditions. No doubt it is also necessary to distinguish varieties of types of such theologising; but this does not preclude significant typical modes in the functioning of the theological process in religion generally.

1. Probably the most basic and invariable characteristic of faith-articulation is its *grounding in and commitment to a particular sacred tradition*, with its rituals, symbols, myths, scriptures, spiritual discipline, community life, and of course its doctrines; doctrines that are often seen as divinely revealed and as much a part of the sacred tradition as any other religious phenomenon. In this interlinked religious life there is, no doubt, the sense of a primal matrix of meaning, and it will be recognised that it is from this primal source that any theological articulation is to derive its directions.

Yet, a crucial question engaging the 'theologians' within virtually all religious traditions raises doubts on this very issue: How far is the interpretation of tradition, whether concerning theological doctrine or modes of life-behaviour, to be directly based on primal tradition? And what other kinds of directives are there for such interpretation? Even a cursory look at various key periods in the histories of Hindu, Christian, Muslim and Sikh traditions, and to a less obvious extent in Jainist and Buddhist traditions, shows that schisms and the development of new movements have usually been characterised by questions about the relationship of *contemporary* life to the primal tradition. In that sections of the Christian tradition have in recent centuries been more exposed to the modern process of change than have most other traditions, this issue has come to the fore more clearly in theological and ethical debate in Christianity than in other traditions. But there is nothing exclusive about this.

The claims of doctrinaire neo-Hindu writers (e.g. Swami Vivekanda, Radhakrishnan) that Hinduism has at every stage of its history both been tolerantly accommodating of all new religious doctrines and cultic life and has at the same time merely been giving further expression to the unchanging *sanātana-dharma*, the eternal Vedic order, have not been wholly wide of the mark. Hinduism *has* cultically been remarkably inclusive, and yet *has* maintained a remarkable cultic continuity, for all the changes that have taken place. In reality, however, those exponents of the diverse strands of pluriform Hinduism who, in each age, have been most effective in directing the course of religious events — cultic, doctrinal, ethical — have been sharply selective and discriminating in their interpretation and re-interpretation of the tradition, as they have been confronted with new cultic, doctrinal and ethical phenomena not explicit in the ancient *dharma*. Typically, 'Hindu' interpreters have drawn on what they have seen as crucial strands of the ancient tradition and have taken these ostensibly as determinative for the new development. This was the case even when strikingly new directions were called for: as in the period of (or communities related to) the Upanishads, later the Bhagavad Gītā, and even later with reforming classical theologians of distinction such as Śaṅkara and Rāmānuja, or even in the case of the reforming theologians of the modern period, sometimes rejoicing in the slogan that 'all ways are equally valid' (e.g. Swami Vivekananda), sometimes appealing for a 'back to the Vedas' movement (e.g. the Arya Samaj movement of Dayanand Sarvasvati), sometimes intent primarily on liberalising and modernising while retaining what they saw as the 'essential tradition' (e.g. the Brahmo Samajis). Each new interpreter was typically steeped in, and in his own way committed to, key motifs in the ancient Vedic traditions, and at the same time was concerned also to respond adquately to the challenge of phenomena outside that tradition yet seen as persuasively powerful.

In the inner experience of many such re-interpreters, of course, what has just been referred to as 'phenomena outside the tradition' may well have been aspects of a sacred tradition that, though not historically part of the ancient Vedic corpus, yet had become vital to their inner perception. Śaṅkara, for example, was clearly indebted to the Buddhist vision of things (to the extent of being accused of 'crypto-Buddhism'); yet his interpretation keeps close to the Vedic/Upanishadic text. Rāmānuja's vision is deeply shaped by an ecstatic love-devotion to God (of the Āḷvārs) and to a system of icon-ritual (of the Pāñcarātra sect), neither of which is explicitly or historically Vedic/Upanishadic; yet the new directions of his theology also express a convincing continuity with this Vedic tradition.

Then, the interpreters of every religious tradition have also assumed that their primary task is to identify and evocatively to indicate the central vision of reality, the core vision of the Sacred, as they perceive it to be embodied in the tradition. The fact that so many distinctive, in some cases dissimilar, perceptions emerge in the evocations of different interpreters even within one general religious family ('Hinduism', 'Buddhism', 'Christianity') has not weakened the intention of theologians to point to their tradition's *true* vision.

2. However deeply grounded the theologian may be in the life of the tradition(s), however convinced that this life provides the creative matrix for all true insight into Reality, *reflection on and interpretation of that life inevitably entails some degree of 'distancing' from the immediacy of vision-experience.* One who merely transmits what has been given in the tradition neither reflects on nor interprets that tradition. There is good reason for arguing that a theologian should also be a 'visionary'; it is difficult to imagine how there can be any authentic kind of faith-articulation without a compelling inner perception of the 'patterns of meaning' demanded of a 'theology'. Even so, to reflect on and interpret meaning to others necessarily entails a mediating role that calls for some degree of detachment from the integrating vision. There is need for a perception of reality in its wholeness that at its most creative point has an intuitive immediacy about it. Along with the creative intuition, however, there is typically in theological articulation also a *critical* apprehension, at least (if it is to be 'systematic') in the sense of providing a *coherent* conceptual account of the apparently disparate dimensions of the tradition; and if it is to be *interpretive*, in the sense of drawing out patterns of meaning previously not explicitly articulated in the tradition's theology.

We do, of course, need to beware of assuming that the kind of critical stance found in some modern western Christian forms of theology is paradigmatic for the conceptual articulation found in all religious traditions. We have, therefore, to distinguish carefully between the very general descriptive categories outlined above and the particular ways the interpretive process is found in the diversity of religious traditions referred to here. All attempts at a comparative typology face a similar problem.

In the case of the wide range of traditions within the Indian religious spectrum there is in general little difficulty in applying categories such as 'critical distancing', 'systematic', 'coherent conceptual account', and so on. Comparable, if not precisely similar, forms of a hermeneutical process can be identified in the various Hindu and Buddhist traditions, including developments in Buddhist traditions outside the Indian sub-continent. To what extent, however, can we speak of a 'critical hermeneutical process' in the case of the Islamic tradition, in which the infallibility and immutability of the primal revelation originating in heaven but recorded verbally in sacred scripture, the Quran, is so strongly affirmed? Similar terms used of the primal Word, such as 'eternal', 'trans-personal' and even 'infallible', in some Hindu traditions do not raise this problem so seriously, and the school (Mīmāṃsā) responsible for giving such great emphasis to the Vedic Word also worked out quite a sophisticated and 'critical' set of principles of exegetical hermeneutics. But what of Islam?

First, we should note the empirical fact of considerable diversity within the Islamic tradition. It is far from the monolithic tradition that the theory of an immutable and precisely expressed written revelation, authoritative for all time and for every context, might lead us to expect. Then, we find that in any case, Islam's doctrine of the three-fold means of authoritative decision-making (Qur'ān, Ijmā', Qiyās) makes it very clear that Islam accepts a process of interpretation by the community and by the individual when the situation demands it; in effect this becomes part of the revelatory process (Cf. Cragg 1986). What is absolutely essential to orthodox Islamic theology is the central vision of the majestic sovereignty of Allah, whose perfect and all-powerful Will calls for the absolute submission (Islām) of humanity. Given this core perception, affirm a number of Islamic interpreters, all other aspects of Islamic theology and life fall into place. In the process of interpreting this 'majestic sovereignty' within the history of Islam, however, we find a kind of transposing of meaning taking place. In the religiously and theologically very significant Sufi movement, the majestic transcendence is transposed into a mystical immanence. We cannot speak of a contradiction here: so transcendent is Allah's greatness and beneficience that only the vision within the inner soul can apprehend these glorious attributes. Thus there is still a systematic interpretation of meaning; but a decisive interpretive move has been made which carries great conceptual and practical ramifications, and which involves a new kind of approach to the primary tradition. Paradoxically, the primary revelation is now both 'distanced' (in the sense that the literal attitude of other Islamic interpreters is left behind) and yet is more immediately interiorised. And it is especially the process of interiorising in Sufi theology that is worked out so systematically.

3. At this point we need to take note of the *dialectic between continuity and discontinuity* in the theologian's relationship to the community tradition. In a

number of religious traditions a 'prophetic' role has been taken up by some leaders/teachers who, in reflecting on the tradition in response to their peculiar context, have so re-visioned its central perception that they have been led to provide radical new directions for the tradition. Throughout the history of many traditions, in fact, it is reflection on the tradition that has led to varying degrees of tension between the orthodox and more original perceptions of the tradition's meaning. Prophets may well be 'without honour in their own country', i.e. among the more conservative interpreters of their own tradition. Where the tension leads to estrangement from the tradition (as with the Prophet of Nazareth and many more) there may be at first a new movement emerging within the old tradition, perhaps as a distinct sect: eventually, in some cases at least, this distinct sect becomes a separate new tradition.

Within the inclusive fold of Brahmanic Hinduism, room has often been found for such 'prophetic' new movements, even for anti-Brahmin movements, as distinct sects, or even as a distinct caste/community within the wider tradition. Thus the Lingāyata movement of Karnātaka in the 12th century, a devotional reform movement with a strong social emphasis, is now a distinct caste/community within the total Hindu social structure. In the very indigenous Buddhist movement 18 centuries earlier (Kosambi 1972: 105-13), with its similar 'prophetic' rejection of Brahmanic priesthood, rejection of its sacrificial cultic system, its Vedic Word, and less explicitly its caste system (as well as its primary way of salvation), such eventual inclusion was not possible, even though various aspects of the Buddhist movement made their impact on Hinduism and were even incorporated into its religious and ethical life. This Hindu willingness to absorb certain parts of Buddhist life was not, however, the reason for Buddhism's eventual decline and disappearance from India as is sometimes asserted. What is clear is that the 'prophetic' new direction preached by the Buddha involved too great a discontinuity with Vedic tradition, an unsustainable inner tension. Further factors in the decline of Buddhism from Indian soil were undoubtedly the over-dependence on patronage in times of shifting loyalties, and the influence of antinomian Tāntrika ideas within Buddhist circles leading to loss of the distinctive ethical emphasis in its primal vision (Cf. DeBary 1972: 110-22).

While this was not the case with the Buddha, many other prophets within various traditions have urged the faithful to 'look to the rock from which you were hewn' (Isaiah 51.1). That is, 'recover the lost vision of your early patriarchs' — a typical prophetic concern for renewal by return to primal roots and original values. Such a concern for primal continuity, perhaps sometimes claimed as a mark of authenticity, appears in many strands of the Gospel record; we find a stress, in differing degrees, on both the newness of the envisioned Way, and on its continuity with the old Covenant. It was seen to be of importance, to the Evangelists at least, to establish that Jesus was of true Davidic stock (or Abrahamic, or even Adamic); this was just as important as to establish the originality of his message and the uniqueness of his person. Later, most Protestant reforming theologians were likewise as concerned to show the continuity of doctrines with apostolic and with early patristic teaching, as to establish a clean break with the 'Babylonian captivity' of Roman teaching and practice. The tradition's cumulative continuity was broken, but identity with both primal vision and its early interpreters was seen as essential to the Protestant 'prophets'.

We should note too the way in which religious traditions typically include accounts of the lonely struggle of the heroic founders of the faith, such as Zarathustra, Moses, Mahavira ('Great-hero'), the Buddha, Jesus, Muhammad, Nanak, as well as a great host of other heroes, many locally recognised. 'Hero-stones' are a prominent feature of local traditions in many parts of South India. In some cases such heroic struggles that typify religious leaders are against a stream flowing even within the community tradition; in other cases the struggle is clearly against those outside opposing the tradition. In the former case, a lesser tradition, a sect or sub-sect will emerge as a result of resistance within the larger tradition, thus repeating, perhaps in less radical form, what the original Founder did. In any case emulation of the heroism of both original Founder and later representatives is typically made an essential part of the practice of the faith. For the interpreting theologian, too, reflective exploration of the meaning of his community's faith involves a similar emulation of the lonely struggle of the pioneering heroes of that faith. Where such 're-visioning' is done in a community that reveres the (re)-visionary as a sacred Guru, or divine doctor, the pioneering struggle and the tension within the community will be minimal. But where the tradition alone, not including its contemporary interpreters, has become identified with the Sacred, the opposition will probably be fierce. And the tension between continuity and discontinuity may well be found within the theologian himself/herself, who will be engaged in self-questioning as to how far and by what criteria reinterpretation of the tradition may legitimately range. Just where is faithfulness to the tradition lost in speculative and idiosyncratic reconstruction? Such questions will be inevitable as long as there are prophetic theologians.

4. There is one further point to be made in this connection. The theologian of a tradition can sometimes *lose grounding in and commitment to the tradition's central vision because of counter-influences* resulting either from an institution-alising of the theological process that emasculates its visionary virility, or from over-accommodation to prevalent cultural values and attitudes, when it is not recognised that the life-attitudes, or the conceptual norms of a prevalent culture are contradictory to the values implicit in the tradition's core-perception of reality. This is not to deny the need for interaction between the sacred tradi-tion and contemporary context if the hermeneutical process is to continue. Nor does it deny that the imagery, and therefore the values, of theologies in most traditions in significant ways reflect the imagery and values dominant in society in various periods of history. Tracing the developments of, for example, the Christian doctrine of atonement shows the inevitability of this kind of interaction between prevalent culture and theological interpretation. It is impossible to envisage any 'pure' religious life wholly separate from the life of larger society, despite the frequent puritanising movements typical at some time of virtually all traditions. But these puritan movements are signi-ficant of the authentic concern that religious vision and the various forms of expression of this vision, social, ethical, theological, be not determined by values and concepts from outside the tradition in any ultimate sense. Many traditions, of course, have coped with this issue by setting up a dual system of commitment within the one tradition, i.e. the 'religious' and the 'secular' (in traditional Catholicism), or those who take the 'great vows' and those who take 'lesser vows' (as in Jainism), or monks and laity (as in Buddhism).

There are various other aspects of the 'institutionalising' of the theological process; indeed, the theologian can never be without some kind of institutional commitment, even if this commitment be to an other-worldly monastic com-munity on the one hand, or to the demands of, say, a secular western university on the other. There is little doubt that developments in modern western Christian theology have been very deeply influenced by the secular university context in which many 'pioneering' theologians have been situated. It is quite possible, of course, that an institutional framework other than the tradition's own community may have a beneficial liberating effect on theological inter-pretation, in turn stimulating renewal within the tradition. The danger is, perhaps, that the theologian set in the university academic context may not adequately recognise the value-orientation that this involves, and may remain more concerned to meet the expectations of secular academia than the needs of religious praxis, with the radically distinct values and life-attitudes expected of those committed to the central vision of a religious tradition.

Karl Barth's vehement insistence that Christian theology must be shaped solely by strict ontological and epistemological commitment to the revelation of God-in-Christ, that is by the transcendent Subject proper to all Christian theological reflection and articulation, must be recognised as carrying some weight for all religious reflection (Barth 1936: 1-25, 330-5). Barth, of course, also recognised the dialectical character of the process, even though his description of what this process involves did not adequately allow for the diverse kinds of *continuity* (with factors 'outside' the revelation) involved in theologising. Thus, in the way Barth described the theological process or method the impression is given that to be faithful to the biblical core vision of reality, there needs to be total *independence* of metaphysical structures that have developed distinct from that visionary matrix, though he did accept that use of current terminology was inevitable (1936: 434). As theological articulation is also bound up with the historical process, it would seem impossible and undesirable to avoid any kind of creative appropriation of aspects of 'other' metaphysical systems. Yet, there is a sense in which in the ultimate analysis some form of 'fideism' epistemologically and methodologically is a necessary part of theologizing if it is to develop in authentic fidelity to its own visionary ground. Barth was certainly serious in his theologising, in some basic respects methodologically akin to the Indian theologian, Madhva, whose school of Vaishnava Vedānta insists on an ultimate ontological difference between God in his self-determining freedom and all else in its God-determined dependence. Thus, for Madhva, as perhaps for Barth and for Islamic theologians too, the final criterion even in the interpretation of the truths of scripture is: 'Does this formulation adequately express the sovereignty of God, the only ultimately independent One?'.

Barth, however, was so committed to the transcendent revelation in Christ that all religion, thus even the Gospel's traditional or ecclesial grounding, is seen as mere human effort, discontinuous with the transcendent revelation of God-in-Christ (Barth 1956: Sect. 17 — 'The Revelation of God as the Abolition of Religion'). This revelational positivism has provided the basis for a number of other theologians, not necessarily committed to Barth's insight concerning the need for epistemological independence, who have tried to develop a *secular* theology in one form or another. Ironically, it was the most famous 'pioneer' of 'religionless Christianity', Dietrich Bonnhöffer, who first described Barth's theology as a 'positivism of revelation'. In common there has been the attempt to desacralise Christian faith and set it free from its grounding in religious or sacred tradition. True, Barth was also able to write of Christianity as 'the true religion', though obviously not in its empirical manifestations: in general his trans-religious view of faith and of theology dominated. And there is irony here that Barthians generally seem to have missed: the more theology is purged of what is seen as distorting dependence on any extra-revelational ontology, or on concepts and values shaping theological formulation that are not implicit in the creative, visionary matrix of the tradition, the more it becomes clear that *the Christian Gospel, and therefore the theological task, is essentially 'religious' in character, and requires a process of conceptual structuring that is analogous to and typical of all religious systems*; and this is pre-eminently because of its grounding in a vision of the very kind of transcendent Focus that the Barthian is so committed to.

One way in which a number of Christian theologians have tried to secularise theology is by 'reducing' the numinous or sacral character of Jesus, by taking his humanness, set in a concrete historical social context, as itself the determining hub of theological reflection. John Vincent's 'Secular Christ' (1968), though effectively depicting his 'strangeness', explicitly denies his 'sacredness'. Significantly Barth too later gave increasing importance to the 'humanness' of God, and on explicitly incarnational grounds. Naturally this is applauded by those theologians who find the numinosity of the Gospel narratives problematic, for whom, for example, the only or most authentic category to be used of the process of salvation in the Christian tradition is that of 'humanisation', seen as 'liberation' from sacral traditions. No one, of course, reflecting on the meaning of the primal Christian vision of God-in-Christ can do other than take very seriously its humanist concern; it is both explicit and implicit. But the special theology-creating character of the humanity of Jesus lies precisely in those features which make that humanity stand out from ordinary humanness, that pointed people to powers, values and a faith-life that go beyond mundane or secular humanness. The Jesus witnessed to in the Gospels (and this applies in different ways equally to Zarathustra, the Buddha, Mahavira, Guru Nanak and other sacred figures) is not a desacralised person (the ideal type of the western secularist perhaps?), but an *outstandingly, if very humanely, religious* person, continually pointing beyond himself and beyond the 'present' secular world to the reality of God and his radically new reign: to God as a transcendent if also accessible and realisable reality. It is difficult to see why 'transcendent' (in Sanskrit the *'paratva'* dimension of 'God') is often assumed to mean a level of being that has no determining relationship to the empirical world, that is the opposite pole of immanental presence; for it is abundantly clear that virtually all religious affirmations about the 'other' realm intend an inclusively relational perception of that 'other'. There is a sense in which even the arch-transcendentalist, Śaṅkara, would have agreed with this, even though he also pointed to an *ultimate* Reality quite unrelated to any other entity.

It is significant of the pervasive impact of western secularisation that even some recent Buddhist apologists have felt it necessary to argue for the 'secular' and 'empirical' character of Buddhism, an issue that we briefly noted in the previous chapter. While it is true that the Buddha's insight into reality included no God, no immortal soul, no priests, and little cosmological speculation, and that the soteriology he announced was based on self-effort (though a self-effort in which there were a number of crucial aids), yet there are certain salvific trans-empirical points in the Buddhist path, and that path leads to the state of Nirvana that is so clearly beyond mere empirical existence; even if we see it as a purified or transposed state of existence which is common to all creaturely life, it still involves a state of being that is quite extra-ordinary. A vision of transcendence is at the heart of Buddhist life. Even the initial refuge-taking — 'I go for refuge to the Buddha; I go for refuge to the Community; I go for refuge to the Right Path' — sets the scene for a typically 'religious' life-attitude. Then the Noble Eight-Fold Path itself, beginning with 'right perception' and ending with 'right meditation', involves a life-style that progressively leads the participant away from an empirical level of being towards that which is beyond the sorrows and frustrations common to all 'composite' existence. The Buddhist 'theologian' (and here we ought to use some other category such as 'dhammalogian' or even better '*dharma-vādin*'), therefore, is to reflect on and articulate the meaning for life of this transcendent nirvanic vision: this too is an essentially *religious* function.

5. That religious *language* is typically drawn from a variety of secular and empirical contexts has led some theologians to argue for the essentially *secular* scope of the content of theology (Van Buren 1963). Moreover, religious experiences, while clearly involving special perceptions and insights, invariably occur in *conjunction with* and are in some way coloured by conditions that are socially, politically, culturally, psychologically delineable. Why not, therefore, *account* for the religious dimension of life by reference to these everpresent empirical factors? A number of 'scientific' studies of religion have attempted just this kind of reductionist explanation. There is every reason to encourage as many analyses as possible of the way these dimensions of life impinge upon religious experience: what we need to recognise, though, is that

when we study the social structuring of religion, or its psychological manifestations, and so on, we are essentially studying human *society*, in so far as it provides the context of religious life, and the human *psyche*, in so far as it manifests the religious consciousness (Pettazzoni, in Eliade and Kitagawa 1959: 59). Yet, this typically conjunctive character of religious experience can never be ignored in any attempt to establish the *sui generis* or autonomous character of religion. In the terms of Christian theology, the classical Thomist doctrine of the analogy of being (*analogia entis*), though in modified form, seems inescapable in theological articulation. Even Barth, while denying any essential continuity between God and the world of creatures, willingly fell back on Calvin's notion of an *analogia fidei* (a term also found in Romans 12.6), in which the transcendent Subject is made the determining point of analogical reference: thus, we can understand the true nature of fatherhood only through the Fatherhood of God, and so on. And language about God is appropriate only 'when it conforms to the essence of the Church, i.e. to Jesus Christ' (Barth 1936: 11).

6. A related aspect of the theological task is the *communication of meaning at diverse levels*. On the one hand this includes the need to communicate to people *outside the tradition and its community*, even though the more primary task will be communication within, more as a domestic activity as it were. What has usually been called apologetics, i.e. the 'defence' of the faith to those not initiated into the life of faith, would come under this category, i.e. communicating faith's meaning to a wider public; but traditional apologetics does give a rather limiting defensive slant to this public role. In other words, an outward looking role for the meaning-communicators within a tradition will also be expressed in a number of different ways.

Common to all such 'public' theology (Tracy 1981: 3-31) is the need for the communicator himself or herself to move outside the limits of the tradition's conceptual world. There is a sense in which every theologian stands between the core-vision and the life of the world, even when it is within the community of faith primarily that the vision's meaning is to be communicated. The more public theologian, or one committed to engaging in dialogical relationship with one or other segment of society outside the community of faith, will make a much more deliberate and conscious effort to find an appropriate standpoint for the communication of the esoteric perception of reality to those who are not initiated into the inner circle. Two extreme opposite responses to this typical religious task are: first, *exclusiveness*, as found in some classical traditions, which denies that the mysteries handed on secretly to inner initiates should be communicated at all to those outside. It is difficult to imagine a person in any tradition with a genuine concern to communicate meaning (to whomsoever), i.e. the typical 'theologian', taking this kind of secretive stance. We might think of the oft-told story of Rāmānuja, the Vaishṇava theologian and 'high priest' of the community's central temple. The Guru who was to initiate Rāmānuja with the traditional whispering into his ear of the ultimately significant Mantra had long been withholding this final blessing from him. When finally the Guru did impart this secret verse, Rāmānuja is said to have climbed up to a balcony of the temple and shouted out the secret for all present to hear (Carman 1974: 39). Admittedly, the exact significance of this story is not entirely clear; what can be concluded in general is that, as one given special insight into the meaning of the Vaishṇava vision of reality, his spontaneous response was to communicate this insight to as many people as possible. And this, of course, was the burden of his extensive theological writings. Indeed, his concern to be a Vedantin (not merely a Vaishṇava Ācārya/Priest) shows very clearly this compulsion to communicate the implicit meaning of the Vaishṇava faith (often without explicit reference to anything esoterically Vaishṇava) to a public that was much wider than the Vaishṇava community of initiates. This is one instance of a dialogical role, even incorporating many concepts and imagery from traditions not strictly speaking his own, when they were found to be appropriate to the task of communicating that tradition's vision-meaning to the wider public.

7. Then there are *numerous levels at which there is communication of meaning within the community*. We might explore these diverse levels by looking at some of the different 'dimensions' of religious life enumerated in Chapter One.

a) While it might most readily be assumed that explication of meaning, in any systematic sense at least, relates primarily to the doctrinal dimension, we shall look first at more *mythic* forms of expression. Not all meaning-explication is systematic or is intended to be such: it is no less theological, for the broad conceptual structuring necessary to be classified as 'theo-logia' need not be in a strictly systematic form. Mythic expression certainly intends to communicate meaning, and in some kind of structured way. In general, of course, in religious life myths are re-told as they have been transmitted rather than created *de novo*. But in the telling of any mythic story, whether as part of a tradition of myth-transmission, invariably there will be some degree of interpretation involved: and at this point myth merges into theology. As we noted in the previous chapter, in any case myth is to be seen as a primal form of theology.

At a level of articulation similar to that of myth we find *poetic* expression (Cf. Hepburn 1970: 75-156). Much classical religious poetry is, in fact, both grounded deeply and often explicitly in ancient mythic stories and other forms of symbolic imagery, and is also reflective in the sense of giving further interpretation to mythic meaning. It may even in some ways be critical of aspects of the tradition, yet it will not typically be concerned to provide systematic articulation for the tradition. In many traditions there has been a process of transition from a primary poetic, metaphorical, perhaps parabolic form of language, to more prosaic, perhaps more literal and conceptually systematic formulation. This latter is systematic theology proper; yet poetic religious expression too is a kind of primal theology, for it too is intended to communicate the meaning of the primal vision. And the former task will always need to include or have constant reference to the more primal theological forms, the more symbolic imagery of the pre-systematic modes of expression.

The process of transition in the New Testament material from the parabolic and sometimes aphoristic form of language apparently used by Jesus, to the theological styles of Paul and John (still within the period of 'primal articulation') is not atypical of theological development in religious traditions generally. From time to time even in dealing with seemingly prosaic (we might think even irritatingly unspiritual) pastoral problems, the generally unpoetic Paul is found to burst into semi-poetic forms of expression, in some cases clearly drawing on material already developed within the community (e.g. Philippians 2). And John's language, while simple prose, still retains as central categories a series of images – word, wind, ladder, birth, bread, water, light, life, shepherd, vine, etc. – drawn from the Judeo-Hellenistic culture of his time, to interpret the Jesus-event.

Quite common in theological articulation in diverse traditions, and especially in the Indian traditions, is the combination of *both poetry and prose*, sometimes one and sometimes the other predominating. In both the great Śaiva and Vaiṣṇava traditions some basic scriptures are poetic upsurges (e.g. Tirumandiram, Nālāyira Prabandham etc.), including both rapture and desolation, of ecstatic devotees of around the fifth to the eight centuries of this era: these are the *bhaktas* whose God-love was a life-transforming obsession (Cf. Hardy 1983). Other basic scriptures (the Āgamas and Pāñca-rātra 'collections') contain sectarian material with perhaps accounts of the great sacred places, iconic, priestly and initiatory ritual, the role of yogic discipline, the daily duties of the faithful, and — more explicitly 'theological' — accounts of the 'greatness of the respective supreme God, his sacred names, manifestations and images, the devotion due to his greatness, as well as the nature of the ultimate knowledge of and union with this supreme Being (Schrader 1973). In both poetry and prose sources, the mythic salvation-histories of the concerned great God are alluded to very frequently. And throughout, myth remains the grounding for theological articulation.

Vedānta Deśika (14th century) is an example from the Vaishṇava tradition of a systematic theologian who writes in both poetry and prose; and both his theology and the perceived sacredness of his person are still living forces in the Vaishṇava community, a tradition which as a whole provides rich resources for ways in which mythic-symbols relate to theological systems, or (to use more historical categories) ways in which the religion of Āḻvār saints and Agamic priestly scriptures became transposed to the Ācārya tradition. Vedānta Deśika was deeply grounded in this tradition that developed around the Āḻvār poet-ecstatics, a visionary tradition that had already been more systematically appropriated and Vedantically articulated in the 11th century by Rāmānuja, and in less original ways by subsequent Vaishṇava theologians. A comparison of the conceptual content of the poetry and prose of Vedānta Deśika is revealing (Hardy 1979). In both he articulates the faith of his Śrī Vaishṇava community within the formative constraints of Rāmānuja's theological structures. In both, therefore, he expresses the primal vision of the universe as the dynamic body of God. This cosmic body is also perceived as the divine 'play' as clearly expressed in a praise-poem of the more specific embodiment of God in the mythic Avatāra ('descent') and Arca ('ritual image') form of Vāmana, the dwarf-Avatāra of Vishṇu (who asked for a boon of three steps of land from King Bali, then enlarged himself to an immense size and bestrode the whole cosmos). Through this praise-poem Vedānta Deśika, with rich use of poetic imagery, is able to express both more appropriately, perhaps more implicitly, the playful divine activity, and more adequately is able to express the 'dialectic dynamism' inherent in the underlying theological vision of the whole cosmos as the divine body (Hardy *ibid*. 306-17).

A further point, more technical, can be made briefly here. Vedānta Deśika is seen in the Vaishṇava tradition's schism as an exponent of the 'northern' school, which advocated the 'monkey-method' in the appropriation of divine grace (thus being crudely analogous to a Pelagian as against an Augustinian stance, to transpose to terms of Christian theological history), and affirmed the need for an 'occasion' provided by human devotional effort, especially an initial cultic act of 'surrender', through which divine sovereign grace can function effectively. Yet in the free play of his poetry his theological position is less partisan; the structure of his theology here did not have so closely 'to conform to any pre-given notional system' (317). Though the poem, as all his writing, is shaped by a 'spiritual vision' that is deeply grounded in the mythically and theologically expressed Vaishnava tradition — Rāmānuja's 'tradition' especially — it is able, probably unconsciously, to provide more unconstrained play for the sovereign grace of God, which was precisely the major point stressed by those thought to have been his opponents within the sectarian polemics.

b) There are, as we saw, levels of meaning-expression in which mytho-poetic forms have been *transposed to more doctrinally systematic conceptualised forms*. As a very significant example we might look again at how this appears in the case of Rāmānuja. In a later chapter we shall look in greater detail at the coherent relation we find between his mythic/ritual grounding and his cosmic vision, again as typifying an essential religious/theological structure. Here we merely note that the central concept of his richly elaborated system (viz. that ontic reality is essentially relational and epistemology is necessarily to be commensurate with this relationality, a position worked out explicitly in contra-distinction from the extreme non-dualism of Śaṅkara) was not a construct of his own inventive intellect, any more than was the inclusively significant analogy we find as the central means of expressing this ontological system (viz. that universal existence relates to the supreme Person as a body relates to its innermost self, for that universe is 'inseparably related' to, is internally controlled by, and is ultimately dependent upon that supreme Person) (Lott 1976: 146-67; 1980a: 21-40; Lipner 1985).[1] The crucial analogy was already deeply embedded, though not yet explicitly prominent, in numerous sources appropriated by the Vaishnava tradition (both those explicitly Vaishnava — Vishnu Purāna, Pañcarātra, Bhagavad Gītā, and to a lesser extent also in the Upanishads, especially in the section on the 'Inner Controller', i.e. in the Antaryāmī Brāhmana).

Thus, typically, a mythically expressed 'vision', or even a whole cluster of mythic imagery, becomes a central analogical concept and the hermeneutical

---

1 I regret that Lipner's outstanding study of Rāmānuja's thought was not available to me before sending the manuscript for printing.

key to, conceptually, a highly sophisticated theological system. Numerous other examples could be drawn from other religious/theological traditions to make the same point.

c) And what of the 'aesthetic dimension' of religious expression? How does this relate to *theological* expression? *Theological* will usually be understood as *verbal* formulations, but a strong case could be made out for seeing certain kinds of non-verbal artistic forms too as theologically potent. In some cases, as with the Tanka-paintings of Tibetan Buddhism, the stylised imagery is used as a focus for meditation on the meaning of the tradition. Even by means of the visual structuring of key-themes in the tradition (especially the theme of the Buddha, perhaps in union with the female Power in all her creative vitality, perceived as the still centre of all the violent agitation of desire-bound existence) the Tanka communicates to the one meditating on it a particular intention, even an interpretation of the tradition's meaning: it conveys a 'theology'. Or, in the Indian-Christian context, in which there will necessarily be a fusion of perceptual worlds (i.e. the biblical and some of the basic life-perceptions of the Indian cultural world), it is especially in the imagery of artistic expression that authentically fused Indian-Christian perceptions of reality will emerge. To a large extent we also find this to be true of Indian-Christian poetic forms, especially the rich *Kīrtana* heritage, the Christian *bhakti*-songs of most Indian languages. Some of the most striking interpretations of Christian faith in the Indian cultural context have been by imaginative artists. In particular we might mention the strikingly expressive 'theological' painting of Jyoti Sahi and others painting and sculpting along similar lines: Sahi does not aim merely to translate essentially *given* Christian motifs into suitable Indian forms; there is rather a deep grounding in both the Catholic/biblical 'matrix of meaning' *and* perceptions of the world and reality from the Indian cultural world (Sahi: 1986). And a coherent new interpretation of the meaning of Christian faith emerges. It may well be through further theological reflection at this level of deeply embedded cultural images, and further verbal reflection on these art forms, that the most authentic Indian-Christian theological articulation will be found.

d) Here we might take further a point made earlier regarding the theological process: is not all theological expression in the ultimate analysis *analogical?* 'Analogy' here need not be understood in the strictly scholastic sense, but rather in the general sense that the sacred focus of religious life typically included a dimension of mysterious otherness, some ineffable transcendence that theologians have always recognised at some point even in their systematic formulations (Pannenberg 1970: 211-31). They have realised that their descriptive language and concepts fail to do full justice to the Other.

Here, however, we have to acknowledge a *divergence* of theological approaches. At least two distinct types emerge: one recognises that language remains ultimately 'symbolic' and can only be indirectly representative of the reality of the Beyond; the other assumes a more fideist realism that takes theological language as authentically expressing that which it describes, though in no fully exhaustive sense. We could illustrate this diverse theological approach from a number of traditions: Indian, Judaic, Christian, Islamic. From the Indian theological systems we will again take the two most outstanding systems, non-dualist and theistic Vedanta. Both recognize the transcendent character of the supreme Being in their differing ways: both, therefore pursue some form of analogical method. On the one hand we have Śaṅkara and the non-dualists insisting that no theological language, not even scriptural words and concepts, can be more than *indirect* pointers to the reality of the Transcendent. For this reason, of primary significance to Śaṅkara and his followers was the Upanishadic text stating that in relation to all texts about 'the formed' and the 'unformed' we can only say 'Not thus, not thus' (Bṛhadāraṇyaka, repeated in several verses). Similarly, another text stating that 'all words turn back' (Taittirīya 2.9) was interpreted as meaning that all our words are powerless to apprehend and communicate the reality of the Transcendent (Lott 1979: 8-26). The 'realists', on the other hand, in general said that there is no reason why appropriate language, especially sacred scriptural language, cannot directly communicate the reality of the character and presence of God. They recognised that none of our words and concepts can *exhaust* the meaning of the Reality. Thus, while Rāmānuja, as we saw, took the scriptural/traditional analogy of the self-body relationship as paradigmatic for an inclusive and very realist understanding of God's nature and his relationship to the world, he still acknowledged that at some points of conceptual comparison the analogy breaks down.

An analogical perspective seems to imply, in either of the above theological poles, some kind of *dialectical approach*. In the Vaishnava tradition, for example, great weight is given to a more straightforward theological 'dialectic' between the 'otherness' (*paratva*) and the 'accessibility' (*saulabhya*) of God — key categories in this system, both of which must equally be presented in conceptualising God (Carman 1977: 77-87), indeed in all our experiencing of God. He is the supremely distinct, incomparable Lord, *therefore* all words and all entities ultimately refer to his being. He is the supreme Self of all, therefore the inmost Self of all beings. The dialectic of Śaṅkara's non-dualist system is more subtle, in part made necessary by the undeniable fact of our everyday experience that things do not seem to be all part of a single identity of undivided Being. Both ontologically and epistemologically, therefore, great subtlety is called for: the ultimate Reality *is* beyond all, yet *is* all: the One Being is unknowable, yet is known to every being: the world is not real, yet is not unreal. Both such systems, therefore, for all their difference, being essentially analogical systems are also *dialectical*, as with similar types of theological system in other traditions.

And this is naturally the case if mythic and poetic forms of expression are eminently apt at the primal level of theologising and if more systematic theologies are to be authentically grounded in the central vision and its primal forms of self-articulation. With creative imagination, though not in some idiosyncratically constructive way, the theologian moves from visionary Focus to the world of 'mundane' images, and back again; no *exactly* corresponding descriptive words and concepts will be found for the theological task. Yet everywhere there will be found images that suggest, that point, that provide reliable indications of the Reality beyond and within. Whether these God-images are seen as *direct* pointers, or merely indirectly symbolic, depends upon the particular perceptual type the theologian belongs to.

e) The role of *scripture* was touched on in the previous chapter in relation to the mythic dimension: here we look at this aspect of literate religious life as it relates to the theological task. Much theological articulation is in fact scriptural exegesis and interpretation, unavoidably so when a set of sacred writings is seen as the repository of authoritative, even infallible, divine revelation: or as the decisive source of testimony to that 'truth' or 'true being' whose realisa-tion the seeker aspires to: or as the reliable basis for the ultimately right way of life that is sought. This list of ways of looking at scripture could be con-tinued (Cf. O'Flaherty 1979). Already it will be clear that there are significant-ly different roles given to scripture, though for the purposes of analysing the theological task it is perhaps sufficient to note that the sacred text, and the interpreter's response to this text, is in one form or another a central factor in the articulation of visionary meaning in all literate religious communities.

In some traditions, however, the *Guru* is relied upon either as the living source of that reality to which scripture also witnesses, or perhaps as the true medium of interpretation of scriptural truth, or as the one who initiates the seeker into the intrinsic sacred power of certain key texts. In the classical Vedantic system, there are three dimensions of, or stages in, the appropriation of ultimate truth; we might even say there are three aspects to doing theology properly: they are, listening, mentally reflecting on and contemplating (*śravaṇa, manana, nididhyāsana*: Brihadāraṇyaka I.4.2). In the first stage especially the Guru's role is all-important, for the 'listening' to the great texts revealing the mystery of Brahman is to be filtered decisively through the mediating guidance of the Guru.

This spiritual preceptor, the Guru, is a figure of immense significance not only in the Vedantic systems, but in the plethora of interrelated but distinct sects and traditions making up 'Hinduism'. As individual guide in the spiritual pilgrimage of virtually every aspirant the Guru is necessary for the interpretation of that meaning appropriate to the particular stage in the journey towards ultimate liberation. We might say then that the Guru is the ultimately exalted form of the figure of the theologian (especially when interpreted as an *avatāra* of God).

Now, in the Sikh religious tradition scripture and Guru have as it were coalesced. The Granth Sahib, or the Great Book, placed as the focal point in Sikh worship, is in itself treated as a sacred object of veneration; thus we see that in Sikh history, at a crucial stage, scripture took over the living role of the sacred Gurus of the past. However, in the development of Sikh consciousness it was perhaps not so much the Granth Sahib as such, but this sacred text as the visual symbolic centre of the community of the True Path. Guruship is integral to that sacred community, especially as it gathers at the Gurdwar (the 'gateway to the Guru'), sings the holy hymns of the past Gurus and shares together in the sacred or sacramental food (Cole: 1982). There is, then, a mystic, sacramental identity of sacred community and sacred Guruship. And that community as a mystic unity now interprets the true Way, even though there are specific functionaries who at certain times are expected to expound the meaning of the scriptural text. There are clearly certain respects in which Sikh religious structuring is analogous to that envisaged by Paul in his concept of the sacred fellowship as the 'body' of Christ, who in turn is the 'embodiment', the true mediator, of God and of divine Truth. The whole body is in one sense to 'interpret' the meaning of Christ: yet there are those with special charismatic gifts who function within this sacred 'body' in special ways ('for the building up of the whole body'). For Paul, however, while there was clearly an important role for scripture (i.e. the Old Testament as far as he was concerned), it did not seem to have the decisively focal position we see in the later

Sikh tradition. That was to come in the Christian tradition too a little later.

Typical of many religious traditions, then, at some stage in their development, is the assumption that scripture (or the sacred oral tradition) itself is a primary mode of *communicating sacred meaning*, at least in so far as this sacred verbal tradition is in living interrelationship with the community of the faithful. In any case it will be seen as central to the theological task, often seen as a transpersonal (in Sanskrit *apaurusheya*) corpus of sacred utterances echoing the creative Word that is the source of all life and all truth; yet a Word whose mystery still needs to be interpreted for those who seek to be within the ambit of its sacred power. Thus, no matter what final authority, or what divine clarity of sacred communication is attributed to sacred scripture, it will typically be assumed in religious traditions that reflective exposition of the text's meaning is called for in the life of the sacred community. It was precisely the Ritual Exegetes of the classical Hindu tradition, with their extreme regard for Vedic immutability, infallibility, and so on, who developed systematic exegesis of scripture within the Indian religious tradition. This *darśana* ('vision'), or school, is the Pūrva Mīmāṃsā, i.e. the 'previous dividers' (or 'ascertainers', or 'exegetes') and the sophisticated principles of exegesis they evolved were then taken over by the 'later exegetes', i.e. the Vedantins, whose varied theological procedures we have good reason to take as of such special significance for understanding how religion and theology inter-relate in the Indian traditions.

There are three issues related to the role of scripture in the theological process that should at least be mentioned: the question of whether scripture is to be seen as an integral part of the sacred tradition or as having a sacred status that places it emphatically above the general tradition; the role of reason in the interpretive task; and the nature of the interaction between text and context.

(i) The *sola scriptura* of the Reformers of the sixteenth century can rarely be more than a slogan in any literal sense, especially when the interpretive task is taken as seriously as with them. But as a way of saying that scripture embodies in a specially focussed form the central vision of the tradition, though itself in the final analysis a part of that tradition, we can still speak of a theology based on *sola scriptura*. What this slogan does not seem to express is the way in which there needs to be dynamic interaction between text and the context of the living community if scripture itself is to be the 'living Word'. Again, suitably modified this applies to all other traditions in their struggle to articulate the meaning of their core vision.

(ii) And what of reason? The 13th century theistic Vedantin, Madhva, on the one hand thought of reason as a 'whore' (Lott 1980: 88) at the service of all and sundry, and on the other hand recognised that in the interpretation of difficult texts, reason in the service of the 'inner witness', is the final arbiter (Sharma 1962). Again, we find similar ambivalence in many other theologians. Śaṅkara, for example, accepts formally the position of Vedanta in denying that we can know anything of ultimate Reality through reason or through inferential argument: Brahman is known only through *śruti*, 'that which is heard', i.e. the Vedic Word. Yet, in elaborating his doctrine of that supreme Being, he quite often introduces inferential argument affirming the necessary existence of Brahman on the grounds of how we experience the world. His arguments are, in fact, very similar to the classical 'proofs' of the Christian tradition, though they mostly echo the classical school of the theistic Logicians (*Nyāya darśana*) of Hinduism. Where Śaṅkara, like all Vedantins, very significantly differed from this school of logic is in never assuming that reason holds some position independent of and superior to the insights of the primal vision. For Śaṅkara especially, the final 'proof' of the reality of the Transcendent lies in *anubhava*, the directly intuited experience or inner perception of that Reality: reason is to be a poor handmaid of that inner vision, however important in the task of expounding and elucidating the sacred text (Murthy 1974). And in one form or another this is the position of all the cultically serious theologians of the Indian traditions. In the final analysis it is surely intrinsic to all authentic theology: the Hindu school of Logic, though significant in many respects, lacks this essential epistemological commitment to the ultimacy of the primal vision. 'Revelation' and 'reason' will of necessity always interact to some degree: but in the theological task as a typical religious phenomenon reason cannot be given a status of superior *autonomy*, thus acting as an independent final arbiter of what is acceptable in revelation. More intrinsic to the theologian's work as meaning-interpreter is the need for *coherent* presentation of the implications of the primal vision, implications for life-praxis as well as for life-perception. But we take up this question of theological *coherence* later.

(iii) There is little formal theory in classical theological discussion regarding the extent to which the *context* of the interpreter is to help shape the interpreted meaning of the *text*. There have been varied hermeneutical theories in the traditions, but few if any picked up the insight given such emphasis in contemporary hermeneutical thought (e.g. Gadamer 1979), viz. that there is a continual and dynamic interaction between text and context in the discovery of patterns of meaning in the text and in the articulation of this meaning in the theological process. Such dependent mutability of textual meaning as just described, would have been problematic for the classical theologians in many traditions, not only in the 'fundamentalist' schools of Islam and Christianity. In some traditions, however, especially in a number of Indian traditions, there has at least been consistent and determining recognition of the primacy of the subjecthood of the interpreter, or rather of the seeker's existential situation, for instance the desire for and need of liberation from bondage. It has consistently been recognised that it is this 'seeking' context that will give meaning as the text is reflected upon; no doubt this is significantly different from the contemporary concern to take seriously the social and political context as needing to shape in an explicit way the meaning of the text.

f) It would be highly misleading if the above point gave the impression that there is to be little response to life-conditions in the theological task as seen by most religious traditions of an earlier age. That interpretation in some sense has typically been 'contextual' becomes very clear when we look at the *ethical and social dimensions* of religious life as they relate to the theological task. Guidance to the religious community as to what its life is to be in the world and what the relationships of the faithful are to be to each other as well as to all other living beings has typically been seen as an essential part of the task of drawing out the meaning of the tradition. Indeed, many would see this as the primary theological task; in many traditions, certainly, it will he seen as an integral part of the Way to salvation/liberation. In most traditions such ethical duties will be seen as intrinsically commensurate with the ultimate goals of life. For example, the concern of many Christian ethicists with *theological* ethics is fully justified, though this should surely not be allowed to hinder *public* ethical discussion.

Any radical distinction between *kerugma* (preaching of primary doctrine) and *didache* (practical teaching) in the Christian Gospel, or in theology, is artificial. Only in extreme transcendentalist systems will there be a radical distinction drawn between what is to be *done*, and what is to be *known* or *inwardly realised*; then ethical action will be seen as concerned with proximate goals, and only inner realisation will be seen as concerned with ultimate goals. In such disparate traditions as Theravada Buddhism and Islam, Jainism and Sikhism, in the Judeo-Christian and other traditions with a high degree of ethical consciousness, instruction in, and therefore interpretation of, the life-duties to be expected of a participant have always been both central to religious life generally and to the articulation of the meaning of the tradition in particular. 'Theologians' have necessarily been ethicists, just as ethicists (within religious traditions) need to be theologians, for all ethical elucidation or exhortation will directly, if not explicitly, relate to understanding doctrinal beliefs.

This interlinking of ethical life-style with doctrinal understanding is typical of so many traditions that it might seem arbitrary to choose examples. We might think of the rigorous, even ascetic way of life expected of the Jaina, especially the monk. Now the sacred Focus for the Jaina, in the early stages particularly, by which soul-purification and ultimate quietude of being are to be achieved, is the image of the Jina, already 'victorious' and purified in the transcendent realm, one of those who has previously 'made the ford across' (as a Tīrthaṅ-kara). Yet it is not only by meditating on his tranquil transcendent quietude that the one still struggling will attain this desired state. There must also be the acceptance of the discipline of life-duties that are thought intrinsically to be commensurate with and therefore to lead to the desired goal: becoming truthful in every way; having no attachment to possessions; being totally chaste; injuring no living thing; limiting the amount of travel and movement; and so on. Yet this life-style is only meaningful because it is placed within a distinctive world-view, with a very distinctive conception of how human action relates to ultimate destiny, of the qualities of the soul and of the universe it inhabits, and so on. Thus doctrinal systems, 'theology', undergird ethical systems, just as ethical systems enable the realising of the transcendent goals aspired to as the culmination of the life-meaning articulated by the Jaina interpreter. Similar kinds of examples could be drawn from the interlinking of *dharma* and *moksha* at least in some kinds of Hinduism, the Eight-Fold Path and *Nirvāṇa* in Buddhism, the *dīn* and the *imān* in Islam; and in every case it will typically be seen that the task of theological articulation of the meaning of the primal vision in the life of the tradition's participants involves ethical reflection also.

g) We have not yet looked at the *ritual dimensions* of religious life and its implications for the theological process. The ritual actions performed in a tradition can aptly be linked with those kinds of specially enabling religious duties that we may call *spiritual discipline* (clearly there has been some reference to this type of religious activity immediately above). Much religious ritual is, of course, transmitted and carried on by a distinct priestly class, or by similar functionaries even if technically they are not thought of as being able to mediate and dispense sacred power or other sacral blessings by virtue of either being set apart sacramentally or born, by heredity, into such a sacerdotal role. Yet, even in this apparently routine process of ritualisation we should not imagine the articulation of meaning by the theologian has no place. In a number of traditions, of course, as we have already noted, there has sometimes been tension between priestly interests and those who are prophetically critical of various aspects of the ritual, and priestly indifference is seen as obscuring the very primal vision the ritual is supposed to be embodying and expressing. Then there will be need for more clear articulation of the true life-goals and the sacred Focus evoking such life-goals; i.e., a prophetic theological interpretation results. We need not look only to the great Prophets of Israel for this kind of prophetic theology (with a strongly ethical dimension too); a number of the *bhakti* leaders of India provide similar instances, perhaps especially the Liṅgāyata movement of Karnataka. Here again, though, prophetic denunciation and theological redirection did not entail an absolute rejection of the traditional ritual practice. Every one of the most important Liṅgāyata leader, Basava's, devotional couplets (e.g. Ramanujan 1973: 61-90) ends with invocation of the manifestation of Śiva found at a traditional Śaiva shrine, Kūḍala-Saṅga (a sacred place at a confluence of rivers).

Then, when aspects of ritual practice for some reason — perhaps changing economic/social factors? — lost their potency and persuasiveness, at least for a significant segment of the community, there will probably be need for *theologians* to provide *new life-directions*, perhaps a new world-view, certainly to interpret new meaning from the old ways. And again this may not entail a total rejection of those old ritual forms. A clear classic case of this is seen in two of the basic sources for the articulation of Vedantic theology; the Upanishads and the Bhagavad-Gītā. Here we shall refer only to the former. At some point in the Vedic period we find groups within that sacred tradition becoming dissatisfied with the elaborate priestly performance of the Vedic ritual, though this was also a *public* performance in which leading householders (or royal figures) usually had an important role. Those given to reflective exercises, however, began to turn more to the quiet retreats of the forests, and to search for a union of one's own self-grounding and the Ground of all cosmic being. Just as the sacred power of the priestly action and utterance was called the '*brahman*', so this Ground of all was still '*brahman*'. And what is striking about so many passages in the Upanishadic books is that it is through meditation on aspects of the Vedic ritual, and the development of corresponding acts of interiorising contemplation, that the key new insights, the new meaning-patterns, emerge. In turn, as we saw, these new insight into the being of

Brahman and of the Self form the basis of India's most elaborate systematic theology, Vedānta ('the *end* of the Vedas'). Similarly in many other traditions, it has often been some aspect of ritual practice that has both provoked a wide range of 'why', 'how' and 'what' questions, and has in some cases led to the practice of spiritual disciplines aimed at interiorising the primal vision that was supposed to have been embodied in and expressed by the earlier ritual practice. Even the radical criticism of the cult has often been the starting point for important new theological directions; it might even be argued that it is the liturgical, cultic matrix of religion that typically provides theology's creative starting point.

Yet, more directly calling for theological explication have been the *spiritual disciplines* that have developed perhaps as supplementary to ritual and liturgy. Whereas liturgy has been corporate (and public in relation to the initiated community), these contemplative practices have usually been more private, though we cannot differentiate them sharply in this way. In Tibetan monastic Buddhism, for example, while there is certainly the practice of individual spirituality, there is also the extraordinarily impressive daily monastic congregational exercises, the reciting of sacred texts and prayers in an orderly corporate form, rather like the Christian monastic discipline of the daily office. What we need to note here, though, is the way these monastic practices are sometimes linked with development of theological (or dhammalogical) competence. The Tibetan Buddhist monks, for example, practice a very vigorous form of doctrinal debate with each other as a means of proving and improving their skill in formulating the meaning of their tradition.

We may look briefly at one other instance of a linking of corporate spirituality with the development of theological insight in a community. The Liṅgāyata Śaiva community, sometimes referred to as Vīra-śaivas, give very great emphasis to their togetherness. As we noted earlier, one of the essential five daily duties of a Liṅgāyat is the nurturing of the devotees sharing the life of the community. And this community also developed the practice of meeting together for mutual encouragement in their 'Experience Hall', which involved a time of exhorting one another in their commitment to the 'Eight Protections' and the 'Five Duties'. A more 'mystical' spiritual discipline is linked with these various activities: there are six 'stages' through which the soul is to move towards its true destiny – intimate union with Śiva in his triple *liṅga*-form; to these forms of the divine there correspond various sub-stages of the inner pilgrimage of the '*aṅga*' (here meaning 'soul'). Some Liṅgāyata teachers identify as many as 101 such experiences. Here we see an instance of theological reflection closely linked with a tradition's spiritual discipline (Nandimath 1979: 120-40).

h) Finally, if we look at the theological task in relation to the *experiential* dimension of religious life, we can assume that just as 'experience' is a sort of hinge-point for all other aspects of a religious tradition, so all levels of theologising need in the final analysis not only to be grounded in authentic ecclesial participation or experience; theology should also intend that participants more clearly see and experience their tradition's meaning and thus appropriate its liberating and life-shaping power. We take up in a later chapter the question of how 'experience' relates to 'expression'; it is agreed that there is a mutual interaction, as each shapes the other in various ways. At this point we shall note only the fact that *contextual* changes too affect the character of both 'expression' and 'experience'. The 'theologian' then has to attempt to discriminate between different ways of experience of the inner life of the tradition as this is affected by attitudes from outside the tradition.

What is at issue is the extent to which the experiencing, the consciousness and perceptual changes of the human community as a whole are to be permitted to shape the way in which a tradition's religious visioning is to be expressed. Perhaps it is the Judeo-Christian traditions that have been confronted more fiercely by this question than most others, in that there has been more rapid change in the cultural values, social habits, and general world-view in western society than elsewhere, as increasingly the secular community in the West develops its norms independently of any ecclesiastical or theological influence. This modernist dilemma, however, is in no sense confined to the West, nor to Judeo-Christianity. All world religions, and primal religions perhaps in an even more intensely threatening way, are in some degree or another now exposed to the challenge of secularisation, to an increasingly technology-oriented culture and the innovative values of western modernity. Most religious traditions have already made some forms of response, no doubt effective to a lesser or greater degree, to this challenge of the modern technological consciousness. Vigorous reactionary assertion of traditional values, as in some Islamic countries, without any responsive interaction can hardly be considered ultimately effective. Nor does it seem likely that the development of a 'two realms' life-style, with a radical dichotomy of industrial, technological values and traditional, family and personal values, as in much Japanese society, will be able to sustain the inner conflict entailed.

The partial assimilation of the innovative values, with appropriate partial modifications of the old cultural traditions, such as is typical of neo-Hinduism,

may to some extent point the way to a theological stance that is both responsible and yet creative, that is faithful to the deepest values implicit in key
perceptions of reality given by the tradition, yet responds appropriately to the
new cultural challenge. Neither absolute rejection of this context of secular
consciousness, nor mere accommodation to its values, can be the way for an
authentic interpretation of theological meaning for such a context. In no
religious tradition can the modern experience as such be *finally normative* in
its search for meaning. Anything less than a response that is sensitively in
tune with the central insights into reality afforded by the 'creative matrix of
meaning' given by the tradition, must in the end be regarded as an abberative
theological stance. Authentic theology will often involve some degree of confrontation, at the levels both of life-values and of world-view, or life-meaning.
The ultimate goals to which the theologian points will necessitate various
kinds of challenge to modes of life that directly contradict the implicit
values of this ultimacy. The theologian is committed to the emerging of a
new consciousness.

Having now attempted this broad-based comparative phenomenological
analysis of the ways 'theology' typically functions within religious traditions,
especially with reference to the various 'dimensions' typical of religious life, by
way of *summary* we might list the *definitive aspects* of this *theological task*.

1) Religious traditions, in their various ways, *articulate their central vision of
reality* and their interpretation of the *meaning* of this world-view and the life-
values and commitments it involves. This is in essence a feature not only of
literate and classical traditions, for primal myths also are ways of verbalising
visionary meaning. In literate traditions, this 'perceived meaning' is expressed
in more clearly conceptualised forms, more explicitly cognitive in content
and at times more systematic in style. The interpretation of meaning typically
occurs at a number of different levels in religious traditions, as well as in relation to the different dimensions of religious life. In many traditions there are
distinct classes of people responsible for the diverse types of theological expression, some even assuming the task of systematic reflection and articulation.

2) This theological task is typically to be *grounded in the ecclesial life of the
tradition*; it is 'ecclesial reflection' (Farley 1978). Its visionary springs will be
found in the creative matrix of meaning — the mythic imagery, the cultic
ritual and liturgy, the doctrines — as well as in the social life of the community

of faith. Thus, the theological process will involve scriptural exegesis and interpretation as an important part. Scripture (or sacred verbal tradition) functions in this normative way because the sacred texts (or oral tradition) are held to embody the core vision in a special way, and this vision of the transcendent Focus is taken as central for theological reflection. Indeed, the theologian's task will be seen primarily to be that of communicating this vision of the Transcendent as that which gives ultimate meaning to life.

3) Thus, one important task of theology is to *identify the ultimate goal of life* for participants in the tradition, and to identify this with the greatest possible *cognitive clarity* (not denying its 'beyondness'), and to provide directions both for a life-style and life-actions appropriate to such an ultimate End. Thus, there are various ancillary forms of theologising that are all part of the total theological task. Despite this diversity, there is a clear integrating factor, at least when there is close correspondence between the primal sacred Focus of the tradition's central vision and the ultimate *goal* for the participant.

4) That theological reflection involves meaning for life and life-values entails its typically contextual character. In that, for the believer, life praxis has the sense of commitment to action and to a life style that are seen as commensurate with the central vision, contextual ethical reflection will necessarily be a part of the theological process. In this matter, though, we find that religious traditions vary greatly in the extent to which this ethical reflective process is seen as intrinsic to the visionary goal of life. In some theological systems, life-praxis is seen as but a preliminary stage on the path to the ultimate Goal. Even in such cases, however, there will probably be basic attitudes or qualities of character that will be seen as intrinsic to the ultimate state of liberation or enlightenment.

5) There is typically a critical dimension in theological reflection, and in two distinct ways. Firstly, 'critical' in the sense that the task of 'reflecting on meaning' intrinsically entails a certain distancing from the immediacy of the focal vision in itself, or from merely experiencing the inner life of the tradition. Secondly, in the sense of critical response to the life-values and perceptions of reality of those not part of the tradition. It has been made abundantly clear that any such 'critical evaluation' will also be a positive appropriating of those aspects of life that are seen to enhance, even to correct, modes of life and thought hitherto expounded by the tradition. And, in the distancing of *reflec-*

tion on the meaning of the tradition's vision, there will typically be the confidence that this vision can provide resources for ongoing revaluation of the context with which it interacts, and itself provide resources for re-interpretation of the theological concepts with which the vision has been interpreted and systematised in the past.

6) In the process of relating the theological process to a context beyond the tradition, there is, typically though not always explicitly, in post-primal traditions the interpretation and communication of the meaning of the tradition's vision *to those outside its life*. This may or may not be seen as an *apologetic* task, and is far more typical of literate traditions, even in highly 'tolerant' Indian religious life, than is usually recognised. Naturally, it is when there is a ferment of religious interaction, as was the case in the sixth century B.C. as well as in later classical periods in Indian religious life, when a variety of distinct religious *darśanas* came into contact with each other, that the task of inter-religious communication becomes most compelling. Although there are different ways of interpreting the term 'truth-claims', there is little doubt that typically in literate religious traditions the distinct perceptions of reality they have expressed have always involved some degree of confrontation, the recognition that some views of ultimate Truth differ cognitively and significantly from others. How religious traditions and their theologians then respond to such a recognition is another matter. But meaning-interpretation always involves some kind of truth-claim too.

7) The task of reflecting on the ecclesial matrix of meaning and systematically articulating this to the community and to the wider public has typically required the theologian *to identify*, as the initial basis of this systematic task, *some image* or analogy, or analogical concept, seen as central to the tradition's vision, as being able to provide the integrating and creative centre for a *coherent conceptual account of the tradition's* perception of reality; yet it will be an integrating centre-point that makes necessary some form of *dialectic* as the only appropriate mode of thus conceptualising a transcendent vision. 'Analogical', 'coherent' and 'dialectic' are all categories that can signify a variety of theological styles and approaches (Tracy 1981: 405-45). Perhaps we might say that typically in theological forms of expression, where the description of transcendence is involved (even though – paradoxically? – a transcendence inclusive of, even in terms of, an immanental dimension) the nature of the 'coherence' aimed for will involve a degree of *paradoxical* expression. The

'major' religious traditions typically attempt to provide *systematic* conceptual articulation, but the theologian will usually also be aware that the very inclusiveness, even elusiveness, of the cognitive range of his concepts, points to their having authentically derived from or developed out of the central images of the tradition's visionary life.

4

Identifying Ultimate Goals: Integrating Lesser Goals

In the previous chapter it was suggested that a religious core-vision always contains within it a perception of some ultimate life-goal, and perhaps also the means to attaining that goal. The supreme aim of life is integral to the transcendent vision at the centre of a religious tradition and experience within that tradition. When theologians draw out the meaning of their tradition, they typically make the goal-means issue crucial to understanding the tradition. The 17th century Westminster Catechism in its opening words provides one kind of example: 'What is the chief end of man? The chief end of man is to glorify God and enjoy him for ever', and goes on to propound just how this 'chief end' is to be attained. But the earlier Christian credal confessions — Apostles, Nicene, Athanasian — were no less concerned about chief ends and chief means, even if less explicitly so. And this normative delineation of what is seen as constituting the essential goals of a tradition has usually acted as a way by which the guardians of the tradition ascertain how 'orthodox' people are in their understanding of and attitude towards the tradition. Clearly more than 'right opinion' will usually be looked for; it will typically be a matter of 'right seeing'.

Almost all Indian discussions of the great issues of life will refer early on to the four 'human goals' (*purusha-artha*): the right ordering of life (*dharma*), the 'economic' dimension of life (*artha*), the satisfaction of natural desires (*kāma*), and ultimate release (*moksha*). Doubtless in most such discussion the finality of the fourth goal, understood especially as release from the binding cycle of rebirth, will be soon asserted. Even in the Indian context of great doctrinal flexibility, the issue of orthodoxy inevitably arose, though it has so often been asserted of late, and to some extent rightly, that being a 'Hindu' is not a matter of giving assent to any particular set of doctrines, but is rather a matter of birth. For many centuries, however, there was a rather crucial divide: between those who saw Vedic scriptures as the basis for *dharma*, as also for the more ultimate goal, *moksha*, and those whose 'dharmic' grounding was in some other set of revelatory insights (i.e. in particular, Jainas and Buddhists). Then both in these *nāstika* traditions, or those for whom 'it is not' (i.e. Vedic authority) and in the diverse paths taken on general Vedic grounding, there is the immediate task of identifying just what are the valid goals of life; what is the true way and its relationship to the final goal? Thus each tradition, or 'vision' within the inclusive 'Hindu' family of traditions, typically begins by affirming the need for 'right seeing', especially right seeing of *tattva*, i.e. that which really is; then this leads up, by a series of spiritual disciplines or 'good means' (*hita, sādhana*), to the anticipated final goal. The structured basis of the Vedantic discipline, for example (i.e. the Brahma- or Vedanta-Sūtras), follows this pattern.

Now can we not assume that if the interpreters of a tradition, or sub-tradition, are more or less unanimous in finding a certain ultimate life-goal at the heart of the tradition, that there is indeed some intrinsic link between visionary centre and identified supreme goal? This still leaves the possibility of great diversity, perhaps even disparity, of goals within a religious community: and, of course, there is the empirical fact of great difference in the kinds of aspirations we find between different traditions. The frequent assertion, almost a slogan, of neo-Hinduism, that there is 'one goal with many paths', that this is the only proper way to look at the multiplicity of religions, has been found to be very plausible to a large number of Indian people in recent years. The point could, however, be equally well reversed: 'One path, many goals'. For we find a great variety of ultimate aims being pursued by such similar practices as, say, the chanting of prayers, counting prayer-beads, fasting, renunciation, ablutions, sacramental food, meditative techniques, and the use of common symbols such as fire, light, water, trees and so on.

Yogic practice may be taken as another example. Used in some form by many different traditions in India, the distinct (and diverse) objectives with which it is practised are often ignored. In the classical school of Yoga, as summarised by Patanjali, the intention is so to yoke the mind that the inmost self can wean itself away from attachment to sense-objects, so that the senses also become stilled, the mind controlled, and the self is set free to experience the pure 'isolation' of selfhood (Dasgupta 1975 (I): 208-71). If God, as the most perfect and liberated soul, can be brought in to serve as an aid to concentration, then the self's ultimate objective is the more assured. But it is *ātma-kaivalya*, or the 'isolation' of the self, that is the final goal of the classically formulated eight-fold yogic path; it is not God, or meditation on God, or union with God as such.

Other ends too can be served by yogic techniques. In the Buddhism of the Elders, as we have seen, there is a similar eight-fold yogic practice that is made the 'Noble Path' to Nirvāṇa. Here, though, there is an adamant rejection of any permanent ontological entity such as the self or soul (Smart, in Wood, 1981: 85). Nor can God, should he exist, be of any help in attaining that desired end. The very thirst for existence is the root-cause of human anguish. Nirvāṇa is, literally, the 'extinguishing' of desire for attachment to or the continuation of ego-existence in the karmic cycle. And the gentle discipline of the eight-fold Path is effective in reaching this blissful goal in which there is no more ego-attachment, desire, dependence, and therefore no more distress. There are certainly *some* similarities between this Buddhist goal and that of classical Yoga, despite the doctrinal disparities.

A tradition with an objective still resembling that of Yoga, but differing in important ways from that of the Buddha, is Jainism (Jaini: 1979). In this system individual souls are sharply distinguished from each other, but (with some exceptions) are equally in need of liberation from material entanglement, and equally destined for an ultimate, isolated state of pure omniscient soulness. Here the difference is, admittedly, seen more in the means employed, when compared to Yoga. Jaina too has its yogic techniques, but is primarily committed to rigorous ascetic acts appropriate for soul-purification. These are calculated first to halt, then progressively to remove the infiltration of karmic matter, which forms like a weighty crust around the soul and prevents its movement upwards to that pure soulness which is its proper buoyant state. In Jainism too, therefore, ontological status determines the particular means by which the supreme goal is pursued. The soul becomes an heroic *jina* (and so 'Jaina') or one who 'overcomes' by his decisive acts of purification.

When yogic practice, however, is followed within the framework of a whole-hearted theism, such as we find in the various sub-sects of Vaishṇavism and Śaivism, its role in relation to the ultimate goal becomes seriously modified. Now, 'union with God' is the final aim, so that yogic techniques necessarily become subordinate to this different kind of *summum bonum*. It is so radically different because the sense of dependence upon the soul's supreme Lord, and the experience of such a dependent relationship with him, is imperative to this kind of theistic perspective. However, in that attachment to the supreme Self is best attained by detachment from all that is other than that Self, yogic discipline comes into its own *at this preliminary level*. Theistic yoga's role is also to be an aid to the soul's meditation on the supreme Lord, helping to concentrate on his many perfect attributes; in classical Yoga this theistic dimension is the preliminary stage and has a lower-level significance.

Yogic practice, then, is used for a variety of purposes and at diverse levels of importance. The common practice does not provide the key to the intention, so that there is as much danger of serious misrepresentation when observers find 'essences' in common external practices as when they assume common goals despite the differences in practice. A far more thorough analysis is needed of goals in relationship to the means employed to attain them. Clearly we cannot say that there are no common goals between religions. It is probably legitimate to classify the objectives of religions into types sufficiently similar to belong to the same conceptual families. And such religious/theological typology is still in its infancy (Biezais, in Honko 1979: 143-160; Cf. Whaling 1985 (I): 97-8).

A complicating factor, as we noted, is that even *within one religion we find such a broad range of goals held by different types of believers.* Indeed, a great deal of the theological debate that takes place within a tradition concerns the question, 'what really is the principal goal, the essential aim, of this tradition?' Such debate can result in reform groups, charges of heresy, breakaway movements, even the emergence of a new kind of tradition. In some traditions, of course, a wide range of goals, of a more proximate, lower-order kind, is permitted, which takes some of the urgency out of theological debate. The great shrine of Veṅkaṭeśvara at Tirumalai in South India has hundreds of thousands of pilgrims each year; they pour in throughout the year. And their motives will be almost as varied as the numbers who seek the 'vision' of the 'Lord of the Seven Hills'. There are those who seek healing, those who want blessings for their marriage, those who just want a jolly outing, those who want success at business (perhaps even black-market business) or at the horse-races; then there are those who seek the gift of ultimate release, and those whose one aim is to experience the Lord's loving presence more fully. All these goals are at differing levels regarded as acceptable. But the Veṅkaṭeśvara shrine is part of the Śrī Vaishṇava tradition, with its clear doctrine of self-forgetting devotion as the most excellent of all goals; and there is little doubt if pilgrims (only few of whom will be Vaishṇavas) were asked what is ultimately the one essential goal of life, a great majority would acknowledge, perhaps somewhat inarticulately, that to know God, to be in tune with God, to be true to God, or some such sentiment, would emerge.

An important task of the theologian of any tradition is not only to distinguish lesser, proximate (though perhaps permissable) goals from the most excellent, ultimate goal envisioned in the tradition; it is also to attempt to *integrate these goals*, to discover ways in which the 'lesser' can be included in the more ultimate, and can help in pointing the way to that final goal, thus becoming in their own way 'means' to the aspired-for End.

There is nothing theologically arbitrary about identifying the ultimate goal, for its ultimacy is inherent in the core-vision. Where the vision is essentially different from that of others, so that a distinct life-goal of ultimate value is required, no doubt a separate tradition, or possibly a sectarian distinctiveness, will emerge.

. Most religions will in practice allow ample room for a number of 'lower' goals, to the extent that in most traditions there are many believers who never reach the theologically (and religiously) desirable level of aspiring to the highest goal. To theologians of the 'puritan' type this will always seem a deplorable state of affairs; others may find such theological inclusiveness and flexibility desirable, perhaps for social, perhaps for psychological reasons. In both Jainism and Buddhism (Gombrich 1971), for example, the laity have a very significant role within the tradition as a whole, even though their life-aims and indeed their life-practices are very different from the goal of ultimate release aspired to by the initiated monks – the 'worthies' (*arhats*), 'alms-receivers', 'perfected ones', 'silent ones', etc. Accepting that they cannot yet aspire to that final goal, the laity seek to do meritorious deeds which will help them on their way to a better birth in the next life. They remain tied to the very life-cycle the enlightened ones seek to escape, and as a means to this limited end the laity make use of the karmic law which is transcended and renounced by the enlightened. But an essential part of the laity's merit is the support of the enlightened by their gifts of food for their sustenance, and in some necessary cases, lands and money for the building and maintenance of monasteries. Thus the disparity of aspiration is resolved by the practical needs of the community as a whole.

Jainism resolves the inherent tension of disparate goals and means between monks and laity by working out a similar life-discipline, but at different levels of application. Thus the twelve Vows of the monk's discipline concerning detachment from property, chastity, non-injury to life and the like, leading on to twenty-two acts of privation, are practiced at a less rigorous, more 'intentional' level by the laity. We might also note that in the Jaina scheme all actions are thought to determine directly the extent to which *karma* (understood as a subtle material) influences the soul. The extreme ascetic actions prescribed by the tradition can result in the soul being fully purified of its karmic encumbrance, so that it can rise up to its proper state of omniscient, aloof soulness. Action as such, then, if of the appropriate kind, is never incongruous within this scheme of soul-purification, though to the outsider it may seem that there is incongruity between the ascetic practice and the aspired end.

It is, then, of great importance to find what is regarded as the supreme aim of life in any tradition, as this will always be integral to the central transcendent vision. How, though, are we to ascertain which is the highest goal in religions where there are numerous goals of importance? The *interpretation of the Bhagavad-Gītā* is a case in point. The 'Lord' Song' is not without claims to be regarded as the most representative of all Hindu Scriptures, even if it does lack some of the esoteric material, especially the Tantric ritual and much of the mythology found in Purānas and traditional sectarian scriptures; perhaps it may be called more 'urbane' in style and more systematic in form than these other writings in the Hindu 'corpus'. But although it is included among so-called 'traditional' (*smṛiti*, i.e. 'remembered') scriptures and is not primary Vedic revelation (*śruti*, i.e. 'heard'), it soon took on the authority of a revelatory Upanishad. Indeed many regard it as the culminating statement of the Upanishadic themes, the Upanishads themselves being the 'end' or culmination of the Vedas (i.e. Upanishad is equal to Vedānta). The Gītā has also managed to include strands from a number of other religious sources, not least from Buddhism. In fact the Gītā might be thought of as a major Brahmanic response to the Buddhist 'threat'. Whatever the immediate cause of its composition, the Gītā is certainly inclusive in style, despite its essentially Vaishṇava theological background. And within a few centuries of its composition it had become so pervasively popular and religiously authoritative that every Vedantic school felt it necessary to have a conclusive commentary written on it, reflecting that Vedantic school's own theological position. Nor was it very difficult for each school to find material by which it felt able to express and find confirmation of its own position, at least to its own satisfaction.

Thus the Gītā's history epitomises the theological inclusiveness (or some would say 'tensions') within Hinduism. The initial introduction of an outsider either to Hinduism in general or to the Gītā in particular is usually a time of some conceptual confusion. So many distinct life-goals are espoused. In the case of the Gītā (as indeed of all Hindu thought) much of the time we are at the level of life operating on the principle of just-deserts; a person attains exactly what he is fit for, he finds just what he is able to seek, he receives what he really deserves. At this level a person should simply aspire to whatever is natural to him. 'What use is there in unnatural repression', says the Gītā (3.33). In other words, karmic law determines the course of events, especially in relation to the individual's destiny.

Cosmologically, too, life-experience is seen as the result of the mixture of qualitatively different strands of the stuff of cosmic creativity (e.g. 2.45; 3.5, 27-9; 7.12-14; 14.5-19). Each person is dominated by one or other of these three creative strands – the purity of light, vigour of passion, heavy darkness; again, *karma* determines how the strands are to be mixed. At the same time the God-believer is able to see this cosmic life-process as God's doing (3.22, 24; 41.3; 7.12).

On the human side, action (*karma*) is to be accepted as an absolute duty (3.5, 8-9); it is an inescapable part of the continual stream of cosmic-life, a stream based essentially on the *brahman*-principle, the mysterious power underlying the ritual sacrifice and through which all creative acts are effected (3.14-33). Indeed, all the presiding deities and spirits of this cosmic life too are dependent upon the eternal sacrifice. Feed these Powers and they in turn will feed human and cosmic life. Here, then, we have a second level of aspiration: to do those ritual deeds that are necessary for cosmic existence. But '*karma*' is not only ritual action: *all* action has its inevitable outworking, its 'fruits' that then have necessarily to be exhausted in either pleasant or unpleasant experience. Yet action must be continued, affirms the Gītā, or there will be cosmic chaos, the 'worlds will fall into ruin' (3.8, 24). This point is really but an extension of the first (doing what is 'natural'); and in both cases there is probably a veiled rejection of the Buddhist call to renunciation of ritual action and of all action that intends ego-satisfaction (but see below).

A third, again corresponding, life-goal is the *integration* (*loka-saṃgraha*, e.g. 3.20), of society and maintaining the dharmic order of things, in particular preserving the well-being of the gentle and those devoted to God. Perhaps here too there was alarm at the implications for the Brahmanic social order if there were further Buddhist advances. Thus, so far, we see the Gītā affirming the first three of the 'four goals of life' – *dharma, artha* and *kāma*.

So far there has been no reference to the life-situation in which the Gītā is set; it is an epic-mythic setting, and of some importance as a grounding for certain aspects of the Gītā's metaphysics. There were two groups of Kshatriya brothers (ruling warrior class), along with their followers, both from the same grandfather. One group of brothers, the Pāṇḍavas, despite a series of conciliatory attempts, including the mediation of Kṛishṇa (even then recognised in a veiled way as the incarnation of Vishṇu on earth) had been unjustly denied their country by their cousin group, the Kauravas. Battle was about to break out between then. As the two armies were lined up against each other, a leading war-rior of the Pāṇḍavas, Arjuna, suddenly decides that he cannot continue with this violent course of action, righteous though their cause might be. The cost in loss of life of his own kith and kin, such violent disrespect towards his teachers on the other side, the disruption of life generally, is not worth this sacrifice. But Krishna happens to be his charioteer, and urges Arjuna to fight as it is the only possible *dharmic* way. Doing one's particular *dharma* is a supreme duty (2.31; 3.35); that is, Arjuna must be committed to action that fits into the total cosmic ordering of things, that particular aspect of the cosmic *dharma* that is manifest in the givenness of one's birth and its natural qualities.

This mythically framed life-situation, then, was the starting-point for the 'Song of God', in effect a rather complex theological treatise. Yet in urging action as unavoidable at this level of life-duty, the Gita immediately brings in a further and higher level of existence, in this case picking up the Buddha's key-principle, viz. that *desire is the cause of all distress in life* (3.37-41). That dharmic action is to be done without any desire (*kāma*) for the benefits of that action becomes a central strand in the Gītā's re-interpretation of things (e.g. 2.47, 51; 4.19-23). Only thus can the person intent on fulfilling the dharmic duties of life remain free from the causal chain consequent on all actions, good or bad. This kind of disinterested action will work itself out in the natural sphere; in his *inner selfhood* the actor will be free. Here, then, is the *fourth* important goal: *desirelessness* and *stillness of inner being*, which seems closely akin to the Buddhist life-goal. For the Gītā, however, no radically new dharmic principle is called for (as the Buddha taught). 'Let each do his own *dharma*, according to his nature, and let him do it for its own sake, not for its benefits': this is a paraphrase of the Gītā's view of what life is at the level of moral imperative. Obviously there are in the Gītā also life-aspirations beyond such an imperative.

Involvement in the life-process at this level of *dharma* leads a person to confusion about his true selfhood. The self, though in essence unchanging, becomes fatally entangled in the mutations and enticements of the natural world. Here again we see assumptions that are part of the Buddhist vision, and assumptions that contradict it. Confusion arising from desire is essential to the Buddhist analysis; but the Buddha could not accept that any unchanging core selfhood was involved in this process. The Gītā's view of such a transcendent inner self reflects the 'vision' of Sāmkhya-Yoga, and to some extent other Indian metaphysical systems. The perceptions of the faculty of mental discrimination (the *buddhi*) and the mind (*manas*, there are in fact a number of organising principles postulated for the complex psycho-physical side of life, all distinct from, though so close to, the unchanging self within) become confused, so that the qualities of the natural, psycho-physical world (*Prakṛti*) are quite wrongly attributed to the unchanging self within (*Purusha* or *ātman*) and the body with its sensory organs is mistaken for the true self.

There is not only an epistemological problem envisaged here. There is also, as we have seen, the traditional Indian cosmic flaw — bondage to the karmic process. Thus, along with virtually every other religious system of India, the Gītā too assumes that the eternal soul or self needs to find *release from its bondage* to the cycle of birth and rebirth. And this is yet another kind of life-goal. Some interpreters have assumed that this is the ultimate goal of the Gītā.

In view of the confusion and the bondage of the self, what is needed is first for the inner self to be disentangled and distinguished from the natural world with all its confusing seductions. To effect this separation the *yogic discipline* is commended (2.39-40, 48-61, etc.). By this 'yoking' of the mind there will be stillness and control of the mind in relation to senses. This in turn means that the inner person stands still in its authentic selfhood. While no such self-hood is envisaged, a similar *tranquil, confusionless 'becoming-Brahman'* was again a key life-goal in the Buddhist vision: to become the very principle of stillness, Brahman (5.21-24; 6.27-8). And so it is for the Gītā, though even yet *not* the ultimate aim.

So we are introduced to another and very crucial theme: the Lord endowed with all manner of great and adorable qualities is revealed in his universal glory (*viśva-rūpa-darśana*, chapt. 11). He is to be loved and worshipped with self-forgetting devotion as the ultimate Goal of life, for he also loves his devotees greatly (4.7-11; 5.29; 6.30-1, 47; 7.23, 28-30; 9.13-14, 24-34; 10.8-10; 12.6-10, 20; 14.26-7; 18.54-62). This is described as the 'supreme secret', a mystery that seems to relativise all prior life-goals (18.63-66). Thus, regarding life's duties, for example: 'Give up all your duties, take me as your sole refuge, I will set you free from all evils' (18.66). In view of all that has been affirmed earlier this hardly means literally renouncing all life's actions. Rather, it is a recognition that all life-actions are in the end offered up to God. And this is the culmination of numerous earlier anticipations of such ultimate God-orientation, a theistic vision of life as God's.

Some interpreters would no doubt argue that the above account is loaded in favour of a God-oriented system; non-dualist exponents, for example, offer a very different interpretation of the same text. Considerable weight, however, must be given to the thematic structuring of the Gītā; the very order in which these various aspirations emerge, even if not in an obviously systematic form, does suggest strongly a stage-by-stage process with a mounting crescendo of bhakti-passages, all culminating in the revelation of the gloriously personal

God and the loving devotion appropriate to him.

Certainly one or other of these life-goals we have found in the Gītā has to be taken, and always has been in the interpreting commentaries, as an *ultimate goal*. Such an ultimate goal has to be seen as either including other lesser goals, or as superseding them, if a convincingly coherent system is to be formulated. In the Gītā's case, as in Indian theistic religion generally (though not invariably, as we can see in the somewhat weak theism of the Logicians and of the Yoga school), the vision of the glorious Lord as the final goal of human aspiration is able to include the numerous more proximate aims of life. We have already noted that the God-believer experiences the cosmic process of just-deserts as God's gift. The ritual sacrificial system is transposed to the offering of all life to God. Indeed the whole karmic process, which could well threaten a theistic system, is seen as initiated by the Lord of all *karma*; the impersonal moral law of cause-effect is made subordinate to, and normally the medium expressing, the personal will of God. In the theistic vision, then, causality operates within the framework of personal grace, though grace will normally operate along justly causal lines. Thus eventually the aim to be released from the bondage of karma becomes *the aim to be in loving bondage to the Lord of the whole process*. And all action, including the sacrificial and other religious action prescribed by scripture, is given a subordinate but ultimately significant role. It is done for the sake of devotion to the Lord (9.27, 34; 12.6; 18.56-7, 65). Thus, karma is ancillary to and included in the *bhakti-*motif; *the supreme goal gives further value to the lesser goal*. This is how at least the theistic commentators elucidate the Gītā's core-vision, with its interdependently formulated concepts.

Although we have been referring here to action and devotion as 'goals', they are often thought of as *means* to some greater end. Traditionally, as we saw in an earlier chapter, there have been three major 'ways' or 'means' listed in Indian discussions on religion — action, devotion, knowledge. Each has been taken as a way to the final end of life. Now it is true that most religious systems will regard the various kinds of actions required by the tradition as necessary to some other end. While neither a Kantian 'duty for duty's sake', nor the modern concern for social action as an ultimate good in itself, are generally typical of the religious outlook, we do find the sense of the necessity, even *ultimacy*, of certain actions as part of a total ritual/cosmic pattern. Often some further religious sanction is expected to undergird and encourage the good works required (even if this is considered morally unsatisfactory by some ethicists). The New Testament, for example, expects righteous deeds of the

Christian on the grounds of a wide range of such sanctions. In some cases, no doubt, the implications are that the desired way of life is good in itself, especially when believers are urged to a certain way of life on the typically biblical premiss that God is holy, therefore his people should be holy, or that Christ was forgiving, loving etc., and so his followers should be forgiving, loving, and so on. By emulating the divine nature their way of life can be seen as a sharing in the ultimate way things are to be. They are children of the kingdom that is to be. It is of interest to find that the Gītā also refers to the need for emulating God in one very important instance: the wise man is to 'perform unceasingly the works that must be done ... (just as) I (the Lord) tirelessly busy myself in work' (3.19, 23), a passage that is rather similar to the statement of Jesus in John's gospel (5.17), though the contexts are very different.

This general attitude of acting in a certain way because God's nature is such and such looks rather like a personalised, and in some instances an eschatologised, form of another strand in the Indian world-view: that the cosmic system functions according to the eternally given order (in the Vedas called *rita*, later *dharma*). Human good, in this kind of perception, lies in acting in tune with the cosmic ordering of things, an order that is microcosmically embodied in the priestly ritual. And in the full-blown priestly conceptualising of this perception of reality (i.e. in the Pūrva-Mīmāṃsā system), ritual action takes on virtually an autonomous life of its own. Sacrifice for life in heaven is effective in its aim not because of divine reward, but because the sacrificial action is mysteriously accompanied by an 'unprecedented power' (*apūrva*) appropriate to that which mirrors the essential ordering of the universe. Thus it is in the ritual action itself that the transcendent dimension, characteristic of all religious perception, is found. And the Ritualists were adamant that ritual action should be done not only for benefits on earth and in heaven — for these are less than ultimate goals — but principally because it is 'to be done' as necessary to the very fabric of things. This imperative quality is its essential nature to which no extraneous divine sanctions can add anything, they felt.

In the Indian tradition, then, even the doing of action can be a supreme goal in itself, and not merely a means to some greater good, though part of a cosmic ordering. For the Gītā, though, such an attitude is included at a lower level than that of the ultimate goal. Those who 'delight in Vedic ritual' only, lack discernment, they 'cling to pleasure and power', 'desire is their essence' (2.42-4). At the higher level of experience the same dharmic actions are required, but 'for my sake', and their consequences are no longer binding for the doer because action and consequences are all handed over to the Lord by whose will all actions bear their proper fruit. This makes clear that *no action, whether sacred or not, is now the supreme goal in itself*. Nor strictly speaking is it a 'means' to the supremely desirable end, for the Lord himself cannot finally be gained by good works, even if there are some passages in the Gītā (as in most scriptures, even of grace-systems) suggesting this. The works-grace issue is always delicately poised between legalism and antinomianism, and generally the Gītā tends more towards the former in its explicit ethics, more towards the latter in its implicit theology (cf. 18. 66). Hence the later split among the Vaishnavas, some favouring the 'monkey method' (with divine grace to be appropriated by suitable action), some the 'cat-method' (divine grace can only be surrendered to). Implicitly, then, *this tradition's* theological position is that the devotional relationship based on a vision of the Lord's love *contains within it the actions desired by the Lord. He, and the relationship with him, has become the supreme goal; action, previously a means thereto, is now an ancillary goal.*

The *reverse order of priorities* is theoretically possible, and has indeed been attempted even in the Gītā's case. The somewhat diffuse, but extremely significant, commentary by B.G. Tilak (1935), an ardent Indian (Maratha) nationalist of the latter part of the nineteenth century, found the 'Gītā's Secret' to lie in its call to action as the supreme good and the supreme goal of life. Devotion is but a necessary aid to this ultimate goal. Undoubtedly this viewpoint has its appeal to a certain kind of modernity, East and West. But exegetically it is less convincing and theologically seems less capable of providing a coherent conceptual system, even allowing the authenticity of such a core-vision.

The other important reversal of goal-priorities is that which makes the devotional relationship *subordinate to 'knowledge'*, the third of the traditional Indian 'ways'. Is the loving worship of God but a useful means to the transcendent end of realising some state of being beyond relational experience? The question is, were the theistic interpreters correct in seeing this experience of impersonal being as merely a preliminary stage on the way to the ultimate goal of God-centredness? First the soul is to realise that despite its contingent, dependent character, it is essentially distinct from the natural world of restless change and mortal decay. Then comes the final 'knowledge' of its proper relationship to the glorious Lord of all, so that 'knowledge' itself becomes an experience of loving devotion, according to this theistic interpretation (Lott 1981).

Whether knowledge as transcendent self-experience, or devotion as a loving relationship to the transcendent Lord, is taken as the central vision, *the final goal of life and the means of attaining it become identical* in both systems based on these visions. And here we have another aspect of that coherence which is a necessary element in any convincing conceptual articulation of a core-vision. Surely the *most convincingly coherent religious systems are those in which the key-perception of reality is expressed in a way that can integrate the ultimate goal with the final means of its realisation.* In such an identity the initial vision retains greater clarity and thus makes a more immediate impact even in its conceptualised form. Subordinate ends and the numerous indirect and ancillary means used in any such system are then seen more clearly as such, even when their relative value is enhanced by incorporation into the theistic vision.

We have already noted that Vedānta is the Indian system that in all its forms has been able most effectively to articulate a primal vision, the vision of Brahman as the integrating power from whom derive all beings, the supreme Self at the centre of all selves, the infinitely perfect One, a vision in which Brahman is perceived not only as the supreme Goal of life, but as the only ultimate means by which he himself can be attained. This is the essential issue at stake in the opening debate of all the commentaries on the primary text, the Brahma-Sūtra (the 'thread' of aphorisms concerning Brahman). 'Then, therefore, the desire to know Brahman', runs the enigmatic first aphorism. And the question is raised, what is the significance of 'then', and what the relation of the implied antecendent to the 'knowledge of Brahman'? If this vision of Brahman is the ultimate aim in the Vedantic enquiry, and thus the ultimate objective of life, is there some means within our reach, such as religious endeavour, by which we can attain that goal? All the great commentaries and their traditions agree that, while religious and ethical actions are ultimately appropriate, (for example as being able to purify the mind and prepare it for the transcendent vision), that supreme Self, Brahman, alone can directly grant the vision of himself. He alone can be depended on as the ultimate means to knowledge of his being. Indeed, such 'knowledge' is in reality the *experience* of his being. Such seems to be the intrinsic structure of a transcendent vision.

Even within the Vedantic tradition in its diverse formulations, it seems possible to evaluate the coherence with which the common vision has been formulated by applying this canon of evaluation: which is able to maintain the most convincing articulation of the means-goal identity? Which is the most coherent from this standpoint? I have argued elsewhere (1986) that I find the presentation of the vision in relational and devotional terms most convincing on this score: God's gracious self-sharing is the means to that self-sharing *prema-*

bhakti which is the goal for the loving devotee. In the conceptual form which makes the goal one of sheer identity, surely there remains the persistent ambiguity of, for instance, how the first movement towards this ultimate experience is initiated. To speak of 'divine grace' in such a theological context, as sometimes even the non-dualist will, seems incongruous.

At the centre of the Christian tradition — and the cause of its most vigorous early debate, the Arian controversy — is a similar issue. In God's saving activity, that is in providing the means by which man can reach his supreme end, or fellowship with God, is it necessary for God himself to take the initiative and in his own person perform the necessary saving deeds? 'Orthodox' faith has always replied in the affirmative. Only God can provide the means by which man can reach him. Thus the God-in-Christ doctrine, even if not the trinitarian formulation of official creeds, becomes inescapable once other Christian presuppositions are accepted.

This position, however, does involve us in another dilemma: does human action itself mean nothing as human destiny is worked out? The *karma*-theory in Hindu thought performs a balancing role here, even if it could also raise conceptual problems for believers in divine lordship and grace. Thus, in their various ways the thorough-going theists had to subordinate karmic law to their God-perception, as we saw. What they tried to do was to show that every human act is both that of a responsible agent and is permitted by the Lord whose grace in the end will prevail. The Christian will need to present his case along somewhat similar lines, unless he feels God's transcendent power and grace to be so freely determined that human actions must be regarded as soteriologically quite insignificant. Again, the vision of a means-end identity would be preserved, but another kind of incoherence would threaten.

5

Drawing Out Implicit Patterns of Coherence

Wilfred Cantwell Smith (1977; 1979; 1981) has argued vigorously for the primacy of inner experiential faith over propositional beliefs. His intention is to redress the attitudinal imbalance in much Western Protestant Christianity, where 'faith', as the means to salvation, has been identified too closely with 'right belief', with assent to some doctrinal formulation. The early Christian experience, Smith contends, was essentially an 'awareness', a 'new insight', a 'recognition', especially in relation to the 'focus of faith', Christ. It was not a new set of beliefs about Christ, God, or the World. Yet Smith does admit that 'the new vision of the world and of themselves was articulated in quite an array of new conceptual symbols'. If we want to understand what was really happening, however, we should not 'concentrate on those symbols, except as clues to something much deeper and more personal. It is not what they believed that is significant, but the new faith that the belief-system gave a pattern to, and was generated by' (1977: 88). In this way the primacy of 'faith' over 'belief' is given great stress (Cf. Wiebe's 'Response', 1979).

In view of the assumption of numerous Christian ecclesiastics and some kinds of evangelicals that true religion is orthodoxy of doctrine, Smith's emphasis is perhaps justified. But his thesis does not seem to allow room for the fact that inner faith has continuing epistemological need both for grounding in and expression through, not merely an 'array of conceptual symbols', but conceptual expression that will always be propositional to some extent. Smith does concede that 'faith' lays an 'inescapable obligation' on the religious person to articulate that faith in coherent form (1977: 99). Certainly the theologian's search for fitting expression of the *meaning* found in faith, and the attempt to communicate that meaning, will entail also a search for an appropriate vocabulary, and a selection of those symbols and analogies of the tradition that seem most expressive of the meaning perceived. Then there will usually be the discursive development of separate themes, and eventually, probably, their systematic formulation into a coherent belief-system. This is all part of the process of fleshing out the core-faith. It will intend to embody the central vision, but will not be directly identified with that vision in its immediacy of self-authenticating perception; 'God', for example, can never be identified directly or fully with the 'God-talk' of theology. Though the vision underlies concepts about the vision (in terms of the inner religious structure), and theology is dependent upon faith, there is also a process of continuing interaction involved between vision and theology; theologies help to shape primal visions as well as being necessary to give shape to that initial apprehension.

There is, then, an interdependence of perception and conception, of 'faith' and 'belief' in the religious life; and this implies that even if the primal vision should be given prior ontological status, the theological process in which the vision is conceptually formulated *can be* an authentic and integral extension of it. The condition for such authenticity and integrity is that theology remains rooted in the primal vision and continues to be oriented towards that central point.

In any tradition, however, whatever steps may be taken to recover the primal vision, there are no certain guarantees that what emerges theologically as the most potent shaping perception is truly that tradition's vital centre. Theologies can fail to do visionary justice to their tradition, which means failing to find appropriate conceptual expression; theologies may, judging from the inner history of their tradition, even positively distort that primal vision in which they are to be grounded. In other words, we can expect some kind of *inner coherence*, in various forms, in looking for authentic theologising, though this will need to be a coherence that does not preclude paradoxical language also; perhaps we can look for 'ecstatic rationality' (Tillich). Historians of religion will in general deny that there are any norms for authenticity; it will usually be said that there is no way of deciding between different forms of theological articulation, all ostensibly based on the same primal sources (but cf. Smart 1958). But it would at least seem possible to propose that some forms of inner coherence be expected if theological interpretation is to be taken as authentic (Macquarrie 1966: vii). What kinds of coherence, then, are desirable or possible?

Firstly, a religion's *key-perceptions and its conceptual system* should cohere in the sense of being seen as *fundamentally commensurable*. If conceptual form or methodological style are not intrinsically in tune with what is central to the tradition's primal perceptions, in the end such inner contradiction will hardly prove plausible as theological interpretation. The whole of Karl Barth's monumental output was just such an attempt to avoid theological incommensurability. According to the key-perception of his early writings especially, such is the infinite distance from the transcendent Subject, that only an unfathomable intervention from the transcendent side can hope to result iñ anything like an appropriate expression of God's true being (Barth 1936: 18-9). The theologian, therefore, is bound by the forms of expression determined by God, and given in the Gospel of Christ. Barth does not, of course, take a literalist biblical position. He does, though, insist that words and concepts can only be analogically useful media for expressing the transcendent Word because God himself has so determined the appropriateness of the language actually used in communicating the Gospel. Language *as such* is quite inappropriate for God-talk.

In this approach to the theological task, however, has the very proper concern for coherence of visionary perception (the 'revelation') and conceptual expression led to a loss of coherence in other ways? The initial gap between these two dimensions of the Gospel is so wide, the dialectic required to bridge the gap so radical, that the detachment of one or other dialectical pole from its moorings becomes inevitable. Naturally it is language and the conceptualising process that suffers from the infinite difference of God and world. Barth's later writings indicate that he himself was aware of the problem; there is more talk of the 'divine *concursus*', and of the humanness of God (though both still seem in terms of Jesus Christ).

It is not only Christian theologians like Barth who have seen that incommensurability must be avoided in talking about the transcendent realities of the faith. Often this is seen as the problem of accommodating revelation and reason. The Logicians (Nyāya-Vādins) of the Indian theological tradition argued for the *primacy of reason* and developed quite an elaborate scheme of proofs for the existence of God (Bhattacharyya 1961). They held for example that the dependent nature of the universe indicates that it is an effect, and as such it must have some cause appropriate in power and wisdom, etc. to that which it has effected. Then the atomic substances comprising the universe would not combine to form this complex creation without someone to set them in motion initially. Nor could the finished product be kept in its created form, and then be destroyed again (in perpetual recreation) without some sufficient Power. And how would words get their denotative power, or scripture its authority, or moral laws their effectiveness, or the karmic process its just inevitability, without the existence of a universal Lord? These are but some of the arguments used to prove God's existence, the inferential method employed being taken as a fully valid way of knowing such divine realities.

Vedantic theologians generally saw a basic procedural problem here; but it was Rāmānuja in the 12th century, who first recognised the need to work out a thorough theological refutation of this rationalist approach to the knowledge of God (Lott 1975: 128-43). Others before him had contended that knowing God cannot be made dependent upon logical argumentation. His main objection concerned the Logicians' assumption that causal activity on the empirical level is in itself sufficient guide for us to understand how the transcendent Lord is ultimate Cause of the whole process. There is, he felt, a fundamental incommensurability involved here. Perhaps for the Logicians there was not such a great gap between the means of knowledge and the Object to be known, in that they believed God to be only the effective cause, the substantial or inner material cause being atomic particles of the elemental substances they included in their primal perception. Thus, for them, the universe was substantially self-existent, only its particular form being brought about by the Lord's will. It was the Vedantic perception of the one supreme Being, Brahman, as the one Cause in every possible way, that entailed an incompatible style of systematic vision-formulation at this point.

What we should note is that this Vedantic theologian was not merely saying that the arguments for God's existence are not quite strong enough to stand as infallible proofs, nor is he merely taking the fundamentalist way out by falling back on infallible scripture as his source of God-knowledge. He is not even being a simple fideist, arguing that faith reveals all, reason nothing. Nor does he avoid 'dialectical' paradox of any kind. Rather he is saying that the style of conceptual elaboration must cohere with and be commensurate with the intrinsic shape of the primal perception, which is that of a gracious Sovereign, Creator of all, pre-eminently distinguished by uncountable glorious qualities. Core-vision determines the formulation of belief-system, or a fundamental incoherence results. And this is all the more significant in view of the 'pan-en-theistic' relational style of his ontology.

This, then, was the approach of a theologian whose conceptual system needed to be commensurate with a vision which sees personal transcendent Being as the one Cause. What of a system based on the transcendent perception of reality as ultimately, irreducibly one? Śaṅkara and the non-dualistic Vedantins also dismissed any inferential proof as a valid method of knowing the supreme Reality. If, however, one is still at the unenlightened level of mediated knowledge, such arguments play quite a useful role. So, as we noted earlier, Śaṅkara himself offered a considerable range of proofs of, or perhaps pointers to, the existence and character of God, the personal Creator. There are arguments from movement, efficient causality, contingency, grades of perfection, finality or teleology (De Smet 1953). To realise the being of the ultimate One, however, neither argumentation nor any other conceivable means can be of direct help. Even scriptural statements can do no more than point in the right general direction. For as scripture itself puts it, in the end words have to 'turn back', powerless to probe fully the meaning of the ultimate reality (Lott 1980: 67-75).

Language and concepts, then, even sacred revelatory language and its concepts, can only provide indirect clues, implicit meanings concerning the transcendent One. In the end only the intuitive experience of that one Being is an adequate and infallible means of knowledge. Thus the 'perception' of the traditional Vedantic 'means of valid knowledge' is interpreted by Śaṅkara in the final analysis as intuited perception in every initial instance. Even in ordinary observation, he says, in the initial moment there is an indeterminate intuition involved; later there may be differentiating cognition, which necessarily distorts the reality to some degree or another.

In the non-dualist system too, then, a serious attempt is made to provide conceptual expression that is appropriate to the distinctive core-vision. But as in the case of the Barthian perception of things, whatever may be theology's need to incorporate some kind of dialectic, we have to ask if in interpreting the 'core-vision', and in the process of attempting conceptual compatibility with it, there is not some fundamental incoherence of another kind introduced. It is not that the conceptual system itself is incoherent. Indeed, Śaṅkara (like Barth) presents his case with brilliant consistency, given the reality of the initial interpretation. But this key perception itself makes necessary the positing of two levels of reality, ultimate and proximate, transcendent and empirical, absolute and relative – the dialectic is all-important. Ambiguity inevitably results: when are we talking about the one and when about the other? This is a strange duality when the intention is to perceive everything in terms of the vision of absolute identity.

Interestingly, a somewhat similar comment can be made about the equally brilliant 'Voidist' system of the Indian Buddhist philosopher of the early medieval period, Nāgārjuna. And it was Nāgārjuna who first attempted to systematise, dialectically, a perception that included two levels of reality. In fact there is little doubt that Śaṅkara (ostensibly an orthodox Hindu) was, historically speaking, deeply indebted to Nāgārjuna's metaphysical approach. On the other hand, perhaps Nāgārjuna too had been influenced by certain aspects of pre-Śaṅkara non-dualist Vedānta. The exact historical sequence is not at all clear.

The suggestion that a certain kind of 'incoherence' arises in these systems could very easily be countered by saying that if there is any such incommensurability between transcendent vision and the conceptualist task, this is just too bad for conceptualism; the transcendent vision must be taken as primary. If concepts prove to be inadequate for the task of vision-expression, that merely shows their essential inadequacy. And this we have to concede to the extent of giving primacy to the great perceptions, and of recognising the need for *some* paradox in all theology. But why have other systems, without losing sight of a vision that in certain respects is equally 'transcendent', managed to avoid at least the extreme kind of dialectical paradox. Is there not something incongruous about the expending of so much energy in the task of conceptualising, if on the conceptualiser's own presupposition the task is doomed to the failure of being fundamentally incoherent?

Secondly, in conceptualising the vision there will be some kind of *coherence of the central Focus of the vision, even though 'transcendent', with all other cosmic existence.* This involves a number of dimensions – epistemological, ontological, cosmological, perhaps even soteriological and ethical. But particular emphasis, or the ways in which each approach is developed in a system, will depend on the nature of the core-vision. Vedānta, for example, carries an intrinsic *inclusiveness* just because the transcendent Object, Brahman, is an inclusive Being. Transcendence in this case includes an immanental dimension; they are not seen as polarities (Lott 1980: 20-6). In Vedānta, therefore, there is not only an attempt to account for all existence as a continuum of being, which makes ontological coherence more obvious. There is also an attempt to provide an inclusive epistemology. The accepted ways of knowing, though operating at different levels, apply to knowledge of both the supreme Object and the world of contingent objects, even though such a system was not allowed to make the very existence and character of the supreme Object dependent upon empirical ways of knowing, as we saw above. What the Vedantins differ about, then, is the extent to which the same ways of knowing can apply to both world and God, that is about the nature of an inclusive epistemology.

Now it might be thought that there are other religious systems, the Buddhism of the Elders for example, which do not seem to involve a cosmological or any other kind of 'inclusiveness'. Their core-vision does not seem to require much discussion of the nature of 'essential being', or of the origin and nature of the universe. The overriding concern is how to put an end to the continual cycle of birth, death and rebirth, and thus how to attain that permanent bliss of Nirvāṇa in which the thirst for existence – the root-cause of the oppressive cycle – is eradicated. There is certainly no time for speculation about the why, when and whence of cosmic origins. But this speculative indifference is far from an ontological or cosmological incoherence. All existence is seen in re- lation to the great goal to which each individual should aspire: the negation or ending of such contingent existence. With this end in view there is then a sustained analysis of the nature of individual existence, breaking it down to its irreducible categories, its component parts, and always seen in relation to the continuing cycle of cosmic existence. Indeed the *dharma* (*Pāli, dhamma*) of an essential category of individual existence is also seen as part of the *dharma* of the wheel of all life; and both are soteriologically 'included in' the *dharma* which is the way of the Buddha, though not in any substantialist sense. In other words, the whole is seen from the point of view of the envisioned goal, even though its style of conceptualising may at first look like some kind of empirical and psychological analysis with little concern for a total view. It is the primary perception that shapes the total world-view, and which will necessarily include such a world-view.

Religious visions, then, are not perceptions of some sheerly transcendent reality, a Being ontologically discrete from all other cosmic realities – neither the transcendence of the radical monotheist, nor that of the seeker for life-transcending Nirvāṇa, can uphold any such position coherently. And this always entails a *mediating stance by the 'theologian' intent on formulating the tradition's core-perception.* To do justice to the cosmic implications of that primal vision of transcendence, he/she has to stand between the sacred experience and the world of mundane experience, between the vision of transcendent reality and secular perceptions of empirical realities. This will sometimes put the transcendent perception at some risk, especially in an age in which secular perceptions appear to predominate. But this possibility of losing sight of the essential perception need not be taken as an invalidation of the whole process of conceptualising and making coherent. For one thing, the theologian (*brahma- vādin* etc.) will also see such a mediating task as an opportunity to communicate his/her perception of reality to those whose perception is different. Points of compatibility will constantly be looked for to facilitate such communication.

The point made by some theologians that the raw materials of a religious perception and a secular perception are the same (e.g. Kaufman; Chapt. 11 below) is undeniable, even if the danger is that the one distinctive factor, i.e. the transcendent Object of religious perception, will then be overlooked. Empirically speaking the believer does not live in a different world. What is distinctive for the believer is a perception of that common world as a world enhanced by, even made a coherent whole by, the transcendent vision. Wherever possible the theologian of such vision will try to incorporate into that vision-determined account of a common world compatible features of investigations from other kinds of world-views, perhaps those more empirically grounded. In any case a degree of inclusive coherence is called for in all conceptual formulations of sacred visions.

Thirdly, one can presume that there must be *coherence in the inter-relationship of concepts and their implications within a belief-system* if it is truly to be a system. This is another aspect in the conceptual task which has been denigrated by some of those concerned for a more determining place to the transcendent character of religious visions. Neat conceptual systems, it is often said, are inhibiting to religion's trans-rational, paradoxical character. And there is truth in this contention; 'coherence' must not be an emasculating enfeeblement of the vitality of primal vision.

Theological expression does take a variety of forms at various states in its outworking. Myths, symbols, parables, images, metaphors, analogies, are all used effectively in the communication of the core-vision. And to communicate such a perception a degree of reflection and conceptual formation at some remove from the immediate experience is inevitable. At its least sophisticated, the initial means of conceptual formation is the mythic story and the symbolic image. Here the implicit concept still remains but is minimally explicated. Essential to the myth, though, is the *intention* that is to be conveyed by the story, and essential to the symbol is the *meaning* that is symbolised. Both would be literally pointless without at least elementary reflection on the perception lying behind them. A purely immediate, purely pre-reflective, wholly non-conceptual experience in religious expression is not an option open to us, though this does not rule out the possibility of immediacy and intuition as an essential part of religious experience.

When we come to expressive metaphors and analogies we have clearly moved even further along the reflective path. Analogical forms of expression, in fact, would seem to be the crucial point of intrinsic stimulus to more systematic conceptualisation. When the theologian looks − consciously or not − for ways in which the transcendent vision is similar to, or is elucidated by, the empirical world, it becomes necessary more and more to reflect on both spheres of experience, to clarify their inter-relationship and so to construct a coherent system. Part of the reflective process in theological systematising will be the recovery, perhaps the replacing, certainly the re-interpretation, of the myths and symbols so essential to primal vision-expression. Thus sometimes very complex symbolic traditions develop, each layer of the symbolising process needing to find its coherent place in the developing system.

To say that *all* religious language is symbolic or analogical (e.g. Tillich 1953: 145, 265-75) is true in the sense that no theologian imagines that the words and concepts used fully exhaust the meaning of the transcendent vision, no matter how impressively the system is elaborated. Every theologian will admit that in some sense the Upanishadic denial of exact conceptual correspondence and adequacy is called for: 'Not thus, not thus'. It is quite another matter to interpret this in terms of an *essential via negativa*, as some theologians in diverse traditions – Hindu, Christian, Jewish, Muslim – have done, and this way of essential negation raises the question again of intrinsic incoherence. As some Hindu theologians put it in rejecting the negating transcendence of non-dualism: 'If you cannot describe God directly and positively, even if not exhaustively, you cannot describe him at all.' Not for them Śaṅkara's analogy of the royal procession, in which the royal person, hid from sight by his courtiers, is 'identified' by progressively eliminating those figures that can be seen (Lott 1980: 73). Protecting the transcendent character of the vision certainly has its dangers.

Fourthly, a somewhat different way of putting the above point is to say that the theologian's task is *to forge into one coherent system the complex conceptual and trans-conceptual forms of expression of the tradition*. They have usually done this by using one *key-analogy*, or *key-concept*, when this is believed to unlock most effectively the meaning of the central vision. The Buddha, for example, made prominent use of the physician-model. A non-speculative, pragmatic approach to the sick patient was called for, as the task of *curing* was of primary importance. To do this, accurate and concise *description* of the patient's condition was the first step. Secondly, there was the need for *diagnosis* of the cause (i.e. desire) of the sickness. Thirdly, a curative course of *treatment* was prescribed (the Noble Eight-Fold Path). Finally, there was the *prognosis* (Nirvana). Thus the four great Truths were incorporated within a model of healing, though to what extent this determines anything other than the form in which these concepts are expressed is hard to say. To some degree this underlying model provided methodological impulse also.

In Islam, as in much Jewish and theistic thought generally, the righteous, majestic, but merciful ruler is the dominant model. Some systems temper this with some further modifying model: the father-son relationship of the Christian faith, the mother's affectionate and effective care in both Vaishṇava and Śaiva traditions of Hinduism. In the elucidation of the Śaiva vision, other mythic symbols from time to time have taken on a determining role, perhaps even given an analogical role. There is Śiva as the Yogi, whose hard-won supernatural powers are effective for all manner of salvific and destructive deeds. Then he is the dancer (*Naṭarāja*) destroying and recreating the whole cosmos in his rhythmic passion. Then, especially of late in the Śaiva Doctrine, he is the one who out of love for his devotees drinks the poison intended for them, and thus becomes the 'Blue-throated' (*Nīla-kaṇṭha*). And, throughout the Śaiva tradition's development, there is Śiva as the Liṅga, once the symbol for the male sexual organ, but in some Śaiva conceptualisations (e.g. Liṅgāyata) made the key-symbol to a quite different doctrinal scheme. In all these instances of traditions seizing on some key-symbol from the plethora of symbols available in the tradition, it is admittedly difficult to distinguish precisely between mythological and analogical usage of the concerned image. When that image becomes the conceptual *key* to the tradition's systematic self-elucidation, however, myth has moved on to, or incorporated, analogy.

In the Vedantic tradition generally it is the *self-model* that provides the crucial insight into the nature of the transcendent Reality, Brahman. As one climactic text repeatedly puts it: 'He (Brahman) is the Self; that thou art'. The various schools of Vedanta are able to pick out differing features of this basic self-model and make that feature the key-analogy of their distinctive interpretation (Lott 1980: 27-37). Thus Śaṅkara found the pure consciousness possible to the self (as in the self's dreamless sleep, or in its state of advanced yogic accomplishment) to be the most appropriate feature by which to interpret and integrate his system based on the vision of transcendent identity. For Rāmānuja it was the self-body relationship that best illuminated his vision of the transcendent Lord's inseparable relationship to the universe, a relationship with loving devotion at its heart.

Madhva found his follow-theist, Rāmānuja's relational perception too threatening to his transcendent vision of the sovereign Lord distinct from all other beings. For Madhva, therefore, the self's volitional potential, its relatively self-determining character was the analogical clue to the absolute freedom and the supreme self-determining that is characteristic of the universal Lord. In comparison with and in relation to that transcendent freedom, all souls are to be reckoned eternally dependent, helpless, other-determined, and in need of their Lord's transcendent grace. This is the key to Madhva's conceptual articulation of his core-vision.

Such analogical modes of visionary conceptualisation *can* be eminently apt for their role. For they include something both of the pre-conceptual vision and indicate the key-concept by which to articulate that vision in a coherent pattern of interwoven doctrines and faith-themes.

Finally, a *coherence of life-practice with doctrinal system* is required of any convincing visionary expression. This is not simply a matter of avoiding an incongruous hypocrisy, as today we might tend to look at this issue. 'Life-practice' here includes religious activities, probably with disciplined procedures for spiritual reflection as well as the social and ethical demands of the tradition. The two great traditions, apart from the Judeo-Christian religions, in which action is perhaps most clearly prescribed and so maintains an integral part of the vision-centred tradition, are Buddhism and Islam, two remarkably different traditions. In both, admittedly, there is a similarly strong sense of the believing community: the Buddhist's initial act is to take refuge in the Saṅgha or congregation of Bhikkus (those who have given up all normal social ties and live off the gifts of faithful laity), and the Muslim's primary duty is to meet regularly with those 'submitted' (Muslim) to the sovereign will of Allah, meeting for prayers, for confession of faith, for listening to the Quranic teaching – all this as an expression of his 'submission' (Islam).

If we look a little more closely at the interweaving of doctrinal system and life-practice in these two traditions, we find that the eight steps of the Buddhist Path (Rahula 1967: 45-50) make it immediately clear that neither right belief nor right practice has a monopoly, and of the various actions required there is equal weight given to both the ethical and the 'spiritual'. Thus there is an initial 'right perception' – especially perception of the Four Great Truths and of the Three Universal Signs (distress, the permanent flux of being, and the lack of immutable selfhood). This is to lead to 'right aspiration' or 'commitment'. Then comes the seemingly common-place 'right speech, action, and livelihood', though each has special significance in the context of the Buddhist's initial perception. This leads on to 'right effort', especially in breaking the five 'hindrances' to attaining Nirvāṇa (desire, lust, passion, anxiety, instability) and the ten 'fetters' (soul-delusion, doubt about the Buddhist way, reliance on ceremony, etc.). From this follows 'right recollection', or control of the mind, and finally 'right-meditation'. And throughout this pursuit of the Noble Path, inner reflection on personal existence is expected, thus encouraging further conceptual patterns of belief.

All this suggests that to describe such a tradition as 'dispositional' rather than as 'propositional' is only partly accurate. It is in fact both, with doctrine and action, assent and attitude, ritual requirement and ethical duties, theoretical concept and practical precept, all cohering together into the one tradition. The *dharma*-wheel (that symbol so prominent in Buddhist and Hindu thought, even if differently understood in each system) or composite tradition of right teaching about universal existence, is made up of the hub of the central-vision, the spokes of conceptually formed beliefs deriving from that vision, and the binding rim of a common practice, ethical and meditational.

To return to the Islamic system, the other obligatory sacred activities, prominent as the 'five pillars' of Islam's religious structure, are fasting, almsgiving to the needy faithful, and pilgrimage to the sacred centre of Islam. A striking feature of this Muslim tradition is the extent to which the primary activities, especially the first two — prayer and confession — serve to strengthen the believer in the doctrines of the tradition. So closely interwoven is doctrine with action that it is virtually impossible to unravel one strand without weakening the other.

The 'theological' task, then in each tradition — and whether the principal concern be with doctrinal confession, with pastoral structuring, or with ethical issues, in every case there is a 'systematic' task involved — is to bring out the implicit meaning of the central faith, to conceptualise both its propositional and its dispositional content, to direct the community of faith into a pattern of life that makes for growth in perception, belief and commitment, and in all this to draw out the intrinsic conceptual shape of the core-vision of the tradition, so that it can be communicated in a coherent formulation that is determined by some integrating key-concept. Theologising of such a kind demands that the theologian constantly seek a clearer perception of the central vision of the faith, so that the conceptualising process also can become more authentic, a more genuine re-vision within the tradition, and thus provide greater coherence, in the fullest sense, for fellow participants in the tradition. Clearly, the symbols, myths and mystic visions of the tradition will have a key role, as the 'matrix of meaning', in this conceptualising process, and to this we turn in the next chapter.

6

Interpreting Symbols, Myths and Mystic Experience

It has now become clear that an issue with very important ramifications both for the study of religion in general and for the theological process in particular is that of how symbols and myths, usually seen as prime components of a tradition's 'matrix of meaning', relate to belief-systems and to interpretations in terms of conceptual formulations. A related issue is that of the cognitive content of religious experience, more specifically, of mystical experience and intuitively perceived realities; but to some extent this can be distinguished from the question of whether such mystical perceptions can properly be given meaning through words, concepts and systematic formulation. That the role of symbols is rather crucial to reflection on how we are to understand religion is clear from the fact that several of the papers in the 1973 conference of the International Association of History of Religions, on methodology, were devoted to this question of how symbols are to be understood (Honko 1979).

1. There is little doubt that Protestant theologians generally, and many philosophers of religion too, have tended to give disproportionate importance to doctrinal formulations in their interpretation of religious life, rarely recognising either their symbolic character, or their dynamic interaction with other dimensions of religious life. To a large extent this reflects the post-Renaissance intellectualism in the major western traditions, secular and religious. A rationalist assumption concerning the nature of religion, and of theological interpretation of religion, has rightly been challenged by, among others, such theologians as Friedrich Schleiermacher, with his emphasis on the inward disposition, Rudolf Otto with his concern for the overwhelming sense of the numinous, to which rationality is radically subordinate, and by Paul Tillich, and numerous other post-liberal Protestant theologians of richly diverse conceptual position; there has also been the continuing trans-rational perspective of Catholic writing. Any understanding of the dynamism of human culture, and thus of the religious life, as essentially intellectual and rational,

with doctrinal and propositional systems as the principal means of understanding religion, has been even more effectively refuted by a wide range of
social sciences — sociology, anthropology, psychology.

Robert Bellah (1970) is one such refuter, arguing both against the re-
duction of the religious dimension of life to categories of the social scientist's
'belief', as well as against the 'objectivist fallacy' in interpretation even within
religious traditions. We need, he argues, to recognise the 'dimension of depth'
in all social and cultural forms, and thus must avoid confining research to
external institutions. His is an approach of 'symbolic realism'. On the one
hand he rejects the assumption of 'symbolic reductionists' that they speak
from some higher level of truth than that of the religious systems they study.
In effect such conceptualists are themselves 'believers': 'All of them believed
themselves to be in possession of a truth superior to that of religion'. The
symbol-systems of religions must, on the contrary, says Bellah, be recognised
as ways of 'apprehending the real', and in the process of this apprehension
great weight must be given to 'tacit' as well as 'explicit' forms of knowledge
(1970: 256-9; here echoing Polanyi's epistemology).

Bellah tries to take us a step further though. With a 'historical background
of unbelief', sophisticated religious people have committed the 'objectivist
fallacy' of equating *cognitive belief* with what is essential to religion (1970:
220). In reality religion is 'beyond belief'. He sees this fallacy as having been
committed only in traditions influenced by the Greek metaphysical outlook,
especially Christianity and Islam. All eastern traditions, he claims, are characterised not only by a less intellectualist outlook, but by an approach to reality
as a 'felt-whole'; all cognitive content, and conceptual systems by which the
intuited reality is depicted, are kept in a radically subordinate place, often
positively devalued. The perception of reality as essentially comprised of
cognitive beliefs about the way things objectively are 'is almost completely
missing in China and India' (*ibid.*: 220). Clearly Bellah is being very selective
in his interpretation of the eastern religious traditions; for there is in a substantial segment particularly of Indian religion, and not only in its 'classical'
phase, an almost compulsive concern for correct belief and for adequate conceptual formulation, undoubtedly intended to be authentic if not exhaustive
in pointing to the objective reality of the Ultimate. Of course, the emphasis
on directly intuited perception of that ultimacy is also very great, even when
there is also a strong epistemological realism. But this does not amount to a
devaluation of the dimension of the belief-system, especially as in virtually
every tradition the 'right way' of looking at things is seen as essential to the

goal of true religious life. 'Belief' is itself a vital part of the creative matrix in the religious life of these traditions.

Bellah's position is that, in essence, of Wilfred Cantwell Smith (1977; 1979; 1981), who as we saw also contrasts 'belief' and 'faith'. It is probably not of great value to follow Smith's historical and lexical arguments concerning the changing meaning of 'belief' (or of 'faith and 'religion'). That meanings of key words in any tradition change is obvious enough; that there is today one prevalent meaning of 'belief' and that this distorts the essential (original) meeting of this word is less clear, though it could be argued that the general loss of the sense of reality in religious traditions in the West is especially reflected in a limited understanding of what 'belief' and 'belief-systems' can be. We must agree with Smith that properly and ultimately religious belief is expected to be an existential act rather than a mere state of mind; it is surrender and commitment and therefore is to be grounded in (as well as to give shape to) an ultimate intuition of reality. Smith recognises, as we saw, that there will be a 'conceptual aspect' to this religious process, and the conceptual dimension will necessarily loom larger for some than for others: but what is conceptualised is not, he argues, 'believed' (in the sense of 'opined') but 'recognised', 'seen', 'discerned', 'known'. We must agree that to draw attention to intuitive vision in this way is necessary; but this *does not preclude or diminish, it rather makes essential, the cognitive, the propositional, certainly the doctrinal dimension of the religious process.* Smith does acknowledge the 'inescapable obligation' that faith lays on a religious tradition conceptually to elucidate what is perceived in 'faith' (1977: 99). The general impression, however, is that not enough room is allowed for the continual and essential *interaction* between a number of shaping factors in the religious process (in spite of his emphasis on such dynamism in his general theory of religious life), an interaction that must include 'beliefs' along with the integrating vision. But we look in more detail at Smith's understanding of the religious process in chapter nine.

2. How then do the conceptually formulated perceptions of reality that we find in religious traditions relate to the *symbols* of these traditions? There is a sense in which the conceptual systems too are 'symbol-systems'; coherently articulated doctrinal schemes do not take the religious person to some level *beyond* the world of symbols and the conceptions afforded through the primal symbolism. But neither do the conceptual systems necessarily take us to a level *lower* than the world of symbolic perception, as is assumed by some interpreters. Belief-systems are *also* forms of symbol-system, though such a des-

cription again raises the question of the relation between symbols and the realities they symbolise. Tillich, whose theological system in general was symbolist, spoke of a dynamic participation of symbol and reality symbolised, and included all theological language, even 'God', 'Christ', etc. as such dynamic symbols. Thus there is 'God beyond "God"' (1957: 14); the reality of God is necessarily beyond that which is symbolised by our concepts about God, or our rituals relating to God, even by our experience of God.

As we have seen earlier, some Indian theologians take a similar view of the theological process. All language and action is at a level of existence (i.e. not at the *essential* level, a distinction which Tillich also held) that can do no more than *point* towards the ultimate Reality. The crucial theological question is, though, how communicative, how truly *symbolic*, is this pointing? How real is the epistemological process? To what extent does the symbol truly share in the reality? And we should remember that here we are talking at the level of theory, of interpretation, of theology. The sincere Hindu who goes to the temple for 'vision' (*darśana*) of God, will perceive, if not 'experience', the image, and the whole temple complex, as a real embodiment of the sacred reality; yet there would no doubt also be the recognition (if there is any reflection at all) that the full reality of God is not confined to such sacred places and sacred embodiments. Indeed, only because there is a reality perceived *beyond*, only because God is perceived as greater than the image is there reality experienced *in* the image. And many theistic Hindus would take a rather similar view of the reality of sacred language; the words of scripture and the sacred songs, truly point to and convey the reality of God, but do not exhaustively describe his greatness. They are *really* symbolic.

The symbolist approach to human culture, and thus to religious life, must give considerable importance to the human need for, and anticipation of, discovering and communicating *patterns of meaning* through our varied symbol-systems. And this in turn necessitates some form of conceptualising. If there is really a symbolic dimension in our cultural and religious life, whether or not we call these ways of life-structuring 'systems', then there is necessarily a dimension of life that is *reflective*, that is perceptive of meaning, that looks to a beyond-dimension. But this is precisely the issue that has been so vigorously debated within anthropology in recent years (cf. Chapters 5 and 6 in Whaling 1985). We cannot here go into the question of whether the 'primitive' mind perceives the universe in a pre-logical holistic way that is essentially distinct from the way moderns perceive. That a technology-based civilisation destroys holistic perception is undeniable; but it might be recalled at least that Lévy-

Bruhl came to deny his earlier thesis of a qualitatively different kind of primitive logic. The human (primitive and post-primitive) mind is after all similar in its functioning and in its structuring of the perceived world. For many life-forms, of course, there is the communication of 'intention', perhaps of a 'beyondness', without conceptualising the 'meaning' of such intention. Birds and insects, for example, communicate a great deal, some of which is easy to decipher, some forms of which seem very mysterious. But in the cultural and religious life of human societies, all symbol-systems entail not only a primal intuitive and integrating perception of reality in the universe and in life within it, or beyond it, but also some degree of awareness of that perception and reflection on the meaning-patterns communicated in the symbol-system (but cf. F. Barth, referred to by Jackson, in Whaling 1985: 215-17).

Melford Spiro (in Honko 1979: 322 ff.), who refers rather disparagingly to anti-functionalist symbolists having a 'Cartesian theory of the mind', also criticises functionalists who ignore the 'cognitive meaning of cultural symbol systems', and who refer almost exclusively to the 'psychological and biological needs of the social actors' and the 'functional needs of their social system', as though there is nothing in the life-process of humans beyond the sheer need for functioning. It is surely almost impossible now to visualise humanness without some degree of reflection not only on the meaning of how and why the life-process is functioning as it does, but also on the direction life is yet to take, i.e. on how to give further direction to life and to our relations with the universe. Reflection on meaning does not necessarily imply a Cartesian dichotomy of rational mind and irrational nature. In the end symbols and myths compel such reflection on meaning. Earlier Hans Penner (in Helfer 1968: 46-57), having surveyed the confusing 'wasteland' of anthropological theories subsequent to Levi Strauss' Structural Anthropology, concludes that both on the functionalist and the symbolist side of the spectrum 'the problem of the cognitive content of myth has been suspended or rejected'. But, 'finally, it is the referent, or object, of myth and ritual as symbolic expressions that remains the central problem . . . ' (*ibid.*: 57).

Although Eliade is one of those who have explained symbols 'by reference to more symbols', by appropriating insights from archetypal psychology and cultural anthropology, he has at least attempted to provide a comprehensive theory of the nature and role of symbols in religious life (e.g. 1959: 86-107). Eliade enumerates a number of motifs that he finds common to religious symbolism, common ways in which 'the World "speaks" or "reveals" itself through symbols', even though the symbol is never 'a mere reflection of objective

reality' (97-8). Firstly, he affirms, through the deciphering reflective consciousness, symbols reveal the hidden reality of the sacred World. This is a reality
that is 'not evident on the level of immediate experience'; its apprehension calls
for the kind of reflection on the meaning of things that is possible, as well as
necessary, precisely through the engagement of human consciousness with the
symbols that confront it. This is not merely rational reflection, but is an 'immediate intuition of a "cipher" of the World'. Indeed, this is how a 'World of
meaning comes to be structured in relation to human consciousness, a World
that is more profound, more mysterious than that which is known through
everyday experience' (*ibid.*: 98). *Secondly*, to this more primal experience
cosmic symbols are religious because they point to an archaic, pre-systematic
ontology, to a reality that is also a way of structuring the world. Eliade sees
this level of engaging in the symbolic as rarely lending itself to formulation in
concepts. *Thirdly*, symbols are multivalent, expressing multiple meanings
simultaneously, and the 'continuity' of these varied meanings is not evident
either in immediate experience or through reflection. However, and *fourthly*,
this multivalent character of symbols allows human consciousness, in its
systematising role, to discover an integrated meaning in the world. 'The
symbol is thus able to reveal a perspective in which heterogenous realities are
susceptible of articulation into a whole, or even of integration into a "system"'
(*ibid.*: 99-100). At the same time, this discloses the fact that the proper destiny
of human consciousness is to be 'an integrating part of the World'. *Fifthly*, and
perhaps the most important function of religious symbolism (especially in view
of developments in later philosophical speculations), is its 'capacity for expressing paradoxical situations, or certain structures of reality otherwise quite
inexpressible' (*ibid.*: 101). While dialectical concepts like 'polarity' and '*coin-
cidentia oppositorum*' have long been part of systematic metaphysical reflection, the initial though dim perception of such concepts was 'not the result
of critical reflection but of existential tension'. There was the encounter with
'the mystery of contradictory aspects of a reality or of a sacrality' that humans
were led to consider compact or homogeneous. Thus, it was through the experience of crucial religious symbols that 'man guessed that the polarities and
the antimonies could be articulated as a unity' (*ibid.:* 102). *Finally*, symbols
always disclose realities that are interrelated with the actual existential situations of human life. At the same time they 'translate a human situation into
cosmological terms' as well as vice versa. It is above all this existential dimension
that distinguishes symbols from concepts, though the unveiling of a 'structure
of reality through symbols by the same stroke brings a *meaning* into human
existence' (*ibid.*: 102-3).

It is clear that Eliade's analysis, even if intuitively arrived at, is of considerable significance for our understanding of religious life, and of the theological process in particular. The assumptions he makes, of course, do need to be tested by reference to the ways in which symbols in fact function in religious traditions. Probably his account does not allow sufficiently for the *diverse levels* at which symbols are experienced; perhaps, therefore, greater weight should be given to Wilfred Cantwell Smith's point (1981: 85) that 'nothing can be (objectively or inherently) a symbol in and of itself', but 'only in relation to some person or persons', and in concrete historical situations; we should not therefore aim 'to arrive at a vision of unchanging prototypes'. For Smith, such is the importance of personal and historically specific experience of symbols that he sees the 'historical evidence' as against any idea of the 'empirical symbol' participating in the transcendent reality (*ibid.*: 87).

It is clear that the 'meaning' of symbols is so very varied in a tradition's history. We cannot speak of *the* meaning of any given symbol, for many meanings can be equally valid; perhaps there is no particular meaning inherent in any symbol. And yet, however much we might agree that 'a religious symbol . . . shimmers with the meaning of the whole universe in relation to man' (*ibid.*: 90) and that no symbol has its 'own meaning', but always signifies a reality other and greater than itself, to see *no* inherent meaning in the great primal symbols seems a rather extreme form of cosmic iconoclasm. While there is some convergence of interpretation between Smith and Eliade, it is their differing emphases that are the more significant; perhaps each serves to correct the other.

Smith also sees some ambiguity in a symbolist interpretation of religious life: it is both necessary (to avoid reifying the religious traditions of others unrecognisably 'into objectively systematised patterns') and yet inappropriate, i.e. for the understanding of one's own tradition; while the outsider should see the Qur'an as a symbol, and thus as a living dynamic force, the believing Muslim is hardly likely to see his sacred book in terms of a 'symbol-system'; though we should go on to ask if a devout Muslim cannot also come to this apprehension of his tradition and still have 'a faith that would save' (*ibid.*: 96).

3. Religious symbols relate closely to *myth* and *ritual*, both of which function as a kind of elaborated expression of symbols. Doctrinal systems are more explicitly conceptual expressions of the meaning intended and implicitly communicated in a tradition's symbol-system. Ninian Smart (1973a) attempts an analysis of the inter-connectedness of these various dimensions of religious

life. He suggests that myth is a more direct and dynamic form of expression of the sacred Focus than is found in doctrine. Myth provides us with a context in which sacred beings are acting; mythic stories are 'moving pictures of the sacred' (*ibid.*: 79). Doctrine provides a more static expression of 'the constitution of the world, of the transcendent', and of other aspects of the world of the sacred. He acknowledges, however, that this distinction has to be 'heavily qualified', and his own analysis of myth, ritual and doctrine shows us clearly that doctrine too has close interlinking with the more 'active' character of the other two dimensions.

Myths are stories, though stories specially pregnant with sacred meaning, about the relationship between the transcendent world of sacred beings (evil beings too) and the human world; and the primary context in which such stories are told meaningfully is that of ritual action. The organic relation between myth and ritual is not surprising, in that by dramatically depicting the character of sacred beings, and their earth-relationship, ritual action is stimulated, whether this is in the form of the worship of such beings, or the means for ensuring their blessings, or acts for warding off evil. These ritual-mythic action-stories are essentially re-enactments of ultimately significant events in the relationship between the sacred and the mortal worlds; thus they are 'celebratory stories' (and different from parables, which do not aim for 're-enactment in a celebratory context') (*ibid.*: 79-82). Myths also have 'explanatory power', sometimes being aetiological by giving an account of, perhaps legitimation for, ritual or social tradition. Then, cosmogonic myths explain the being and character of the world in terms of dependence on sacred power, and in a way that usually confirms the perceived relationship between that power and humans. The re-telling of myths in a ritual context is significant, showing that the power of the celebratory events they describe is repeatedly available and repeatedly redemptive (*ibid.*: 87). Smart recognises that myths assume two distinct 'worlds', though he is unhappy with Eliade's sharp distinction between the two worlds of sacred and historical time, corresponding to sacred and profane space, with mythic action all taking place within sacred time and sacred space. Examination of the mythic dimension of traditions such as Hindu and Christian shows more inter-action. Thus Smart prefers to use the terms 'macro-cosmology' and 'micro-cosmology' to refer to these two levels of perceived reality, with a 'meso-cosmology' as typifying the sacred geography depicted in some mythic stories (*ibid.*: 84-5).

Then with an illustrative analysis of the Easter story and celebration of Christ's resurrection, Smart proposes the following dynamic relationship between myth and ritual: 'The myth, uttered as an element in the ritual, is the central aspect in the way in which the original is replicated'. There is a principle of *likeness* involved, so that the 'words themselves as uttered contain something of the power of the original. This feature of sacred language is characteristically applied to names of sacred and numinous objects, which thus become signs or part of what they stand for' (*ibid.*: 93). Smart hastens to add that while there are certain typical features in 'the dynamics of divinities', and the 'mythic-ritual milieu operates with its own principles of numinous power', we should not overlook the complex interaction of a great variety of factors. He sees myths as like 'collages', 'assembling contingently given elements into patterns structured by the described dynamics' (*ibid.*: 102-3).

Having thus shown the typically close interconnection of myth and ritual, with the 'numinous' as the linking factor, Smart then goes on to consider 'the role of mythic stories where the ritual and numinous elements in religion are not of ultimate importance' (ibid.: 104). This proves to be extremely illuminating — and my own interpretation here goes considerably further than Smart's — regarding the role of reflective and largely doctrinal insight as the means by which *myth is transposed to a different level of meaning*. Theravāda Buddhism, in its classical Pāli form, is taken by way of example. For in this tradition, 'the ultimate aim is not salvation to be derived from a divine (numinous) being, but rather the stilling of those forces which make for rebirth and the attainment of supreme peace and insight' (*ibid.*: 104). It is not worship and sacrifice that are now the means, yet there is still a strong mythic dimension, with gods and demons in dramatic interaction with humans. The role of myth is somewhat ambiguous, for even in this dramatically depicted world it is by special insight that the Buddha, 'prototypically', then followed by other 'worthies', proves victorious over the temptations of Māra the seducer. Māra constantly tries to defeat these 'awakened' ones by misleading them with *false* knowledge. Thus, although there are many typically mythic features in these Buddhist stories, there are also highly significant trans-mythic elements. Smart suggests that the power of the presence of the numinous in other kinds of ritual-mythic tradition corresponds to the superior power of the Buddha's special insight into the meaning of life. And this insight is very explicitly doctrinal and ethical in content: first, the four noble truths covering the human condition, actual and potential; the three universal marks of existence; then, the clearly delineated eight-fold way to be walked, with its almost equally balanced ethical and meditational requirements.

It is quite true that the Buddha 'transcends the gods, just as nibbana transcends the heavenly regions, and the knowledge of nibbana all numinous powers'. It is true too that in this way 'the higher values of the Buddha's path have an ambiguous relation to the mythic-ritual realm' (*ibid.*: 106). But a strong case can be made out for seeing the still constitutive *meditational requirement as corresponding closely to the previously expected ritual*, especially the Vedic sacrifices to the gods; and the *mythic dimension is transposed into a new doctrine, a new perception of the ultimate structure of the universe*, and of the Powers of the universe in relation to the human condition and human destiny. This tends to confirm further that a *mythic story is always a doctrine-shaped story*; it incorporates a perception of the way things are in the universe. The transposed form of the story in this Buddhist case retains many mythic features at a lower level of meaning, and replaces ritual with meditation. This is, as Smart also mentions, almost exactly parallelled in post-Vedic, i.e. Upanishadic developments. Similar kinds of transposition – forming varying types of 'collage', to use Smart's term, perhaps not a term that adequately expresses the dynamism that he obviously intends (cf. Smart 1984, and Duraisingh 1984: 169-78) – can be seen in a variety of other traditions. The Old Testament Israelite tradition, for example, in its transposition from the Yahwist, Canaanite and other antecedent traditions, retains some of the mythic dimension, but it is far less prominent and given less directly revelatory status; at the same time the numinous element is enhanced as a central feature of the ritual. It is, however, the prophetic and priestly interpretation of a salvation history, forming a new theology, a new pattern of perceived meaning, that becomes all-important in Israel's destiny and in the attaining of ultimate life-goals.

To what extent, in all these religious traditions, is it the *mythic-ritual grounding*, in other words the focussed symbolic dimension, that forms the 'creative matrix' for the discovery of new insight and thus for the conceptual articulation expressing this newly discovered meaning? If we look at the whole process of the developing Buddhist tradition, particularly if we include Greater Vehicle Buddhism, or the development of Hinduism in its puranic forms of expression, we see the mythic matrix over many centuries still bringing forth conceptual offspring, still proving its doctrinal fecundity. Yet, in helping to shape new doctrines we can in some cases discern only very subtle perceptual correspondence, in others more obvious 'coherence' between mythic motifs and emergent doctrine. It would seem for example, that doctrines incorporating a *body*-motif (e.g. the *tri-kāya* doctrine of Great Vehicle Buddhism, the central body-analogy of Vaishṇavism, the Śiva-body doctrine in some forms of Śaivism,

the Christ-Church-body motif in the Christian tradition) are one highly significant way, in very varied religious contexts, of expressing more innate perceptual correspondence.

Another aspect of how this process works out in Theravāda Buddhism is
seen in what Smart calls the 'congruence' between its trans-mythic attitude to
the ultimately liberating Focus, and its treatment of cosmology: 'Thus the
elaborate series of upper worlds, impermanent heavens, are correlated to differing stages of jhana or meditation. This equation between place and psychological state prepares the way for seeing the "end of the world" (nibbana) as
something to be "seen" and "tasted" by the saint at an even higher level of
contemplative insight' (Smart *op. cit.*: 108). At the same time, mythically, the
heavenly realms are very prominently depicted to exhibit 'the previous locus
of the Buddha before his descent to earth, the loci of the various gods and the
rewards of good conduct, bringing one upwards towards the highest spirituality' (ibid.: 108). In this way myth and meditation (the transposed form of
ritual) still interlock, though mythic truth is now recognised as of 'symbolic'
value in the light of the reflection on the new goal of existence. Conversely,
of course, we might note that new symbols emerge, or more correctly, old
symbols emerge with new power acquired from the perception of new meanings. The Bodhi tree for example, is now primarily the sacred place of 'awaken-
ing' (*bodhi*); yet it retains some of its more 'primal' significance as the centre-
point of cosmic existence, though now with an ambiguous existence; for the
tree often in Buddhist symbolism indicates that life-sap, or thirst for ego-level
existence which has to be utterly uprooted.

Eliade's interpretation of the sacred tree as a hierophany of the archetypal
Cosmic Tree, therefore, fits to some extent, but only when we take into
account Eliade's further elucidation that symbols are also multivalent in meaning. And the more we try to fit all mythic symbolism into archetypal patterns
the less significant is the 'milieu-transformation' of which Smart speaks (ibid.:
106), or the transposition of traditional material into new situations, where
there is interaction of myth and milieu, and where new interpretations are
called for. It is this process of response to and participation in the realities of
historical and cultural change that Wilfred Cantwell Smith has given such
weight to in his interpretation of the role of symbols, though his rejection of
all 'inherent meaning' on the one hand, and his underplaying of the shaping
power of doctrine and belief in this process on the other, can be questioned. If
we are to see a tradition with all its diversity as a 'mythic whole', and if at each
stage of this historically conditioned existence this mythic symbolism is to

provide liberating meaning, the interpretive process, necessarily a process of conceptual articulation and belief-formulation, is an essential shaping factor in the tradition.

This need for mythic meaning, and thus for convincing elaboration of doctrinal belief in response to the changing cultural milieu, implies other key dimensions in the religious life: the *life*-significance and the *ethical* dimension, as well as the *spiritual* practice involved in such meaning-interpretation. Smart calls this the 'practical and experiential dimension of religion', with which, as he points out, 'doctrines' as systematisations and analyses of divine and worldly reality, have to retain connection' (*ibid.*: 116). Even the 'rather abstract-sounding doctrine of transcendence' in theistic religious traditions can directly impinge on religious experience and practice, 'when it is related to the experience of God as the Other', or as the creative power on which the world depends, and when it is related to 'the mythic-ritual screening of the Holy' (ibid.: 117). This impingement upon life-practice by the doctrinal dimension in Theravāda Buddhism stands out very clearly, as we have noted earlier. The primary doctrine of the three universal marks of existence, for example, actually results from, or at least is confirmed by, the Buddha's own life-experience. But the path set out as the way to overcome these existential realities that so blight the human condition, is the *Dhamma*, which most distinctively in Buddhism is the right way taught by the Buddha, with its precise ethical and meditational requirements. Practice and doctrine are very closely co-ordinated; the doctrines are not merely speculative and ungrounded metaphysical affirmations, but are rooted interdependently with Buddhist life-experience, a life-experience that in turn is perceived in the light of these undergirding doctrines.

4. Thus, in the end we face this question of how *religious experience* relates to doctrinal affirmation and to the concerned tradition's conceptual formulations. Does doctrine, evoking as it does religious expectation, determine what people, whose consciousness is shaped by their particular social world, come to perceive and experience in their religious life? Or in the final analysis is it the way people experience their religious tradition that shapes the way they express its meaning theologically? This is a complex issue, and perhaps we are mistaken even in attempting to disengage experience from expression, but differing responses are found to the question:

a) If we want to stress the importance of 'popular' religious life, official and

classically formulated doctrinal positions will be given little experiential significance. And it must be recognised that far too often accounts of religious
traditions, especially interpretations by theologians, have tended to overlook
less sophisticated and perhaps more primal perceptions of the 'commoners'
within a tradition. In historical material there is usually the problem of having
no such perceptions available; the interpretations of such elitist groups as the
priesthood, the recognised teachers, or perhaps the charismatic leaders, in any
case *cognoscenti* with some community standing, are often all that remains
recorded. As we have stressed throughout, these 'recognised' interpretations are
of the utmost significance in our understanding of any tradition. But they are
not the whole story. An account, for example, of Theravāda Buddhism in Sri
Lanka, as Gombrich has shown (1971), is incomplete without also recognising
that the cultic practice and religious perceptions of substantial numbers of
people, rural people especially, within the whole Buddhist community differ
considerably from orthodox Theravāda Buddhism; there is much that is in
common in folk-tradition almost universally. Orthodox Theravāda would no
doubt see such folk-religion as needing to be transposed to the true Buddhist
level of insight, and would thus be relegated to a lower order of truth.

In a number of traditions any strict distinction between 'classical' and 'folk'
perceptions is somewhat artificial; the mythic matrix, or key motifs in the
basic mythic symbolism, perhaps a cosmic symbolism, will at least to some
extent converge; for example we find within Brahmanic Hinduism many primal
motifs (about the Earth-Mother for instance) that will be common perceptions,
though differently termed, of rural India generally. Then, the doctrinally initiated will feel able to interpret such primal motifs in an orthodox theological
mode; though in this process of interpretation there may well be meaning-
perceptions that are not part of the perceptions of the 'uninitiated'.

b) In view of this last point, another response to the experience-expression
dilemma is to give greater weight to 'the interaction of myth and milieu' that
we noted earlier. The changing cultural context of a religious tradition, the new
perceptions resulting from interaction with life outside the community of the
initiated, compels reinterpretation of the tradition. Thus experience, we might
say empirical life-experience, affects doctrinal expression; the interaction with
context evokes new perceptions and new expression of the meaning of the
ancient myths.

c) When we look at the great formative moment in the emergence of new religious communities, or traditions, according at least to their own interpreta-

tions of their histories, experience is often seen as *prior* to doctrinal expression. The Buddha contradicted major strands in the received wisdom of the increasingly prevailing Brahmanic heritage in his background, including doctrinal themes as well as religious practice, because he came to experience reality differently. Just how totally original was his conceptual world is historically debatable, as with most great reformers and initiators; continuity and discontinuity are often delicately interwoven. Certainly key concepts in his worldview, such as *karma* (the potency for good or evil of each one's action), rebirth, insight into a transcendent level of being, a yogic meditative discipline, liberation from the fetters of samsaric existence, and so on, were already part of an important section of the Brahmanic world he did not accept. Yet his interpretation of these doctrinal themes and liberating practices, and thus his reinterpreting of previous conceptual symbols, was quite distinctive, a distinctive new direction that seems to have been based on his distinctive experience of life and his insight into the meaning of life; there was a new vision of human destiny.

Similar comments could be made, though recognising quite variant religious worlds, about Christ and Muhammed. In the case of the emergence of doctrine about the 'Christ-event' we find even from the apostolic age that interpretive doctrinal formulation was shaped primarily by the apostles' response to and thus experience of what had happened to and through Jesus. In the Prophet's case there is in the Islamic tradition greater emphasis on what is 'revealed' from above through the Prophet, rather than what was existentially disclosed through experience of the 'Companions' with the Prophet. But the basic pattern is the same: while there is interaction of the doctrinal and the experiential dimensions in both, there is also at least the intention that expression and interpreting tradition 'follow' the Founder's life-experience.

d) In many religious traditions, however, it is the classically formulated doctrines, however much subject to reinterpretation in changing contexts, that have proved determinative for the typical forms of religious experience. Perhaps we have to make a distinction here between the creative religious genius of the Founder, Prophet, Enlightened One, Ford-Maker, etc., and the disciple, the believer, the participant, the initiate.

5. Related to the above is a subject of crucial import in the interpretation of religious life. What is the nature and significance of *mystical experience* within religious traditions? In addition to the question of how mystical experience relates to doctrinal formulation (or whether it is essentially ineffable, to be

expressed only in radical paradox; cf. Moore 104f, in Katz 1978), there has been extensive debate concerning types of mysticism: What is essential to mystical experience? A further, more ontological question sometimes is: Is mystical experience to be seen as the authentic culmination of religious life? Or, does such experience in some way authenticate the truth of religion? In this brief section obviously we cannot refer to the whole range of recent debate (cf. esp. Zaehner 1961, 1969; Katz 1978; Woods 1981; Almond 1982), but will confine our discussion to the questions of how we are to calssify mystical experience and how this relates to doctrine and interpretation. Otto's early comparative study of Śaṅkara from the Hindu tradition and Eckhart from the medieval Catholic tradition, both monastics, tried to identify a single type of religious experience bridging these two historically very distinct traditions. Interpreters such as Radhakrishnan, on the other hand, asserted that while in essence there is only one kind of religious experience, this is to be found most authentically in the mystical experience of undifferentiated oneness of Being and Consciousness. R.C. Zaehner, however, identified three types of mysticism:

a) *Panenhenic*, which is an experience of unity of being that includes especially a sense of oneness with nature; it evokes a sense of being in touch with the reality of the world.

b) *Monistic* mysticism, which is interior experience of a transcendent identity of being evoking a sense of 'the isolation of the soul from all that is other than itself' (1961: 165). Almond (1982: 32) summarises the distinction thus: 'While both the panenhenic and the monistic experiences involve abrogation of subject-object polarity, and thus are unitary experiences, the former includes the "world" whereas the latter excludes it'. The monistic experience, however, can be *expressed* in different ways (ibid.: 33) – and here is the hinge-point of much of the discussion. Zaehner also sees monistic experience as possibly emerging from the panenhenic experience. The latter can be distinguished as transcendence of space and of time (cf. Almond: 34), and it is from the convergence of these two that monistic experience emerges.

c) *Theistic* mysticism, in which there is a sense of exalted and inclusive union of love with God, who yet remains distinct from all else. Zaehner clearly saw theistic mysticism as the highest form of religious experience, and this normative perspective has been criticised by Smart, Staal and Almond.

Central to this debate about what is to be labelled 'mysticism' is the question of definition, though in the end it may not prove to be so very important in gaining understanding of key types of religious experience; arbitrary definitions of what makes a mystic may not preclude understanding what is definitive of his/her experience, though this will tend to confuse the typological task. Zaehner defined mysticism thus: in mystical experience 'sense perception and discursive throught are transcended in an immediate apperception of a unity or union which is apprehended as lying beyond and transcending the multiplicity of the world as we know it' (1961: 1989).

As examples of 'panenhenic' mysticism Zaehner quotes the Chāndōgya Upanishad passage (3: 14) referring to the great Self who 'encompasses' all beings, the whole universe, who is 'the self within my heart, smaller than a grain . . . greater than the earth . . . '; also (8.1.1-3) the 'tiny space' within the 'tiny lotus-flower' indwelling Brahman, which is also a wide space within the heart, and within which 'everything is concentrated' (1961: 137, 200-1).

In the case of theistic mysticism we have the problem of deciding whether in fact there is an *experience* of utter oneness that is then *interpreted* in terms of relational distinction of God and soul merely because orthodox doctrine (in the concerned theistic tradition) requires this. Is this what has happened in the case, for example, of Al-Ghazali? (Zaehner 1961: 157-8; Almond 1982: 39-40). This is how he describes the Sufi experience:

> The mystics, after their ascent to the heavens of Reality, agree that they saw nothing in existence except God the One . . . all plurality entirely fell away. They were drowned in pure solitude; their reason was lost in it . . . nothing was left to them but God. They became drunk with a drunkenness in which their reason collapsed. One of them said, 'I am God' (the Truth) . . . But the words of lovers when in a state of drunkenness must be hidden away and not broadcast. However, when their drunkenness abates and the sovereignty of their reason is restored – and reason is God's scale on earth – they know that this was not actual identity, but that it resembled identity . . . This condition is metaphorically called identity . . . but in the language of truth (it is called) union.

Almond comments: Al-Ghazali admits 'on the one hand that phenomenologically the experience is one of undifferentiated unity and that therefore it appears as if a monistic interpretation is valid, yet he alleges on the other hand that the proper interpretation is one of union between the soul and God . . . presumably for the apologetic purpose of giving certain Islamic experiences an orthodox flavouring'. Almond hastens to add that while what is phenomenologically in this case monistic mystical experience is theistically interpreted, such need not be the case with all theistically interpreted mysticism. However, is it quite so clear that Al-Ghazali has admitted 'phenomenologically' that the experience is trans-theistic monism? All he has admitted is that in the state of 'drunkenness' the *language* of utter unity is used, but that this must be taken 'metaphorically'; the reality, the 'language of truth', is different. What they had seen was 'God the One', in union with whom all other 'plurality entirely fell away'. There is, though, some ambiguity about the status of reason (God's 'scale on earth'), by whose 'sovereignty' the mystic comes to know that 'this was not actual identity'. Is reason here seen as on a lower level of truth than the Reality of the 'ascended' mystical state? This is more usually the position in mystical language interpreting experience, when typically there is a lower-order role given to rational articulation of the mystical state, and paradoxical language is often used. But this does not mean for the mystic that paradox is utterly irrational, or that rational interpretation has no 'truth' or 'reality' (cf. Staal 1975).

Smart (1964, 1975; reprinted in Woods 1980: 78-91) has been rather critical of Zaehner's typology. Phenomenologically, he argues, panenhenic mysticism cannot stand as a distinct type of religious experience, for it is not delineated as such clearly in mystical texts; and the mystical strand in both monistic and theistic mysticism is essentially the same experience. We are justified, phenomenologically, only in speaking of one type of mystical experience, though this may be interpreted in different ways. Smart gives great weight to a two-fold typology of religious experience; one type is experience of the Numinous, in which there is a sense of a transcendent Object, usually theistically interpreted, as beyond one's own being — a transcendent Object on which one is ultimately dependent. Here Smart makes use of Rudolf Otto's well-known description of religion (though for Smart only one possible type of experience) as experience of the *numen* which is the *Mysterium, Tremendum* and *Fascinans*; i.e. the numinous Object of religious worship which fills with awe, which is 'overpowering' in its might and majesty, evokes 'a feeling of personal nothingness and submergence before the object directly perceived'; there is too the sense that the Numinous alone is the one great reality; and the wholly other character of the Numinous induces a sense of 'blank wonder, an astonishment that strikes us dumb' (Otto 1958: 26). Inextricably mixed with these feelings is the *fascinating* side of the Numinous, which evokes longing, desire, love. And what is experienced in the contemplative religious type is something quite different from this. Here there is the inner unitive experience, or realisation, of what one essentially is; there is contemplation of the depths of one's own being, whether this is understood in terms of an eternal soul, as in much Hindu and Christian contemplative experience, or along with the denial of such an unchanging entity within, as in Therevada Buddhism.

The term 'mysticism', Smart argues, should be reserved for contemplative experience only; it should be classified according to phenomenological type and without the varied interpretations of this experience that we find in Advaita Vedanta, Buddhism, Jainism, and so on. When either the Hindu Yogi or the Muslim Sufi experience transcendence within, however they may interpret this — whether as merging or union with God, or as realisation of inner soulness in all its depth and immutability — as a phenomenon their experience is the same as that of the Monist, the Theravada Buddhist, or the Yogi in the 'enstatic' state of *samādhi*. It is a single type of contemplative experience of inner transcendence to which absolute significance is given, and within which great emphasis is given to immediacy and to meditational practice.

We must, Smart argues, make a very clear distinction between mystical experience and its interpretation. Different interpretations have differing degrees of 'ramification', i.e. greater or lesser dependence upon religious doctrines and conceptual systems, that are not directly connected with the experience as such. Interpretations of mystical experience, therefore, are given from differently ramified points of view; sometimes they are auto-interpretations and sometimes hetero-interpretations; sometimes within one tradition there will be both types of interpretation, though this will entail a priority schematising, so that one will be seen as the other. Thus, there are systems which are predominantly and typically mystical, but which incorporate the theistic and numinous experience as a lower-order strand, as in *Advaita*. Or there may be the reverse structuring, as in theistic Vedanta (cf. also Smart 1964). In any case, he sees the variety of auto-interpretations (of one phenomenon, mystical experience) as accountable by the interplay between these two distinct and non-reducible types of religious experience (Almond 1982: 50).

Despite this recognition of a complex interplay in view of the many different kinds of interpretation of what Smart sees as one typical mystical experience, are we justified in attempting to restrict the meaning of 'mysticism' to this one simple type? Steven Katz (1978), for example says 'no', and has argued, as probably many other historians of religion would want to, that the particular conditioning or 'mediating context' (26) of the tradition that forms the grounding of experience must be given more weight; and the interpretation will most probably give direct expression to that 'mediating context'. We surely need to avoid giving the impression that when it comes to mystical experience doctrinal and cultic context, and therefore theological interpretation, have no integral connection. Much of Smart's argument in fact is intended to show that there is just such an integral inter-connection. He tries to show, for example, that mystical experience is typically the result of a carefully structured spiritual discipline aimed precisely at attaining that kind of experience (Smart 1958: 40-1). (Numinous experience, on the other hand, is said to be more unexpected, more confrontational). We should not press these conditioning factors too far of course; for many mystics will make the point that in the end the beatific vision can in no way be controlled, and theists do have their own kinds of spiritual discipline: 'I was in the temple, and I saw the Lord...' (Isaiah 6).

While Smart's thesis of a basic contemplative/numinous typology is quite convincing, we need to recognise that:

a) Each of these basic types is significantly modified and reshaped when dynamic features of the other type are incorporated. It is true that priorities pertain within the new fused religious structure; there will not be *equal* weight given to, for example, both unitive contemplation and the numinosity of God. But a God-worshipping, God-loving theist who incorporates the practice of meditating on that God as the inmost self of all (e.g. as the Vaishnava bhakta probably will) so modifies his theism that it is difficult to see why this cannot be called *mystical theism*. Or the non-dualist who yet gives a dynamically significant role to *bhakti* (e.g. Madhusūdana Sarasvati in his commentary on the Bhagavad-Gītā) has so modified his contemplative stance that it can aptly be called a *bhakti-advaita*. Priorities remain, but it would seem more true to the dynamic interplay of the religious process if we take the mystic-theist typology as but a very basic framework that should not preclude the emergence of both theistic-mystics and mystical-theists; and in each case the qualifier significantly remoulds the type.

b) Given this possibility there would be good reason to allow greater authenticity to the interpretations given within religious traditions of their typical experiences. There is no need to go to the extreme of saying that each person's self-interpretation must always be right. This kind of phenomenological infallibility is hardly convincing, for individuals, even theologians, and religious *groups* too presumably can be mistaken. Yet, community theological interpretation of typical religious experience within a tradition must surely be given the utmost respect. Even when the ineffability of the experience is stressed, and paradoxical forms of expression, we can assume that something important is being described (cf. Moore, in Katz 1979: 101-6; cf. also 1-6 ff. on the interplay of experience and interpretation). Literal and total inexplicability is obviously not intended, or silence alone would be appropriate; and paradoxes are clearly not meaningless. The point would rather seem to be, typically, that in the end conceptualising the mystical experience just cannot do *full* justice to it. Staal (1975) also argues that mystical experience need not be regarded as irrational; post-mystical 'discernment' in Buddhism, for example, is an orderly discernment of meaning.

c) Special weight does need to be given to the macro-microcosmic dialectic in at least some mystical experiences, including much theistic mysticism. This panenhenic vision does seem to be typical, for example, of the Bhagavad-Gītā and of many other expressions of religious experience in Indian traditions. Such a panenhenic structure may not be explicit in all clearly mystical texts, but it would seem justifiable, despite Smart's criticisms on this point, to include it as a distinctive mystical type, though often found as a dimension of other mystical types too. Again, we need to note the reshaping dynamism here as different forms of experience, and different types of doctrinal undergirding and interpretation interact one with another. Our typologies should not remain static and oversimplified, though we do need to continue to search for and give whatever visionary Focus that mystical (or indeed theistic) tradition identifies as central and determining.

This 'Focus' will, as has been affirmed above, also have interdependence with diverse other metaphysical doctrine and interpretation. We might take the classical Yoga system of Patañjali as an example, as it often features in discussion of mystical types. There are interpreters of this yogic experience who assume that the interpretive concepts Patañjali and other classical yogic teachers make use of are peripheral to the yogic experience. The interpretive difference between Patañjali's Yoga and the system of Advaita have, for example, been called 'merely technical' (by Swami Prabhavananda and Isherwood); in essence, it is said, the two systems are the same kind of mysticism, and the non-dualist interpretation is taken as the more authentic. An analysis of the process involved in Patañjali's Yoga by David Bastow (1980) shows rather conclusively that the distinctive doctrines are essential to any authentic interpretation of the experience. Now the doctrines concerned are derived largely from the Sāmkhya system; the question is, do these doctrines 'play a subsidiary, derivative role? Can the true goal of the yogin be stated in non-Samkhyan terms?' (*ibid*.:102).After a carefully sustained analysis of the material Bastow concludes: For Patañjali and his commentators, 'metaphysical knowledge is an integral and central element in their path to kaivalya. They do not think of this knowledge as being ineffable, beyond the reach of concepts or philosophic understanding; thus they are committed to a metaphysical system that is distinctive'. He goes on: 'This commitment is not a peripheral matter, an afterthrought; on it is based the structure of the path as they describe it' (*ibid*.: 118).

It is true, of course that the yogic technique, in variously modified forms, is capable of appropriation within religious paths that have other goals than that of the Patañjali tradition, as we have seen in Chapter Four. In each case, however, it is the distinctive goal, closely identifiable with the distinctive sacred Focus, which makes necessary a distinctive accompanying interpretation, which will have, explicitly or implicitly, metaphysical, certainly doctrinal dimensions. What results will be a distinctive experience, the interpretation of which within the concerned tradition (if not by individuals) is essential to the experience itself. There is a mutual interaction of experience and expression: the doctrinal features of a system do shape various other dimensions of that tradition; including especially the meaning for existence that is found through the core-experiences of the tradition. It is necessary in religious studies, therefore, to examine comparatively various types of religious experience, perhaps focussing on core-experiences that have some mystical features, but to examine them in relation to the various other dimensions that help in the shaping of these experiences. It will undoubtedly be found that the doctrinal dimension, and the conceptual systems within these traditions, will be of great significance for the way the meaning of the experience, and thus the meaning and goal of existence, has been understood. That both experience and interpretation deeply interconnect with the mythic/ritual/symbolic matrix of religious traditions will be rather obvious.

7

Coherence of Cultic Practice and Cosmic Vision

In this chapter[1] we take up a further aspect of the inner coherence to be expected in the theological process, looking in more detail at one major Indian
religious system. Both in Western Christian and in Indian religious thought a
similar though distinct kind of polarisation has taken place in the recent past.
In India, religious studies tend to be of two very different sorts. There are
studies of a particular tradition – its rituals, scriptures, doctrines, community
life, and so on – usually done by a person belonging to the tradition. Then
there are those philosophical or literary studies, which aim to rise above all
cultic considerations. University theses are more likely to be of the philosophical variety, as there are very few departments of 'comparative religions' in India.
Students wanting to do research on the non-philosophical aspects of religion
can only do so indirectly, by making their study suitable for a history, language,
sociology, or anthropology department. In a land richer than all others in
religious resources this is a strange anomaly, but probably reflects both the
nineteenth century style of religious education in the West, which India came
to adopt, and also the reluctance of traditionalists in Indian religions to allow
their sacred subject to be handled in non-sacred contexts.

Obviously, there is a valid place for internal cultic description, without phi-
losophising about it either from within or from without. And there is a valid
place for philosophical studies that, even if religiously oriented, have little
explicit reference to cultic traditions. Yet the fact is that in the Indian tradition a great deal of philosophic thought is, directly or indirectly, reflection
about cult-oriented life, religious life. The presuppositions underlying most
Indian systems of philosophy often derive from such cultic traditions, even
when unconsciously held presuppositions. Ignoring the dynamics of this

---

1 An earlier form of the main ideas of this chapter was published in *Proceedings of the
Seminar on Temple Art and Architecture*, edited by K.K.A. Venkatachari (Bombay:
Ananthacharya Indological Research Institute 1981), pp. 30-46.

undergirding cultic life is a weakness in such otherwise excellent analyses of Indian thought as that of, for example, Karl Potter (1963).

It is in Vedanta in particular that we can see most clearly the integral connection of practised cult and conceptual system; yet this inter-connecting is usually ignored in Vedantic studies. Vedanta's basic source, the Upanishads, for example, makes little sense apart from the background of the acient Vedic cultus. One very important Upanishad (*Brihadāraṇyaka*) begins with a meditation on the inner significance of the royal horse-sacrifice. Another (*Māṇḍūkya*) is devoted entirely to reflecting on the meaning of the 'seminal' cultic utterance, AUM (OM). Then the opening statement of the Brahma-Sūtras, the aphoristic summary of the Vedantic system at an early stage of its development, is: 'Then, therefore, enquiry into Brahman'. This has always been taken to mean that the system of Vedantic *knowledge* of supreme Reality presupposes the system of Vedic *action*; there is an inner connection, but Brahman-knowledge does not depend directly on any prior action. *Veda-anta* means, literally, 'the end, the intention, of the Vedas'. Even more clearly, after the system (in the Sūtras) has dealt with the question of the nature of the supreme Being and the universe of souls and matter, we are led to think about the life-duties, meditative practices and so on, issues directly concerned with community and cultic life.

There is a widespread fear that unless Indian philosophy can be shown to transcend and supersede all cultic or sectarian influence, its validity, especially its universal significance, is questionable. Radhakrishnan (1929 (II): 445) seeks to depict Śaṅkara's system of non-dualist Vedānta (*advaita*) as 'pure philosophy' even though Śaṅkara himself says categorically that there can be no knowledge of the ultimate Reality apart from the revelation of scripture, which is hardly the basis one would expect to be posited for a purely philosophic system. A recent work (Bhatt 1975) on the theist, Rāmānuja, claims that he was virtually uninfluenced by the Vaishnava cultic system in the formulation of his theology of 'non-dualism-with-distinctions'. He is said to be a purely Vedic thinker. Significantly, it is argued that in some of his doctrines (notably his idea of the celestial form of the Lord) Rāmānuja allowed himself to be influenced injudiciously by 'anthropomorphic concepts', 'mythological fancies', 'narrow orthodoxy'. As a philosopher, it is argued, Rāmānuja should have been above such 'superstitions', even if there is scriptural basis for them (ibid.: 53-5).

It has to be acknowledged that Śaṅkara did sit rather lightly to his sectarian tradition, though certainly not rejecting it. And to some extent even Rāmānuja's formal Vedantic writings do not give free expression to the Vaishnava cultic forms in which his daily temple and personal life was steeped. For the sake of Vedantic recognition and the compulsion to wider communication, no doubt, certain conventions of style and even modification of content had to be observed. But this does not mean that Rāmānuja regarded cultic life as a lower-order reality than the more conceptual articulation of Vedantic ontology and epistemology; the very structure of his Vedanta indicates just the opposite. There is good reason for contending that his tradition's cultic life was the most creative factor in the formation of Rāmānuja's viewpoint as a Vedantin; and there is no intrinsic reason for thinking his a less universally valid form of Vedānta. Indeed, that Vedānta in which cosmological viewpoint can be seen to cohere with important aspects of cultic life, in which worship-experience and conceptual system are most effectively integrated, should surely be reckoned the most *authentic* form of Vedānta (Lott 1986). Such a criterion of internal coherence of cultic life and conceptual system is intrinsic to the Vedantic tradition; indeed a similar case can be made out for the inner integration of, for example, Buddhist cosmology and meditational practice, of Liṅga-devotion and the soul's pilgrimage in Liṅgāyata Śaivism. If there are to be criteria for evaluating any theological system, these should surely include such internal coherence.

Rāmānuja, then, shows very clearly the intrinsic relationship that does exist (and therefore should exist?) between icon-worship and cosmic vision. The temple at Śrī-Raṅgam in Tamil Nadu, with its central image of Raṅganātha, obviously played an important part in Rāmānuja's life as the great preceptor (*ācārya*) of the Vaishṇava community centred there (Carman 1977: 33-8, 233). He was also the director (*Śrī-kārya*) of the temple, in which capacity he had to resolve a number of tensions that had developed in supervising the temple-life. Despite a lack, in his writings, of many *direct* references to sectarian ritual and literature (either to cultic practice or to the poetic ecstasies of the Vaishṇava saints), Rāmānuja most certainly continued the earlier policy of fusing the two great traditions of his religious heritage, Vedic and Vaishṇava. Thus the practice of both symbolic meditation and direct image-worship were essential in the cultic life for which he was responsible. There was, too, his personal devotion to his household icon, symbolising Varadarāja, the deity of his previous temple-home, Kāñcīpuram.

It is true that Vaishṇava cultic tradition speaks of two levels at which the divine becomes present with his devotees — as the 'manifest' and as 'unmanifest'. The latter are the transcendent, the emanationary and the interior levels of divine existence and activity. Essential to sharing in these levels of the divine Being, however, are the incarnational and the iconic manifestations. Conversely, all the divine embodiments are intended to lead to a sharing in the unembodied forms, though in an inclusive way, for there is no intention of superseding these divine embodiments.

There are at least five ways in which we can see an integral relationship between icon-meditation and the understanding of reality that is conceptualised in Rāmānuja's system. This inner coherence would lead us to suppose that it is cultic life which provides the creative springs of Rāmānuja's vision (darśana). While cultic derivation can also be attributed to most other religious systems in India, perhaps in no other is the cult-concept relationship so integral.

Firstly, there is his concept of the *divine embodiment on earth*. Indian temple cultic life revolves around the icon, with myths recounted and rituals performed in connection with it. Thus the central image is the focal point of temple life, the most effective point of access to the tradition's sacred power, the place where the tradition's vision is most tangibly expressed. Each temple tradition recounts its peculiar mythological origins and the 'glory' (*māhātmya*) of that 'divine place' (*divya-deśa*). Its sacred myth seeks to confirm the distinctive holiness of the divine embodiment at that sacred spot. Indeed, the temple itself is seen as shaped in the form of the body of God.

Clearly there was a shift of understanding when we compare this with early Vedic religion, in which the altar, constructed for the sacrificial occasion, formed the focal point of the sacred world. The sacred sacrificial fire, the embodiment of the god Agni, the 'house-priest' of the three-worlds (earth, sky, the higher heavens) was probably the nearest counterpart of the later divine icon. In this later iconic cult the one divine Person becomes experienced as most immediately accessible to the devotee precisely in the act of image-ritual.

Closely linked with this kind of iconic faith in Vaishṇavism is faith in special personal incarnations, again mythologically recounted; the image too is said to be such an *avatāra*. About this form of divine embodiment Rāmānuja writes as follows in his introduction to his Gītā-commentary, though I can here only include parts of the passage:

> The Lord of Lakshmī, He who is the opposite of everything that is evil . . . who is distinguished from all things other than himself . . . who is a vast ocean of countless auspicious qualities . . . such as brilliancy, grace, fragrance, tender softness, beauty, and youthfulness . . . who is adorned with countless divine ornaments of various kinds . . . who while remaining in his own form was not directly accessible through meditation, wor-

ship and such other devotional acts . . . being a vast ocean of boundless
mercy, affability, affection and generosity, he made his own form in conformity with the configurative nature of each of the several species of
beings, without giving up his own essential nature; and thus descending
again and again into each of their regions . . . and under the pretext of
removing the burden of the earth (but really) for the purpose of becoming
the Object of refuge even to people like us, he descended to the earth
and made himself visible to the eyes of all men . . . having refreshed the
entire universe with the nectar of his looks and words, pregnant with
boundless compassion, friendliness and love . . . he promulgated the way
of realising God through love, which is fostered by knowledge and works,
which has himself for its Object and which is declared in the Vedanta as
the means for attaining emancipation of the self, the highest of human
goals (Sampatkumar 1969: 1-4).

It is precisely this conviction that the transcendent Lord has made himself
accessible to his devotees that informs Rāmānuja's whole Vedantic viewpoint,
even if not always so obviously expressed, so that *supremacy* (*paratva*) and
accessibility (*saulabhya*) become the two determining conceptual poles in his
system (Carman 1974: chapt. 5). However much the details of iconic ritual
have to be taken as implicit, there us undoubtedly a constant interaction in
Rāmānuja's thought between the experience of the iconic divine embodiment
and the incarnational (*avatāra*) divine embodiment. It is the doctrine of incarnation in this broadest sense, therefore, that is central in the conceptual process
and which accounts for the continual emphasis on God's 'accessibility'. Even as
we read his account of the 'surpassing beauty' of the incarnation (as Kṛishṇa)
in the above passage, we are led to think that Rāmānuja could just as well be
describing the *iconic* embodiment; each provides the impulse for the other.
Another passage in his Bhagavad-Gītā commentary (4. 11) suggests the same
continuity of embodiment-experience:

It is not merely by incarnating myself . . . that I give protection to those who seek refuge
in me. I show myself to them . . . (so that) they keep on experiencing my form, my
essential nature which is really beyond speech and thought even to yogis, experiencing it
with their very eyes and other sense-organs . . . (Sampatkumar *ibid*: 119).

Rāmānuja seems to have in mind here a continuity of experience of the divine
presence, extending from the special embodiments of the divine 'descents'
(*avatāra*), through the more general embodiments of the icons, to the experience
of those with peculiar ability to 'image' the divine presence in their meditations.

Secondly, there is Rāmānuja's concept of the *whole universe as a divine embodiment*. Far more openly and frequently expressed in his Vedantic writings is this doctrine of the universe as the great body of God, a body to which he is the inner controlling Self (cf. Lipner 1984; 1986). This universal embodiment forms the *macrocosmic* aspect of Rāmānuja's vision of reality. There were, of course, numerous scriptural passages that he could turn to in confirmation of his self-body analogical understanding of the God-universe relationship (Lott 1976: 18-48). The important Inner-Controller passage in the Upanishads was one such, and there were numerous parts of the Gītā, especially the statement that is repeated in various ways in the all-important eleventh chapter with its glorious 'vision of (Krishna) in universal form'. 'Behold, the whole universe . . . all unified in my body' (11.7, etc.). But in themselves these texts do not provide a ready-made key to Rāmānuja's cosmological perception, even if in some cases (e.g. the Vishnu Purāna) they are quite important in the Vaishnava tradition. It is rather his primal vision of reality that had gripped Rāmānuja and guided him to the use of these texts instead of others for his principle of interpretation.

Are we not justified in assuming that it was the practice of continual icon-meditation as the mode of devout and loving 'recollecting' ('like a flow of oil' between soul and God) of the divine nature – the 'way' that Rāmānuja perceived also as the ultimate goal – that prompted this prior vision? It is one of the principles of both 'orthodox' Upanishadic and 'non-orthodox' Tantric meditation that one becomes like the object upon which one meditates. It does not require greatly sophisticated psychological theory to suggest that once the mind is concentrated on an objective image to the extent that inward consciousness is filled with it, then this interiorised image is likely to determine perception of the outer world. Conversely, the divine body upon which concentration is focussed will be seen as including the whole objective universe. This is not an attempt at a reductionist 'explanation' of the meditative process. Whether such a description fits or not, the resulting 'vision' need not be any less of an ultimate revelation of the nature of Reality. I merely wish to stress that Rāmānuja's primal perception, his key-doctrine of the whole universe as the body of the supreme Self, coheres innately and consistently with the iconic devotion and inner meditation that was so prominent in his cultic tradition.

Thirdly, the ultimacy Rāmānuja ascribed to cultic devotion provided a basis for an *ontological and epistemological viewpoint that is essentially relational*. His self-body analogy (*śarīra-śarīri-bhava*) is far more than a mere cosmological metaphor. It provides a fundamental model for understanding both the nature of reality and the ways in which we apprehend that reality. In other words, the organic and 'inseparable' relationship of body and self afforded a comprehensive key for unlocking the ontological and epistemological mystery of the universe, as Rāmānuja saw it. As psycho-physical beings we are eternally in an inseparable relationship with the supreme Self; we are his body.

As this point a pertinent counter-question could well be asked, especially in an Indian context. Why, in Rāmānuja's system, does the divine 'Object' of worship and meditation not so fill the meditator's consciousness, that subject and object become indistinguishably one? Why not go all the way and advocate pure non-dualism, a vision of pure consciousness, as Śaṅkara did? Why this 'non-duality-determined-by distinction'? Why in interpreting a Gītā-passage (6: 29-31) which speaks of a meditating yogi 'seeing his self as existing in all beings and all beings in his self', and which speaks of God likewise as seen in all, with all beings seen in him — why does Rāmānuja contend that the text affirms an essential 'similarity' (sāmya) only and not an identity of being? It is surely because of his fundamental and continuing conviction that in the relational act of worship and devotion the soul is in touch with ultimate reality: the reality of its own individual selfhood and the reality of the supreme Selfhood. For Rāmānuja it is a reality of the most absolute kind that is disclosed in the proper relationship of these two, a loving relationship that can never be superseded. Hence he can bring out the full force of Krishna's statement in this same passage (6.30): 'I am not lost to him, nor is he lost to me'. It means, says Rāmānuja, that the continuing reality of the relational mode of existence is assured because there is similarity and not identity between meditating souls and worshipped Lord, as they are 'within sight' of each other.

Early in his major Vedantic commentary, too, Rāmānuja had argued that there can be no valid knowledge, especially knowledge of the supreme Being, except by way of relationship. None of the Vedantically accepted ways of knowing (pramāṇas) — scriptural testimony, perception, inferential argument — can operate without the interaction of subject and object. Knowledge of that ultimate kind cannot completely supersede the knowing process itself; transcendent goal and the means of its attainment must have a fitting commensurability. Thus the ultimate knowledge that liberates the soul can never be the pure consciousness of non-dualism. Consciousness must be seen as the attribute of the knowing self. And in the case of God-consciousness it means that by which the soul can cognise and participate in the Object of its worship.

What Rāmānuja also claimed was that within this mediated, relational process of knowing the supreme Self there an *immediacy* of experience, a directness of perception, such as would be the case in the lover's knowledge of his beloved to a lesser extent. Immediacy is possible for all devotees because it is the supreme Self who is found to be the inmost Self of all finite beings. Corresponding to the macrocosmic dimension of the universal divine embodiment there are *two microcosmic foci* – the iconic embodiment mediating the vision of reality, and the finite self which is the knower of the Other, a finite self that is also 'inseparably related' to its body. In both foci the supreme all-present Self is the inmost Self, thus making an immediacy of experience possible within the relational life of meditative worship. But this immediacy of inner vision can never do away with the mediation of embodiment and iconic meditation. Underlying the whole Vedantic process of 'knowing the supreme Person' and intrinsic to that process, argues Rāmānuja, is a relational view of knowledge and of the reality to be known that precludes any sheer identity of consciousness or of being.

It has been claimed that in this system of Rāmānuja's, epistemology determined the nature of ontology (Bhattacharya 1936: 23-4; Sircar 1927: 3). While it is true that these two dimensions are remarkably integrated and interdependent in his thought, what is more determinative is the key-vision of all things cohering in the supreme Self as body related to self. And the originating factor here is surely the iconic embodiment central to the cultic experience.

Fourthly, the *devotional attitude focussed in the cultic life provides the cohering stimulus for the conceptual process*. By way of example we may again take the problem of clarifying the relationship between the three great 'ways' of religious life – action, knowledge and devotion (*karma, jñāna, bhakti*) – each as we saw, being given a place of primacy by one or other of the traditions. Rāmānuja makes it clear where he stands. He strongly disagreed with Śaṅkara's contention that the liberated, realised person has no further concern at all with the doing of action, even though he agreed with Śaṅkara that the ultimate goal can never be realised by human effort alone. Both conceded that the prescribed duties done in the right spirit can help to purify the mind, so that it becomes partly prepared for the liberating experience (Lott 1980: chapt. 10).

What Rāmānuja stressed in addition to this was that the person who is lovingly devoted to God will delight in performing all the good deeds he can as an offering to his Lord; this in turn God also delights in. In other words, it is the devotional attitude, or rather the love-relationship, that makes all the difference in the performance of action. Similarly with knowledge, the other

great religious way. Very early in his Vedantic commentary Rāmānuja makes
it clear that what he understands by liberating knowledge (so emphasised by
Śaṅkara, and indeed an essential feature of the Vedantic tradition) is the experience of adoring meditation on and intimate acquaintance with the supreme
Person. For, he taught, the essence of meditation required by the ancient
tradition is *bhakti*, trustful devotion, loving adoration, dependent sharing in
the being and nature of the Object of meditation. In other words, this inclusive
kind of devotion is not just one of the 'ways'. It is rather *the way* which alone
can integrate both action and knowledge, and which at the same time determines their role in such a synthesis.

It was in his more esoterically devotional writings that Rāmānuja brought
out a more typically Vaishnava way of talking about the devotional life. The
devotee is to delight in being a slave of the Lord, in seeing his whole life as
an act of 'constant service'. An incident recounted in the tradition about the
life of Rāmānuja (Carman 1974: 29), when he was still being initiated into the
Vaishnava way, gives some indication of how this servant-attitude was believed
to have been first instilled in his mind. Just after he had broken with an early
teacher (Yādava Prakāśa) of a certain kind of non-dualism, Rāmānuja's mother
advised him to seek counsel from Tirukacci Nambi, a non-Brahmin disciple of
the great Vaishnava teacher, Yamuna. It is said that Tirukacci Nambi instructed
Rāmānuja to carry a pot of water every morning from the well up to the
temple of Lord Varadarāja. When Yamuna, near death, heard that Rāmānuja
had broken with the other teacher and was performing this lowly service in
the temple — says the tradition — he sent for him to come to the Vaishnava
centre, Śrī-Raṅgam. Presumably he recognised that here was a man who was
not only an intellectually suitable student, but whose acceptance of the 'con-
stant-servant' role showed his eminent suitability for the post of temple
director and of teacher of the ontological realities implicit in the cultic action
central to temple life.

Those who have written polemic against Hindu 'idol-worship' — and this
includes a number of reformers and iconoclasts within the Hindu tradition —
often ridicule what they see as the 'anthropomorphic' idea of God being
dependent upon human help. Why should the supreme Spirit need waking,
bathing, feeding, garlanding, and so on, as is assumed by the devotees who
perform the fourteen 'service-aids' to that Spirit in his image-form? It is
certainly not my task to attempt an apologia for icon-worship. It may well be,
though, that the idea of God's helpless dependence on his devotees' service is
theologically nearer the truth than my missionary forefathers recognised, and

that the tension between transcendence and accessibility that other theologies as well as the Vaishṇava's see in the divine nature is most strikingly expressed in this kind of incongruous dependence of God upon human help. Rāmānuja, at least, was not afraid to say in his Gītā-Commentary (7.18) on behalf of Vishnu: 'The support for my existence is under the control of my enlightened ones. Why is this so? Because the enlightened one, my devotee, is not able to sustain his soul without me . . . Therefore I cannot sustain my soul without him' (Sampathkumar). Later in this Gita-commentary (9.29) Rāmānuja speaks of Vishṇu treating those who have intense love for him as though they were his superiors.

Picking up a similar sentiment, a later leading Vaishṇava teacher, Piḷḷai Lokācārya, speaks specifically of God in his iconic incarnation as being 'dependent upon the worshipper for all activities . . . (there is an) interchange of position as between lordly owner and dependent property. He appears as if ignorant, as weak and dependent' (Tattva-Traya III. 202). This has been further commented on in the Vaishṇava tradition:

This is the peculiar privilege of the devotee when he can constrain the Lord of the universe, as it were, to dwell in a particular image . . . This is the greatest grace of the Lord, that being free he becomes bound, being independent he becomes dependent on his devotees for all the service he receives. In other incarnations man belonged to God, but behold the supreme sacrifice of the Lord – here the Almighty becomes the dependent property of the devotee. He carries him about, fans him, feeds him, plays with him. Yes, the infinite has become finite, that the child-like soul may grasp, understand and love him. (Yamunacharya 1974: 208).

In Rāmānuja's writings, of course, a much more persistent theme is the devotees' utter dependence upon God, just as a body is dependent upon its controlling self. And this, too, fits coherently with Rāmānuja's faith in the enduring validity of turning to God's presence in meditative devotion. Ontologically it is the devotee, not God, who is in need and who acknowledges his need by turning to the great Self of all for 'refuge' (*saraṇāgati*), 'throwing himself' (*prapatti*) in utter resignation at the feet of his Refuge who has graciously made himself accessible. In their original language the terms used in this sentence would introduce us to some of the most significant, as well as the most controversial, terms in the Vaishṇava tradition. But note how they are eminently suited to the iconic symbolism – 'taking refuge at the feet', 'throwing oneself at the feet of'. Admittedly, Rāmānuja himself *wrote* very little about this 'surrender' concept which has led to such painful schism in the Vaishṇava community. Without trying to take sides here, surely we can say that when human dependence upon Vishnu's grace and his accessibility has been made the conceptual context for a devotion-based style of religion (as is emphatic in Rāmānuja's writings), the only fitting attitude with which to carry out these devotional acts is that of 'falling' before this gracious Lord, accepting One's status as a 'surrendered one'. In the devotional attitude there is a sufficient focus for a wide range of conceptual systematising.

Finally, in Vaishnava thought *the heavenly world too is perceived in terms of the temple experience*. Theoretically, as in many other religions, the temple is taken to be a replica of heaven; it is known as 'earth-heaven' (*bhū-vaikuṇṭha*), the sacred centre of the world, the focal point of Vishnu's sovereign presence in the midst of the mundane. There seems little reason to doubt that in empirical terms the process is the reverse: the celestial realm is envisaged in terms of the temple, with the glorious icon-manifest Lord as the central figure in the heavenly courts. Either way the icon is heavy with symbolism of the life of heaven.

The question of whether God possesses a body, and the theological implications of this, frequently came up in Indian theistic debate. One well-known argument was that it is quite incongruous to think of God as a creator of the world (after the manner of a potter or carpenter), for to create he would need a body like theirs to function with. (In fact, Rāmānuja himself argued with great force against the possibility of proving by inference that God is creator, using, inter alia, arguments similar to this). To possess a body would make God equally subject to the law of karma, and so on. There is no need here to go any further into this complex debate. What we can note, however, is that while most theists, Indian and Western, have felt it necessary to affirm that in an ultimate sense God must be without bodily form of any kind, Vaishnava theology boldly asserts not only that the whole universe is related to God as his body, but also that he possesses a celestial, supernatural body, though a body not determined by karma as is the case with others. Rāmānuja's emphasis on this eminently beautiful and supernal form certainly puts strikingly his rejection of the non-dualist view that all descriptions of the ultimate Being in terms of 'name and form' must be limited to the empirical sphere and cannot be ultimately real. Thus he takes to the extreme his contention that God is essentially 'one-with-distinct-qualities'.

Other schools, however, accepted this ultimately personal nature of God, but rejected the idea of his supernatural body. What Rāmānuja constantly stressed was that the Lord's 'one permanent heavenly form is (entirely) suited and appropriate to his being'. Or again: 'He has an infinite variety of superlatively glorious ornaments that are suited to his form', just as are his amazing weapons, his gracious consort, his infinite realm of attendants, and 'his infinitely great realm manifesting his glory . . . (and his) celestial abode the essential nature of which is beyond the grasp of thought or speech' (Vedārtha Saṃgraha par. 127). Rāmānuja does not explicitly describe the celestial forms as made up of 'pure light matter' as was later taught in his sect. He merely affirms that their God's celestial form is wholly fitting to and integral with his eternal nature as supreme Lord. Thus his heavenly body is as much part of his divine sovereignty as are the 'glorious qualities' so beloved of Vaishṇava doctrine; this body is quite transcendent to all material bodies.

Even so, Rāmānuja's description of this transcendent body includes qualities of such a rich visual beauty, almost sensual in style, that are reminiscent of the visual, aesthetically pleasing beauty of the Vaishṇava icons (H.D. Smith 1969). In fact the terms 'beauty' and 'beautiful' are among the most characteristic of his descriptions of the divine Person. If the experiences of the earlier Vaishṇava saints (the Ālvārs) and the later teachers are truly indicative of the Vaishṇava tradition, then it was the icon-form of Vishṇu that captivated his devotees and evoked such ardent admiration of the divine beauty, for these other writers are even more explicit than Rāmānuja on this issue.

Rāmānuja's somewhat more cautious attitude probably reflects his continuing concern to give adequate expression to the *transcendent* dimension of the divine character, perhaps even more than to the divine accessibility. Thus he contended that only the supreme Person in his infinite perfections can be the proper Object of meditation when various symbols are employed as meditative aids. To the question, Can these symbols be thought of as carrying the *essential nature* of Brahman, the supreme Self? Rāmāuja replied that no absolute identity can be made: 'What is to be meditated on is the symbol only, not Brahman as such; Brahman enters into the meditation only as qualifying the way it is looked at . . . so that something that is (known as) not Brahman is looked at as Brahman' (Śrī-Bhāshya IV. 1.4).

Now this may look very much like a version of the non-dualist's viewpoint, but Rāmānuja makes his position quite distinct from Śaṅkara's. Looking at objects which are, in themselves obviously *not* the supreme Self with a 'Brahman-view' is very different, holds Rāmānuja, from taking such objects as in reality the one Self, but a oneness on which some objective image has been superimposed. 'To view a superior person', wrote Rāmānuja (*ibid*), 'a prince, for example, as a servant would be degrading to him. On the other hand, to view a servant as a prince would be exalting to the servant'. The ultimate Object in all meditation, then, is God himself; all symbolic forms are to lead to the knowledge of his great qualities as supreme Person, hence to the intimacy of self-forgetting devotion.

It is interesting that Rāmānuja did not interpret the symbols as direct representations of the supreme Person's presence by being present in them as their inner Self. Later this was precisely how Madhva, even with his more radical concern to stress the *difference* of God from all else, did interpret them. Perhaps it was simply in order to make his position quite distinct from that of the non-dualists that Rāmānuja overlooked an opportunity to make use of his general hermeneutical key, the self-body analogy. Even so, his understanding of meditation and worship as mediating the immediacy of God-knowledge and God-experience is not negated. What happens in the cultic life corresponds to what happens in the heavenly life.

It has been the main contention of this chapter that the *outer image and the cultic experience surrounding it shapes the development of inner perception and thus the emergence of conceptual systems*. Hence the need to examine doctrines in cultic settings. Rāmānuja's system in particular shows with great clarity the continuity of this process, with its intrinsic and proper coherence of cult, perception and conceptual system. The influence, however, is far from one way only. However wholehearted cultic devotion may be, as soon as believers begin to reflect on the meaning of their tradition and formulate their concepts systematically, *an interaction of outer and inner images begins*. At this point — and we can assume that this is true of all religious traditions — theology begins to determine inner consciousness as it is focussed on the cultic practice, the very practice that helped to create the inner consciousness. When this cult-concept interaction takes place it is the task of the theologian to ensure the continued coherence of the two interacting factors. This Rāmānuja has done with remarkable perception and conceptual skill.

8

Ways of Investigating and Interpreting Religion

a) Historical, Behavioural, Analytical Approaches

In the next three chapters we shall look, by way of a rather selective and rapid overview, at a variety of ways of attempting to understand religious traditions. We begin with what some have called a 'hard' investigative approach and move on to a more 'soft' style of understanding (Dudley 1977: 31-4): the former may be more rigorously empirical forms of description, in which 'objectivity' is perhaps an explicit aim, as against approaches that may attempt to move beyond neutral description, or perhaps give a more significant role to the subjectivity of the participants. Or the significant differences may be in the fact that the latter aim eventually to work out a systematic 'science of religion'; whereas in general those giving more weight to one or other of the 'hard' scientific disciplines, with their greater emphasis on empirical particularity, find it difficult to accept the validity of any integral 'science of religion'. This will be regarded as yet another 'theology of religion', in which the integrating principle is probably seen as normative interpretation of what religion *should* be, as not inclusively appropriate to all the varied manifestations of religious traditions.

Or perhaps the most significant polarity may be in the conscious acceptance by the 'hard' approaches of an interpretive or category-framework that is taken from a discipline other than that of religion itself; the 'soft' approach may be more concerned to avoid any kind of 'reductionist' explanatory categories. In other words, the reasons for any polarising of approaches are more complex than is sometimes recognised.

On one thing there is general concensus from virtually all scholars in religions: so diverse and wide-ranging are the phenomena found in religious traditions that no *single* approach is competent to deal exhaustively with everything that constitutes religion without recourse at all to other disciplines, or to other forms of approach. Religious phenomena include tribal myths and classical texts, mystical ecstasies and metaphysical philosophies, elaborate rituals and rigorous ethics, ancient symbolic imagery and contemporary cults – the list is almost endless. Such rich diversity calls necessarily for investigation from a variety of approaches. Similarly, the fact that phenomena usually identified as peculiarly *religious* are typically manifest in conjunction with and as part of the historical and human cultural process, in socially institutionalised contexts, or along with psychologically identifiable mental states and patterns of human behaviour, makes it inevitable and only proper that the dynamics of religion should be investigated from the perspective of the disciplines appropriate to these dimensions of human existence. No one will dispute that at various behavioural levels such studies are essential to the task of understanding the life of religion in all its diversity. What is not as generally accepted is whether there is a further, more integrative approach which affirms that, while various aspects of such separated disciplines are needed, in the final analysis no one such fragmented empirical study goes far enough, or provides authentic understanding either of any one religious tradition, or of those patterns of life that are typically 'religious' in all traditions.

At this point we might look again at the question of *definition* of religion (cf. Baird 1971). Basically there are three courses we can take: we might decide on a definition that has merely a *functional* status (*ibid*: 16-27), and pursue our study of religion rigorously within the conceptual constraints such a definitive framework may place on the subject. This means consciously accepting a particular perspective that may make certain aspects of religion more prominent and give less importance to others, this being inevitable in view of the great diversity and complexity of data found in religious traditions, and in view of the methodological need for some kind of perspectival starting-point. Being a merely functional approach, rather than attempting to define the essence of religion at the outset, such a definition does not call for continual modification; rather, it may be discarded and another functional definition adopted if the former is found sufficiently inadequate in view of the evidence. It has been argued, however, that even the process of testing through the examination of data does not prove or disprove the truth or legitimacy of the adopted definition, but merely its *'applicability* and *usefulness'* (Baird 1971: 7). Such merely functional definitions are 'semi-arbitrary' in that it is recognised that there are many other meanings which the term 'religion' might be given, and such a perspective is *not intended* to provide insight into the essential character of religion. Other functional approaches tend often to assume that religion itself is essentially functional in nature (e.g. Malinowski 1948; Whaling 1985: chaps.

3-5). In any case a form of reductionism would seem inevitable in this kind of deliberately perspectival approach; whether it would be a temporarily useful kind of reductionism, prior to a more integrative and inclusive approach (and understanding) is another matter. Definitional focus will certainly imply some kind of methodological slant, functional or otherwise. but precise use of terms in itself will not preclude, and may not wish to preclude, assumptions about the essential nature of religion.

A. *second* approach to the definition of religion is to take one's *intuition* about the essential nature of religion (cf. Baird *ibid.*: 2-5), not merely as a starting point, but as a definitive guide to the way in which the great range of religious phenomena is accounted for. The patterns of religion then are based on what is presupposed intuitively of religion's essence. This will usually mean that large areas of religious traditions will either be given lower-order placing, or will be ignored as not of ultimate significance for understanding the essence of religion. Once such an intuitive-essentialist perspective is adopted, then even though there may be an ostensible intention to check this position against historical and empirical evidence, the intuition usually proves to have remarkable endurance.

A *third* approach will be to acknowledge that any preliminary definition will be in part intuitive, though intuition based both on the accounts that others have given of religion and on one's own observations up to that point of outstanding features in the great 'world religions'. From the beginning it will be recognised that any such definition is *provisional* and, while giving a constraining framework for the time, will require *further refining and continual modifying* in view of further experience of the complex ways in which religious traditions shape themselves. For, increased understanding of what definitively constitutes the life of religions in all their diversity will not necessarily come from increase in empirical data (essential though this may be) but rather with increased insight into the inner structuring of those diversified phenomena. It will be on the basis of what we conclude to be the essential features and inner structuring of those traditions universally recognised as 'religious' that we will decide, for example, whether Marxism, humanism, nationalism, fascism and other such socially structured and shared world-views are also to be seen as 'religions', or as surrogate religions, or as traditions that are quite distinct from religion. In this general approach to defining what religion is, the preliminary, partly intuitive, 'definition' can do no more than provide some general direction as to the nature and range of the subject. There is, of course, difference of opinion as to what a definition's function is; in any case it is not possible to *begin* with a fully formal definition of what constitutes the essence of religion, even though some preliminary perspective is unavoidable. That this makes for less than 'precise' procedure cannot be helped. Terminological precision, with exact logical definition of terms, may not in the end make for the greatest descriptive adequacy.

These different attitudes as to whether we need a precise definition to begin with and regarding the ways definitions are arrived at echoes the very diverse methodological attitudes found in religious studies. The two most basic types of approach, which were not referred to very explicitly in the opening paragraphs of this chapter, have often been classified as *descriptive* and *normative*; but this is hardly adequate in that each 'descriptive' discipline or behavioural science inevitably works within a theoretical framework of some kind. It may well intend that its theoretical assumptions ensure the greatest possible descriptive rigour; it may aim at eliminating as far as possible all subjective value-judgements, all normative theory. It is doubtful if this is ever possible. Whether the desire for detached objectivity is actually *desirable* is another matter. In any case such a commitment is itself a kind of normativity.

Moreover, when we turn to the 'soft' end of the religious studies spectrum it is quite clear that there is a very prominent *descriptive* concern here also. Those who give primary importance for example to the inner intentions or experience, or to the interpretation of the participants within a tradition, whether to the non-professional *illiterati*, or to the well-informed *cognoscenti*, whether to their spontaneous outbursts or to their systematic formulations, are in their different ways attempting a *descriptive* approach, whatever other 'normative' assumptions they may make as part of the theoretical framework they adopt for this descriptive task. But neither is it merely a question of who gives the more importance to external manifestations of religion as against its inner dynamics, its unseen factors. Phenomenologists, for example, will necessarily focus primarily on that which is 'manifest' in religious life, even if they go on to look for patterns, essences, types that seem to account for, or that lie behind, these manifest forms. And it could be argued that systematic theologians can have a very 'positivistic' attitude towards external revelatory phenomena — scriptures, doctrines, creeds, formulations. On the other hand, 'behavioural' scientists such as psychologists of religion will obviously be very greatly concerned about participants' inner feelings, their mental/emotional states, and the unseen forces that affect their outer behaviour.

A further complication to be noted briefly is that even within each scientific discipline related to the study of religion there are always considerable differences of approach; each will have exponents who would like to direct their discipline into a more rigorous ('hard') method; some, on the other hand, may be concerned for more integration with other disciplines, or for an inclusiveness within the discipline, or for less commitment to extra-religious explanatory theory (cf. Whaling 1985). We began by setting these three chapters within a hard-soft typology; the limitations of such a scheme will now be clear. What we in fact will do first is discuss a *few* of the issues emerging in the historical, behavioural and philosophical approaches to religion, noting more especially points at which questions can be raised when they adopt a more 'hard' approach to the life of religious traditions.

1. The term 'History of Religions' is probably more often used than any other in the English-speaking world to refer to the systematic investigation of religious traditions, so we first look at the *historical* approach to the study of religion. The majority of books written on 'world religions' adopt a more or less historical account, though perhaps not often within a very rigorous historical method. Yet there is usually the attempt to trace chronologically the origins of each religion, mainly by reference to ancient texts and the traditions' founders, as well as taking some note of developments that took place in the various periods of their histories. It has been pointed out (Rudolph 1981) that it was a 'quite specific period of western intellectual history, namely the Enlightenment' that 'decisively determined the nature of the discipline' of *Religionswissenschaft* (*ibid*.: 96). Along with other traditions religions too became the 'subject of rational, scientific research' and it was 'especially the historical and philological disciplines' that 'fleshed out the first beginnings' in the study of religions (*ibid*.: 97). Philology gave 'methodological support' and ethnology, an 'equally historically oriented discipline... fertilised theory formation' (*ibid*.: 98). And these two, it is argued, should 'continue to play an unimpeded role' in the development of religious studies, though Rudolph acknowledges (and more fully so in Honko 1979: 98-109) that there is also the need for a more inclusive comparative or systematic 'mode of working' (we shall return to this point); for *Religionswissenschaft* is 'an historical *and* systematic discipline having as the object of its reflective and reconstructive investigation sets of circumstances which are part of human culture in the sense of tradition..' (*ibid*.: 99). Thus, while asserting that any hermeneutical approach is of very limited methodological value it is acknowledged that the diachronic data of 'objective historical perception' need to be 'complemented' and 'interlocked with' as 'wide a range of analogical and parallel phenomena as possible', which results in a systematic 'typological' method (*ibid*.: 106).

A basic question engaging those committed to the historical method is that of *what kind of objectivity* should historical reconstruction attempt. One side from which there is a radical critique of the historical method as traditionally pursued is that of the existential/hermeneutical movement. Hermeneutical philosophy (e.g. Gadamer 1975) would see all attempts at human understanding of the past as a process of dynamic interaction between tradition and contemporary context, with the subjectivity of the interpreter as it were intermediating meaning from these two converging 'horizons of meaning'. The 'emergent meaning' is neither precisely that objectively found in the tradition, nor that of the interpreter's subjectivity. Historical research, perhaps especially the study of religious traditions from the past, inevitably involves this dialectical hermeneutical process; we can no longer think of 'history' as a rationalist reconstruction of the objective facts of the past. Yet, in response to this denial of any objective recovery of the past, we still need to face the question of how we arrive at the most authentic possible understanding of human traditions which can be assumed to have their own reality quite apart from subsequent interpretations of them. The historian rightly asks: How do we best avoid the distorting projection possible in our subjective assumptions? And this is obviously a question of serious import to the historian of religions.

Then there is a more specific though related question. Just how important is it in the attempt to understand our traditions (as part of human history) to establish plausible and rational patterns of a *cause-effect sequence* in those traditions? Some kind of causal principle will be as important for historical methodology as for any scientific discipline if patterns of historical meaning are to be discovered. In the historical approach to religions this causal principle raises a rather crucial question of *explanation* (cf. Wiebe 1981: 61-81). For the historian is not concerned merely with plausible chronology or sequence of events. There is the search to understand the phenomena of the past in terms of the historical context in which the preceding and adjacent factors that explain given events can be historically identified. 'History' is in this sense interpretation through explanation; the historical context, or sequence of events, is thought to be able to provide the framework for perceiving meaning in any given history. Are not those committed to a rigorous historical method committed to explaining and accounting for any phenomenon seen in this history — whether part of a religious tradition or not — in terms of factors equally part of the historical process? And does this involve an *unacceptable reductionism* for the religious person committed to realities existing in some sense *transcendent* to such an empirically accountable process? Is the historical critical method in the end an anti-religious reductionism, as fundamentalists have in their own doctrinal terms long argued? It is quite possible, however, with an interpretation of religious history that takes the causal process seriously, while not attempting to draw out any trans-empirical factors to account for this process, yet to allow for an *ultimate* trans-empirical explanation, thus seeing various *levels* of causality (as indeed 'theologians' often do). Another possible 'theological' interpretation is, like Nagarjuna, Śaṅkara, and some Idealists, to find all causal relations as obscuring what is ultimate. The point is, acceptance of 'historical' explanation for a religious tradition does not in itself preclude the trans-historical dimension. 'Sacred histories' are possible along with secular histories, seen as in dynamic conjunction with the secular causal sequences in the historical process, perhaps as distinctive, meaning-shaping 'perspectives' of that secular history (Harvey 1966).

And yet — if all historical interpretation entails explanation, and thus some interpretive theory by which patterns of meaning can be seen, from the point of view of participants in a religious tradition it becomes important that such explanatory theory is *compatible* with the key concepts or the patterns of meaning seen as implicit in the tradition's inner or 'sacred history'. It is just not acceptable to religious commitment that the compatibilities or adjustments *all* be in the other direction, that theologians alone be expected to re-vision their world view to accommodate their tradition's meaning to contemporary 'scientific' explanations. Interaction of 'perspectives' will be necessary unless incompatible reductionism is taken to be the only rigorously historical path, and religious insight is given no place in the interpretation of the concerned religion.

2. In the study of religion through the approaches of the *behavioural sciences* — sociology, anthropology, psychology — we find a great deal of convergence and interdependence. Yet the key to how religion is understood does differ in each discipline; social structuring, cultural forms, mental processes — each is seen as the most significant factor in deciphering the *hidden* dynamics of religious life. Indeed, our understanding of the complex ways in which there is interplay between religious phenomena and diverse kinds of structuring in human life — social, political, cultural, psychological — is in many ways dependent on these disciplines. For the shaping of religious traditions has much to do with these dimensions of human life; understanding this interplay contributes so much to understanding the dynamics of religious life. What, however, when a behavioural science assumes, as it often does, that religion is to be

studied in all its manifest forms *essentially as no more than a human cultural phenomenon*? Have we to assume that it is on these grounds that empirical investigation is not only appropriate, but is of *decisive* importance in understanding what is really happening in religious life, as it were transcendent to the deluded level of theologising? This does not mean that behavioural scientists never take religious life with very great seriousness, nor that they can only see it in a non-realist, reductionist, functional way, as we shall see.

The most formative sociologists of religion, Durkheim and Weber, for example, both saw religion as providing the key to understanding human society as much as the converse (cf. Whaling 1985: chaps. 3-5). But these two formed their questions about society in very different ways, as well as understanding the dynamics of religion differently (Baum, in Eliade and Tracy, 1980, to which the following is considerably indebted). Durkheim's theories were of remarkable seminal importance to the conceptual development of both sociology and anthropology, to some extent even of psychology. For Durkheim the primary issue was: How does society hold together? What is the basis of its coherence and its sense of identity and continuity? For Weber the primary issue was: what are the dynamics making for the transformation of society? What are the key factors in society's continual changes? But both found the answer to their questions in religion. Thus religion was seen by both as essential to understanding human existence.

For Weber, religious systems provided that matrix of meaning by which social systems emerge and change, and through which they can be interpreted. The social process in itself, however, does not exhaust religion's meaning. Religion's matrix is in some sense trans-historical, and includes a socially transcendent dimension, though participation in this religious dimension of the human historical process is not inevitable. It is the 'virtuosi' who are most clearly in touch with this transcendent Focus of religion. Weber, moreover, felt that there was in human society diminishing sensitivity to the transcendent dimension (he claimed to be religiously 'tone-deaf' himself) which has resulted in the increasing secularisation of our time. To a large extent the seeds for this de-sacralising process are found in Protestantism, with its rationalist spirit and capitalist ethic. Thus, for Weber, religion has ontological reality, but human culture is not necessarily based on or oriented to the dynamics of religion.

In Durkheim we find some very different assumptions. He saw the complex cultural symbol-systems that comprise religions as essentially those self-projections of society that are necessary to human continuity and self-identity, but have functional reality only. Because religion serves a continuing functional

need for human existence, religion in some form or another will always continue. Naturally, these symbol-systems by which human society adapts itself
to changing conditions will go on changing. Yet, for Durkheim, the primal
totemic type of religious life, in whatever adapted form, will always serve to
integrate societies, creating a corporate consciousness within them, and making
ultimate demands beyond the individual and his/her needs. Thus morality too
is created through the totemic corporateness, calling for those eminently
religious ideals, sacrifice and surrender, as the other side of social participation.

These two, then, have been of seminal significance for the development at
least of the sociology of religion, and for many anthropological assumptions in
the case of Durkheim. It would be useful, however, to look briefly at more
recent representatives of those who have approached religion, perhaps a 'science
of religion', from either an anthropological or a sociological stance, or were
strongly indebted to the behavioural approach, in one way or another. *First* we
note the theoretical framework that Th. P. van Baaren adopted in proposing a
'science of religion' (1972: 35-54). Van Baaren's initial definition of religion
reveals his anthropological perspective: 'Religion is a function of culture
and is connected with and interacts with other functions of culture' (*ibid*.: 36).
'Culture' is taken to mean 'all that is learned' as humans 'satisfy their biological
and social needs and adapt themselves to their environment' (*ibid*.: 37). However, Van Baaren hastens to explain that he does not 'deny religion its own
specific character within the framework of culture', nor does he neglect the
fact that 'religions claim a supernatural cause for their existence' (*ibid*). Thus
he does not intend a full-blown functionalist account of religion, but rather
wishes to emphasise that religion does in fact function in culturally identifiable
and determinable ways. He recognizes that in the final analysis religion cannot
be determined by anything other than itself; thus Van Baaren's 'ultimate'
dimension saves him from a 'reductionist' account, as he himself argues: 'Reductionist theories of whatever kind give insufficient attention to the fact that
for most religions the belief in the reality they postulate is essential for the
consciousness of . . . ' (*ibid*.: 39).

In passing we might note here how close Van Baaren comes to an ecological
account of religion, which may well become more prominent in religious
studies as the need to recognise human participation in the whole bio-process
of the earth, as essential to human existence, becomes more pressing. To date,
apart from general philosophies of life and of science, such as Capra's writings,
a conscious 'ecological' approach to the scientific study of religion has tended
to be mostly geographical, i.e. noting how types of religious systems have

developed in conjunction with particular types of geographical environment. Clearly there are many other aspects of religious traditions, as of human cultures generally, that relate directly to human adaptation to environment and to the challenges of human dependency upon the bio-sphere. Growing out of American 'cultural ecology' (e.g. Steward 1955; Sahlins 1968; Harris 1968), Scandinavian scholars in religions, such as Hultkrantz and Bejerke (in Honko 1979), have begun the task of systematic interpretation along these lines, while explicitly avoiding the limitations of any strict functionalism.

Van Baaren accepted in general the socio-anthropological definitions of religion postulated by Clifford Geertz and Melford Spiro, the latter's being as follows: It is 'an institution consisting of culturally patterned interaction with culturally postulated superhuman beings'. Van Baaren does emphasise the role of belief-systems in general, and in particular of belief in divine beings or powers, objectively postulated by believers, by which the life of the world is explained. Beliefs are not necessarily prior to religious behaviour, but Van Baaren contends that they have a right to be considered first because believers themselves usually see things in this order: 'I do this because this is the kind of faith I have'. And while religious actions will all be meaningful in some way to the community concerned, they will only be so within the framework of the tradition. And internal explanations/interpretations cannot be given any 'higher value' by a science of religion; that is, there is nothing ultimately significant in self-understanding. The 'meaning' behavioural disciplines see in a tradition's actions will involve very different categories of explanation. 'In science under-standing can only be used as a special form of explaining' (*op. cit.*: 45). Thus, to understand a religion, from a scientific perspective is to be able to explain it in terms of the concerned science. There must be no 'theological absolutism'.

Van Baaren sees the difference between a 'systematic science of religion' (grounded in the basically socio-anthropological approach he adopts) and theology in the essential *normativity* of theology. The science of religion limits itself to the 'empirical study of religions as they are' and thus aims at 'objectivity' or 'impartiality' (*ibid.*: 42-4). Each religion's theology, on the other hand, will see its own symbol-system as 'the sacred model' of and for the divine reality, i.e. as *true*. For the science of religion, the theological distinction between true and false religion makes no sense. No religion is more than a human model of reality, so that the most the scientific approach will acknowledge is that 'in a certain historical situation or social context one religion functions better than another one' (*ibid.*: 43).

In response to Van Baaren we might agree that this kind of neutral attitude to questions of truth would seem, at least at certain levels of investigation, to be necessary for *any* scientific approach to religion; but we find that the particular ontological status we give to our 'model of reality' is crucial in our interpreting of what kind of meaning and at what level of meaning this 'model of reality' intends to communicate. If methodological agnosticism and neutrality has, perhaps unintentionally, built into it a methodological *atheism* (i.e. that the 'model' has no ontological correspondence to 'reality') it is difficult to see how any understanding based on such an approach can be compatible with the tradition's own interpretation. As another anthropologist has put it: 'The very nature of religion alters depending on whether one applies, for example, a positivistic or a theological paradigm'. There is an inherent tendency for religious studies (studying the religious as phenomenon) 'to reinterpret, even reconstitute, the religious in terms of paradigms which cannot be justified with respect to intra-religious criteria' (Heelas 1978: 1, 7).

This seems to be the dilemma of the behavioural approach: to be scientific in approach religion will necessarily be interpreted and explained in terms of the 'paradigm' found acceptable by the concerned science as a way of discovering meaning, and thus it must be to some extent reductionist. Perhaps interpretation from *any* systematic perspective will always involve some form of reductionism, i.e. explaining the 'meaning' of the concerned religious life from some perspective other than it's own. The very least we can expect, however, is that the 're-constituting' of religious life through the behavioural scientist's interpretation will neither ignore that phenomenon which the concerned tradition (and analogously religion generally) perceives as its central, integrating Focus, nor will it assume that sacred Object *not* to be ontologically real. That such an Object *is* a perception of the concerned community, and *is* therefore a *human perception* cannot be denied. No doubt, too, behavioural sciences will need to limit their 'frame of reference' to what is behaviourally, i,e. empirically, investigable. But to make this frame of reference a positivistically interpretive theory within which to understand religious life raises serious methodological questions.

There is, of course, a fine line to be drawn here. What, for example, are we to make of Cliffore Geertz' now well-known socio-anthropological definition of religion? (1973: 90): 'Religion is a system of symbols which acts to establish powerful, pervasive, and long-lasting moods and motivations in men by formulating conceptions of a general order of existence and clothing these conceptions with such an aura of factuality that the needs and motivations seem uniquely realistic'. In anthropological terms this is no doubt a fine statement, and Geertz offers important insights into cultural realities and for the interpretation of religion as a 'symbol-system'. And Geertz does give crucial importance to what religious people say they believe, and thus to the meanings, and metaphysical systems derived from these perceptions, that they affirm. Given, then, that we take religious participants' perceptions of their sacred Foci as the basis for our understanding of what religion is, why at the same time assume that the 'factuality' of those sacred Foci is merely an 'aura', a *seeming* reality? It is quite possible to take the 'symbol-system' paradigm as a way of looking at religion without in this way so undermining the participants' sense of the reality of their sacred Foci, without explicitly making it a 'seeming' reality. Or is this 'seemingliness' intrinsic to interpretation by way of 'symbol-systems'?

In some of Peter Berger's writings more serious methodological doubts arise. Berger's thought is of great importance to us not merely because he is so racily astute in theorising both on sociology of religion and on theology, but more importantly because in attempting to delineate the differences of approach involved he illuminates, intentionally and unwittingly, the crux of the methodological problem of trying to be both scientific and theological in religious studies. Berger's sociological position is clearly Weberian (and in a limited sense Marxian, i.e. he is not committed to Marxist ideology). It is interesting, however, that he has collaborated closely (especially in the writing of *The Social Construction of Reality*, 1966) with Thomas Luckmann, who is much more functionalist in approach and more in the tradition of Durkheim. Significantly, they differ quite markedly in their definition of religion: Berger, from a sociological perspective, sees religion as 'the human enterprise by which a sacred cosmos is established'. Religion is 'cosmization in a sacred mode' (1969: 36). Luckmann's definition is more inclusive and 'purely functional': 'Religion is the process of transcending the individual existence of man in a structural meaning, which is, in most cases, a culturally given system of meaning . . . . . In other words, religion can be handled as being equivalent to socialization', and should include political ideologies, etc. (Kehrer and Hardin, in Whaling 1985: 168).

The theoretical framework within which Berger seeks to understand the social process involves a dialectic of three 'moments', the dialectical nature of which is the key to understanding, for 'society is the product of man' as much as 'man is the product of society' (1969: 3). There is:

a) Externalization, as a process in which humans construct their worlds of meaning, a process of 'continuous outpouring' of human subjectivity into the external world. Thus, the human has to 'make a world for himself', for the human-world relationship is not something given (1969: 5).

b) Objectivization, in which the 'product' or 'construct' becomes a 'reality that confronts its original producers as a facticity external to and other than themselves' (*ibid.*: 4).

c) Internalization, or the process by which the constructed world, social institutions and cultural products, are experienced as 'subjectively real' (*ibid.*: 17). This involves a process of 'reappropriation', in which the objectified worlds of meaning that human society has produced in turn act upon humans, thus making them products of society.

In this process every social construction, with its normative *nomos*, or sacral order, entails a 'transcendence of individuality'. And insofar as such a transcendent world has 'sacred' character, it is a religious world. Religion, therefore, is seen as part of the process of socialization, cosmization and *nomos*-making. As a sacredly transcendent world it will also involve a *theodicy*, that is a theoretical system that attempts to explain the nature both of the ordering and of any 'anomic' factors that seemingly would contradict the order; thus theodicies, and their sacred orders, act as *legitimations* of the way things are in and in relation to the sacred order. 'Every nomos confronts the individual as a meaningful reality that comprehends him and all his experiences.....The nomos locates the individual's life in an all-embracing fabric of meanings that, by its very nature, transcends that life. The individual who adequately internalizes these meanings at the same time transcends himself' (*ibid.*: 54). Rites of passage, for example, which aim to cope with painful as well as pleasant experiences of life, and involve an implicit theodicy, function in just this meaning-giving and 'transcending' way. The *karma-saṃsāra* complex of Indian systems is taken as an outstanding instance of 'theodicies of great rational consistency', in which every possible 'anomy' can be integrated within an all-embracing interpretation of the universe (*ibid.*: 65-6).

In this process Berger sees an intensified *masochistic* attitude involving 'self-denying surrender to society and its order' typically accompanied by ecstasy at thus being dominated by the other. Essential to such masochism is the experience that 'I am nothing – He is everything – and therein lies my ultimate bliss' (*ibid.*: 55-6). In the religious form of this ecstatic self-negation, 'the other of the masochistic confrontation is projected into the immensity of the cosmos, takes on cosmic dimensions of omnipotence and absoluteness, and can all the more plausibly be posited as ultimate reality . . . The sadistic god is not handicapped by empirical imperfections. He remains invulnerable, infinite, immortal by definition' (*ibid*.: 57); there are none of the 'contingencies and uncertainties of merely social masochism — for ever'. And in Berger's understanding of religion's function, 'plausibility', undergirded by 'plausibility structures' by which to experience reality and meaning, are key categories. Part of the plausibility seems to be the introduction in various ways of factors that 'mitigate' the masochism; Berger sees such 'mitigation' in Christology for example (*ibid*.: 76f.).

Another key category in Berger's theoretical framework is that of 'alienation' (and here we see more clearly the convergence with Marxian and Freudian thought); religion has been probably the most powerful agency of alienation' (*ibid*.: 87). For, in all cases when social or religious constructs are seen as having their own 'facticity' the result is an alienated world as a phenomenon of consciousness, especially of false consciousness. An essential quality of 'the sacred as encountered in "religious experience" is otherness, its manifestation as something *totaliter alier* as compared to ordinary profane life. It is precisely this otherness that lies at the heart of religious awe, of numinous dread, of the adoration of what totally transcends all dimensions of the merely human' (*ibid*.: 87). A vivid example of this is the climactic vision of Krishna in the Bhagavad-Gītā.

At this point Berger introduces a methodological point of great importance, one that fits the kind of theoretical stance to which we have seen him committed, and one which must surely be questioned. As we shall see, it seems in fact to contradict certain but not all aspects of his own later account of religion and his theological stance in later writings. He contends that within a sociological or scientific frame of reference the assumption that the experience of the 'sacred', the 'other reality' which impinges upon the empirical world, is 'genuine', cannot be allowed. Not only is the 'ultimate epistemological status' of such experiences to be 'rigorously bracketed', the assumption must be made that such 'other worlds' are 'only available as meaning-enclaves within *this* world'. They are 'elements within the socially constructed world . . . Empirically they are products of human activity and human signification — that is, they are human projections. Human beings, in the course of their externalization, project their meanings into the universe around them. In this way, 'the "objectivity" of religious meanings is *produced* objectivity, that is, religious meanings are objectivated projections. It follows that insofar as these meanings imply an overwhelming sense of otherness, they may be described as *alienated projections'* (*ibid.*: 89). Berger is not quite willing to *equate* religion with alienation, yet because 'religion posits the presence in reality of beings and forces that are alien to the human world', we must, he argues, recognise the 'alienating power inherent in religion' as responsible for much of its world-building and world-maintaining enterprises. In this sense, we can 'associate religion with false consciousness' as often manifest in history. He sees the 'mystification' of religion as equal to such 'falsification'; what are in reality human symbols become 'dark symbols of the divine' (*ibid.*: 90), and this prevents their comprehension in human terms.

Berger does go on to allow that within the social/religious process there may be not only the ultimate ratification of the given norms, but also their transcendence and relativization. That is, 'de-alienation' *can* take place too, and religion does manifest itself in history not only as world-maintaining, but also as world-shaking. Within religion itself, as found for example in the Old Testament, there are 'debunking' motifs. The transcending factor moves beyond legitimation to criticism of institutions previously seen as sacred (*ibid.*: 96-100). In any case, religious projections can only be investigated sociologically and scientifically on the basis of *'methodological* atheism'.

There is a rather obvious question to ask of Berger's position here: Why methodological *atheism*? Why not a less committed 'agnosticism'? (cf. Smart 1973b). But it is not merely a matter of terminology here. For it will have been recognised that the theoretical 'frame of reference' Berger has adopted for his sociological description is implicitly and explicitly 'atheistic'. The term he himself uses for his methodological approach is not misplaced. Even though in the appendix to this book he argues that we would be mistaken to conclude that there are either theological or anti-theological implications in his approach, that it is 'strictly within the frame of reference of sociological theory' (*op. cit.*: 179), and that it is just a matter of a sociologist asking different questions from a theologian, Berger can hardly justify his claim that all he has done is 'bracket' throughout — 'externalizing', 'projecting', 'alienation', 'masochism-sadism', etc. — is not the language of the phenomenological bracketer; his theory is far from that of neutral description. It is just not the case that any sociological theory 'must, by its own logic, view religion as a human projection' (*ibid.*: 181). This is not necessary to a sociological approach as such; it is but one possible sociological theory, and one providing a paradigm for understanding that clearly 'reconstitutes' religious phenomena in a way that evokes a very different, generally negative, understanding of their 'meaning'. It is significant that in a previous book, *The Precarious Vision*, Berger had differentiated between 'religion' and 'faith' (i.e. Christian faith), in a somewhat Barthian style, though this distinction is given up here, where he argues that such a theory of the socialization of religion is quite compatible with faith. 'Projected meanings may have an ultimate status independent of man'. It *may* be 'that man projects ultimate meanings into reality because that reality is, indeed, ultimately meaningful, and because his own being (the empirical ground of these projections) contains and intends these same ultimate meanings' (*ibid.*: 181). This is rather well put – but leaves us with a much longer leap of faith from the 'empirical' to the 'ultimate' than seems to be necessary or perhaps even possible for most believers; the theological explanation of things will seem far less 'plausible' once the Berger-style 'empirical' explanation has been adopted. And, as was asked above, just how 'empirical' is such a sociological theory?

Then to say that the theologian, *qua* theologian, 'should not worry unduly over anything the sociologist may have to say about religion', for there is no real 'methodological' problem, does not resolve the issue. Sociological theory in the Marxist/Freudian tradition *does* raise methodological questions; in essence these are questions of ontological compatibility. For Berger there is no incompatibility, though we then have to look at the particular theological stance he takes; and he does acknowledge that some theologies are less 'immune' to scientific critical analysis than are others. But in terms of 'empirical' description/explanation, to what extent should this be the case? That by the bracketting of ontological status we cannot relieve religion of any kind of critical examination has to be accepted: ethical questions, for example, cannot be ignored, though they need to be handled with great cultural sensitivity. Is it proper, though, for our descriptive frame of reference to have built into it explanatory theory that will necessarily favour certain kinds of religious structuring over against others? We would certainly need to ask to what extent such a theory had, albeit unconsciously, built into it a particular theological stance. Is it possible, for example, that in Berger's case a Lutheran doctrine of 'the two kingdoms' (as well as the Lutheran epistemology of 'in, under and with') plays some role here? (Though no one could accuse Berger of being a traditional doctrinaire Lutheran). The considerable gap, though dialectically related no doubt, between the 'empirical' and the 'ultimate', naturally means that theologies making a similar distinction are more 'immune' than others to the implicit threat of Berger's sociological theory.

Turning to Berger's more explicitly *theological* writings, we may briefly note that in *A Rumour of Angels* (1968) he had been critical of theologising in terms of 'translation'. This refers to theologians concerned to articulate a more 'secular' theology, who attempt to translate 'the traditional religious affirmations' into 'terms appropriate to the new frame of reference, the one that allegedly conforms to the *Weltanschauung* of modernity' (1968: 35). Paul Tillich and Rudolf Bultmann are seen as examples of this approach. Berger is surprisingly critical of these kinds of attempts to make theology more plausible to modern modes of thought: 'The supernatural elements of the religious traditions are more or less completely liquidated, and the traditional language is transferred from other-wordly to this-worldly referents'. Such attempts are self-defeating claims Berger: 'For most people, symbols whose content has been hollowed out lack conviction, or even interest. In other words, the theological surrender to the alleged demise of the supernatural defeats itself in precisely the measure of its success. Ultimately it represents the self-liquidation of theology and of the institutions in which the theological tradition is embodied' (*ibid.*: 26). Sociologically, Berger is explicitly critical of the 'double standard' involved here: while the past and its tradition is 'relativised in terms of this or that socio-historical analysis', the *present* and its assumptions 'remain strangely immune from relativization' (*ibid.*: 51). Berger sees it as a positive theological gain that sociology of knowledge debunks present projections and perceptions equally as much as past traditions. 'While other analytic disciplines free us from the tyranny of the past, sociology frees us from the tyranny of the present', i.e. from that 'vulgar progressivism that sees one's own moment in history as history's pinnacle' (*ibid.*: 57).

Berger believes that a 'viable theological method' lies in responding to the sociological challenge that all religion is human projection by dialectically inverting it. There is no need to go the Feuerbachian way of reducing theology to anthropology. Rather, it is 'logically possible' to accept the theory of religion-as-human-projection and *also* to see this projective process as a 're-flection of divine realities' (*ibid.*: 59). A proper theological method, therefore, will not look for 'religious phenomena that will somehow manifest themselves as different from human projections. Nothing is immune to the relativization of socio-historical analysis'. The meta-empirical cannot be conceived of as a kind of 'enclave within the empirical world ... the theological decision will have to be that, "in, with, and under" the immense array of human projections, there are indications of a reality that is truly "other" and that the religious imagination of man ultimately reflects' (*ibid.*: 59). For Berger this implies an 'inductive faith', a theological method that 'begins with experience', then 'moves from human experience to statements about God'. 'Deductive faith', on the other hand, improperly and implausibly moves 'from statements about God to interpretations of human experience'. Properly, anthropology is to be the 'starting point for theology' (*ibid.*: 65). On this basis, Berger affirms various 'signals of transcendence within the empirically given human situation', signals that are to be taken as 'prototypical human gestures' (*ibid.*: 65). He mentions the argument from order (e.g. as when a mother reassures her child), from play, from hope, from damnation, from humour. Only this kind of inductive approach 'makes faith plausible' (*ibid.*: 95).

As we would expect, this allows only a somewhat passive role to the 'tradition'. Indeed, it is not easy to see just how Berger here differs very greatly in methodological approach from the secular theologians of 'translation' he so roundly condemns, though his exposition of these 'signals of transcendence' found within empirically given life is very persuasively written. As with the secular theologians, though, the religious traditions are all to be 'confronted'. Our present pluralistic situation first highlights and clarifies our 'contradictory options' (*ibid.*: 101); e.g. there can be no possible convergence between Buddhism and Christian faith. The 'confronting' is by way of a search for 'whatever signals of transcendence may have been sedimented in' the traditions. This entails 'an approach grounded in empirical methods of inquiry . . . and free of dogmatic a prioris' (*ibid.*: 103) (Here Pannenberg's emphasis on 'empirical history' and 'empirical anthropology' is strongly endorsed). We have to throw off any 'already achieved' attitude. For example, 'to speak of "revelation" before one is sure just where one may speak of "discovery" is putting the cart before the horse' (*ibid.*: 103).

At this point it is clear that the dialectic Berger has referred to is not one in which there is continual interaction between our grounding in a mythic/cultic tradition (including 'revelation') and the impingement of the 'empirical' world, out of which interaction 'discovery' emerges. His analysis here does not seem even to be of a piece with his sociological theory of the dialectic between externalization, objectivization and internalization. Berger does, however, go on to acknowledge that 'the theological enterprise will go beyond the empirical frame of reference at the point where it begins to speak of discoveries and explicate what is deemed to have been discovered – that is, at the point where the transcendental intentions in human experience are treated as realities rather than as *alleged realities*' (*ibid.*: 104). Naturally, such a transition 'from empirical analysis to metaphysics is in itself an act of faith . . . it is absurd to speak of "scientific theology" . . . if transcendence is to be spoken of *as* transcendence, the empirical frame of reference must be left behind'.

However, whether theology is to be called 'scientific' or not, this assertion that the 'transcendent' dimension affirmed by religious traditions can never be taken as such in any scientific description raises in stark form the great dilemma posed by the whole scientific approach to the study of religion. That a methodological 'switch in frames of reference' (*ibid.*: 104) has to be made cannot be denied; that such a transition has to be in the Berger manner can be questioned.

It is perhaps significant that in a later work (*The Heretical Imperative: Contemporary Possibilities of Religious Affirmation*, 1979), while a number of the earlier positions are still maintained, some important modifications are to be seen.

a) While theology is elaborated much more systematically, with substantial critique of such theologians as Barth and Bultmann, a more deliberately *phenomenological* stance is taken throughout. Thus greater emphasis is given to religious tradition and to distinctive religious experience, both being described with considerable evocative skill. Indeed, it is assumed that 'at the heart of the religious phenomenon is prereflective, pretheoretical experience' (*ibid.*: 34). All 'metahuman explanations' of this experience have for the time being to be set aside if there is to be a truly 'phenomenological' investigation; but it is to be looked at 'in terms of the manner in which it appears in human experience'. Great emphasis too is given to the communication of such specific religious experience through distinctive symbols. This locates religions in a 'specific body of symbolism that has a history and a social location' (*ibid.*: 47). Empirical investigation is therefore entirely appropriate.

The 'human projection' theory still stands, but it no longer seems to be set within the more loaded theory of 'methodological atheism'. 'Alienation' is now seen as linked with the experience of 'modernity'. Being communicated through human symbolism and language, *'religion can be understood as a human projection . . . But this very communication* is motivated by an experience in which the metahuman is injected into human *life'* (*ibid.*: 48). This religious experience 'insists that . . . the gods inhabit a reality that is *sui generis* and that is sovereignly independent of what human beings project into it.' And for religious experience it is not human projection that is finally important in interpreting reality. Thus, 'the human world in its entirety . . . is itself a symbol – to wit, a symbol of the divine . . . (it) stands for something beyond itself' (*ibid.*: 113).

b) Considerable importance is given to 'development of theoretical *reflection*' within religious traditions (*ibid*.: 48). And this includes both sophisticated doctrinal systems and reflection that is embodied in myth. Berger sees it as a human compulsion to reflect about experience; but in addition to this basic humanness, 'a religious tradition must develop reflective thought because of the social requirement of legitimation'. However, both the process of tradition-embodiment and theological reflection have to be relativized. While the need for 'authoritative accounts of the original experience' is inevitable, 'the distinction between religious experience and religious reflection is crucial' (*ibid*.: 49). This means that interpretive reflection, just like the embodying of experience in traditions, is 'inevitably distortive', a dilemma that theologically makes both for difficulties and for opportunities.

c) The plurality of *world-views* has become far more prominent, with especial importance being given to two primary contestants, the 'Indian' and the 'Jerusalem' polarities. Berger bemoans the fact that 'few Christian theologians show any interest in the non-Western religions' (*ibid*.: 151), when there is such a crucial difference of religious perception at stake. For Berger 'contestation means an open-minded encounter with other religious possibilities on the level of their truth-claims... To enter into interreligious contestation is to be prepared to change one's view of reality' (*ibid*.: 152). The crucial question is whether the divine is to be experienced in *confrontation* or in *interiority*, though it is recognised that these are merely ideal types, with great diversity being found in the empirical life of religious traditions. Perhaps it is also possible that '*both* types of religious experience are true.' In any case, much work needs to be done in exploring earlier attempts to deal cognitively with different types of religious experience. Thus, what is important for theology in the West, is no longer to be in such 'awe of modernity'. For there is 'a different "other" than modernity' that can be 'a more fruitful stimulant for Christian theology. . . . It is immensely more fruitful to delve into the Upanishads than into the latest product of contemporary ideologists. In sum, *to turn from contestation with modernity to the contestation with Benares is to break through the impasse of contemporary Christian theology*' (*ibid*.: 169).

d) As a final comment we may note that Berger now provides a far more elaborate typology of theologies. In addition to his earlier deductive-inductive typology, he also refers to the 'translation' model as a 'reductive' type. His commitment to the inductive way of theologising is still as strong, but there is now clearer recognition that 'faith and inductive reasoning stand in a dialectical relationship to each other: I believe — and then I reflect about the implications of this fact; I gather evidence about the object of my faith' (*ibid.*: 129). It is still doubtful if this is quite what is required of, or indeed phenomenologically typical of, the theological process.

By way of conclusion of this section, I would repeat that even if our task is seen as that of description alone, to be authentically descriptive of the life of a religious tradition we have to incorporate as primary data in the interpretive process, and as evocatively as possible, what it is that the participant experiences, what these intentions, ecstasies, life-goals, ways of perception and so on are. But above all, what the *essential features of the sacred Focus is and how this interrelates with all the other phenomena found within that tradition.* At least we might hope that behavioural science will go on becoming more interested in 'other people's belief-systems . . . as being worthy of investigation in their own right' (Beattie 1964: 29).

3. It is difficult to be at all precise about the role of *philosophy* in religious studies, mainly because the philosophical approach can range so widely — from speculative metaphysics to linguistic and logical positivism. Despite, in recent years, the virtual eclipse of explicit metaphysical theory, except for some neo-Hegelianism, in philosophical schools, and the emphasis on analysis — logical and linguistic — and on clarity of reflection on all intellectual endeavour, especially in the British and American empiricist movements, there is no reason to rule out the possibility in the future of a revival of metaphysics. The philosophy of science in particular seems likely to confirm the need for new models of reality, and of the epistemological process; in any case, it is now again clear that theology and religious systems in general cannot exist without some undergirding with metaphysical theory. As we have noted, even in the Buddha's approach to the religious life, often classed as pragmatic and anti-speculative, there are a number of assumptions about the structuring of cosmic existence that can only be called 'meta-physical'. It is just not appropriate to 'theological' systems, or to 'faith', even when the attempt is made to set 'true faith' over against religion, to attempt to eliminate metaphysical dimensions and theologise on a purely secular, non-transcendental basis. Even in the physical sciences the interpretive role of the theoretical framework, with its necessarily subjective dimension, means that a thoroughly myth-less objectivity has itself perhaps only a mythic existence.

Despite the possibilities for new metaphysical directions, it would seem most profitable at this juncture in our response to the various 'scientific' or systematic approaches to the study of religion to focus primarily on *philoso-*

phy's analytical and critical role. The most distinctive contribution of the philosophy of religion in the past 30 or 40 years has been its ability (at times) to provide analyses of the logical structuring of meaning-patterns in religion (cf. innumerable articles in the journal, *Religious Studies*; or the writings of Frederick Ferre, for example). In its analytical role philosophy of religion suggests primarily a 'hard' approach. It may serve mainly in clarifying the logical status and the cognitive meaning-implications of religious statements. And clarity in understanding is important; it is not necessarily destructive of the performative potency of religious language.

Moreover, analytical clarity too functions at a number of different levels. It can involve the dis-covery of the 'internal logic' (Smart) of religious life and of its conceptual systems in particular. Beyond this more preliminary role it may function in a hermeneutical role, helping in the interpretation of religious meanings, perhaps in those terms most readily comprehendable in contemporary thought-patterns and in the formulation of more coherent expression of meaning-patterns. Or it may involve the interpretation of the significance of the findings, or perhaps the theory-framework, of the behavioural sciences in their approaches to understanding religion. Philosophy of religion thus stands as an interdisciplinary discipline, and is able to make a distinctive contribution to understanding between various sciences in the ways they are able to relate to each other. While philosophy of religion can, and perhaps often does, serve as the apologetic arm of theology, its more essential role would seem to be as a neutral assistant to the theological task in its broadest sense. Its specialist role, however, means that it is not to be identified with theology. Van Baaren (1972: 44), strangely, dismisses philosophy of religion as a 'discipline which cannot be assimilated by science of religion'; it is too akin to theology, he finds.

Wiebe has recently (1981) raised again the question of whether religious studies, and the philosophy of religion in particular, should not be concerned about the *truth*-issue in religion. Most scholars in the religions' field have argued that only theology raises or should raise this concern, and that any scientific study of religion concerns itself only with the *meaning* of religious traditions. Wiebe does not agree; one of his strongest arguments is that if religions are ontologically committed, making definite truth-claims with implicit if not always clear cognitive content (and this surely is the case), then any serious (rigorous?) investigation of religious life must also concern itself with the truth-question however problematic this may be in view of apparently conflicting truth-claims. Others (e.g. W.C. Smith in Hick 1974) have argued that religious traditions do not make 'truth-claims' in the sense of objectifiable propositions; their ontological statements, some would assert, are not intended to be literal descriptions corresponding cognitively to the way things objectively are. Perhaps it may be said that religious 'claims' are 'dispositional' rather than 'propositional', or perhaps 'indicative' rather than 'informative'. No doubt these warnings against over-literalism should be carefully reckoned with, especially in the sense that religious utterances are intended to be evocative of realities greater than can be literally described. And all theologies will in some aspect of their articulatory task make this 'beyondness' clear. But this is not what is meant by those who argue against religious statements having any 'truth-claim' in them.

Given, then, that in some sense religious traditions do make 'truth-claims' which carry some kind of cognitive content, and if the analysis of these truth-claims and their diverse meanings is to be one important part of religious studies, this will clearly be the task of philosophy of religion. And we might go one step further: the analysis of divergent meanings in religious systems will probably make inevitable at some stage, though in the most cautious and tentative ways, some kind of plausibility-*evaluation*, which amounts to *truth*-evaluation. There is no way that philosophy of religion, or any other approach, can judge in any ultimate sense what kind of ontological reality there is in this or that religious tradition. The 'truth-evaluation' possible cannot be decisive for the ultimacy of any tradition, but rather concerns the *plausibility* of the conceptual ways in which a tradition expresses itself. Moral philosophers and ethicists will naturally be concerned mainly with the ethical values and their consequences for human and cosmic life implied in religious traditions. And ethical evaluation, providing it is done with a thorough cross-cultural awareness, cannot finally be avoided in our study even of sacred systems. The very fact that these sacred systems continually modify, to a greater or lesser extent, their forms of ethical life, makes it both necessary and legitimate for moral philosophers even outside the concerned tradition to be part of this process. Informed sensitivity is essential however.

When we speak of 'plausibility of the conceptual ways' in which religions express their vision of ultimate reality and its outworkings in life, the question of the *coherence*, the inter-relationships of various parts of the systems, the integrated nature of conceptual systems in particular, becomes important. And the kinds of coherence to be envisaged we have discussed in Chapter Five.

In affirming these various goals for the philosophy of religion we also have to acknowledge that the philosophical approach can so easily 'degenerate' into theological apologetics, whether consciously competitive or covertly judgemental from one particular religious perspective. There is no doubt a valid place for explicit theological apologetics, but this needs to be distinguished from any evaluatory task philosophy of religion might attempt. The line of demarcation here may not be very definite. Indeed, there is a sense in which just because philosophy of religion is in some respects close to various forms of theology, especially systematic, moral, and even apologetic theology, it must also work out its stance the more carefully and rigorously *independent* of any ultimate theological commitment. And it can only do this if there is a far more thorough knowledge of the various religious systems it is to analyse and 'evaluate' than has usually been the case with philosophers of religion. In the past, much philosophy of religion has been of the culture-bound type that speaks ultimately in the language and with the assumptions of Christian faith, or perhaps the neo-Vedantic or the Buddhist faith, or has sought a speculative stance transcendent to any recognisable religious tradition; this has been in effect a new form of speculative theology, though a 'theology' without grounding in one or other matrix of meaning essential to theological articulation. It can avoid both these stances.

9

Ways of Investigating and Interpreting Religion

b) Phenomenological, Comparative, Dialogical

1. The phenomenological approach to the study of religion in a systematic way can in some respects claim to be the most significant overall contribution to understanding religion. However, this would be disputed by many who favour a more rigorously historical or empirical method. We can only justify such a claim if we understand 'phenomenology' in the broadest sense as meaning a basic *attitude* towards religious phenomena. In the way this approach developed as a distinctively identifiable 'discipline' (again, disputable according to some), it bears a rather tenuous relationship to the phenomenological philosophy of such diverse thinkers as Kant, Hegel, Husserl and Heidegger. It was P.D. Chantepie de la Saussaye, the Leyden historian of religions, who in 1887 first outlined the principles of a 'phenomenology of religion' in which he made it clear that he sees the need for *historical* investigation into religious traditions to move on to the higher plane of *phenomenological* investigation of the essential inner structures of religion (Waardenburg 1972: 15-17, 105-17). Ever since then it is the relationship of the historical to the phenomenological that has been the central issue. Later exponents of this phenomenological approach pick up two technical terms proposed earlier by Husserl as part of his 'science of pure consciousness', in which phenomena are to be apprehended in their pure objectivity. These two technical principles are *epoché* (i.e. the 'bracketing', or 'suspension' of judgement regarding the phenomenal object), and eidetic vision (i.e. the intuitive, undistorting grasp of the 'essence' of the object).

It was, however, G. van der Leeuw who (in 1925 and more fully in 1933) first developed these phenomenological principles into systematic and now almost 'classical' form, with extensive reference to materials from ancient religious traditions, in his *Religion in Essence and Manifestation* (1938: esp. 671-8; cf. Waardenburg 1978: 187-248). His seven basic themes, in paraphrased form, are: (i) There is the assigning of names to the phenomena as found in their manifest forms. Of one type of religious phenomenon we can say, 'This is sacrifice', of another. 'This is prayer', and so on. Thus, on the basis of analogous phenomena in a variety of traditions we identify common essential forms of religion. At the outset, therefore, we find that 'eidetic vision' is called for. We can also see that phenomenology assumes the validity of a comparative method (though in English-speaking studies Comparative Religions was usually identical with History of Religions and its predominantly historical approach). (ii) Then there is the interpolation of each phenomenon into our own experience, that is, allowing the objective phenomenon to speak for itself in our consciousness. Thus 'prayer' becomes not merely that which we have known hitherto as 'prayer', but prayer as manifest in the devotion of Muslims, Sikhs, Vaishṇavas, and so on. (iii) There is the exercise of *epoché*, 'bracketting' the phenomena as far as their ontological status and the question of their ultimate truth is concerned. This calls, of course, for a temporary bracketting also of our own beliefs and ontological commitments. (iv) We can then clarify the phenomena by comparing and contrasting them with phenomena of similar structural type found in other religious traditions. (v) There will then be authentic *understanding* of what has been observed. 'Understanding' (*Verstehen*) is obviously a category with rich meaning and of crucial significance for Van der Leeuw (Waardenburg 1978: 234-5), as indeed for most post-Heidegger phenomenologists, and we return to it below. (vi) Our perceptions can then be checked, and thus controlled, by reference to a variety of empirical data, provided by philology, archeaology, etc. (vii) There will, finally, be *objective knowledge* of the concerned phenomena, knowledge in which their authentic subjectivity is apprehended. Then, 'the subjectivity of the object is the objectivity of the subject'.

C.J. Bleeker, another exponent of the phenomenological school and, though once a colleague of Van der Leeuw, rather critical of his approach (1971: 15) wrote of this method as 'an empirical science with philosophical aspiration' (1959: 103). This makes it necessary for him to play down to some extent the principle of 'eidetic vision'; he claims that phenomenology only uses the term in a 'figurative sense', for it is not intended to be a vision of 'essences' as in the metaphysical sense of Idealism. Nor is there intended any 'science of the essence of religion' (*ibid.*: 104). Rather, from time to time phenomenology 'manages to detect the structure of a greater or smaller complex of religious phenomena'. However, in the three principles Bleeker suggests for a more viable phenomenological approach we find that the first of these is very similar to eidetic vision; this is *theoria*, the unbiased, direct looking at objective phenomena so as to discover their distinctively religious significance. Then there is the search for *logos*, 'manifest in the structure of both the historic religions and of religion as an idea', for each religion has built into it its own logical structuring. The four elements of these structures are: constant forms, irreducible factors, points of crystallisation, and types. Then, thirdly there is the principle of *entelecheia*, 'the course of events in which the essence is realised in its manifestations' (*ibid.*: 110).

Bleeker goes on to stress (a) the conviction as expressed by Kristensen, that 'there is no other religious reality than the faith of the believers . . . if our opinion of a foreign religion differs from the meaning and evaluation of the believers themselves, then we have no longer to do with their religion' (*ibid.*: 106-7). There is necessarily 'a limit to our ability of understanding'; (b) the need for a close 'correlation' between history and phenomenology. On the one hand the phenomenological approach depends upon the historical approach for the material from religious traditions which form the basis of phenomenological systematisation. This forms a 'necessary control on all too wild speculation'. On the other hand, the phenomenological approach acts as a 'safeguard against barren specialisation', which can result in 'a jungle of facts' (*ibid.*: 108). Only a phenomenological approach to religion is able to transform 'the chaotic field of the study of religions into a kind of harmonious panorama, a typological survey . . .' (1952: 150).

Van der Leeuw, and later Joachim Wach, expounded an elaborate theory of 'understanding', that brings in also the way phenomenology relates to theology in his thought; here he is clearly indebted to the philosophical and hermeneutical theories of Dilthey, Spranger and Heidegger. This involves the conviction that structures of reality are meaningfully organised, and that discovering this meaning requires an interaction of subject and object in a process of reconstruction. 'Understanding' is not merely a single unitive vision of meaning, but extends over a number of such moments of 'experiential unity', so that there emerges a wider understanding of ideal types of reality-structures (Waardenburg 1978: 235). Thus, the *Verstehen* of the outsider is as much an authentic religious experience as the primal experience of the participant. In this way, 'by making his interpretations not only in theology but also in phenomenology in view of an ultimate meaning, Van der Leeuw arrives at a frank absolutisation of the whole notion of meaning. The significance of the phenomena is cut off from the people for whom it is or was valid and there is neglect of the role of human inter-subjectivity in any understanding'. Incidentally, Van der Leeuw held, perhaps as necessary to his general theory of *Verstehen*, that only a religious person can reach understanding of religious phenomena (*ibid.*: 236).

Van der Leeuw saw a close interlinking between phenomenology of religion and theology. There is little doubt that his Christian faith was normative for him in his study of religion, though we need to note carefully what was his understanding of Christian faith and its theological task, especially what he understood by 'phenomenological theology', both as the culmination of authentic theology and the link between phenomenology and traditional theology. Needless to say, by incorporating his theological stance as an integral part of the phenomenological task, and vice versa, his position was unacceptable even for many fellow-phenomenologists.

Waardenburg (1978: 127-30) has listed a number of criticisms made of 'classical' phenomenology of religion, before going on to suggest a 'new phenomenology'.

a) Phenomenology's almost exclusive concern with trans-traditional types of historically manifest religious phenomena, virtually irrespective of historical context (i.e. its synchronic dimension), has been unfortunate. Equal weight should be given to 'religious' and 'non-religious' factors; thus religious phenomena should be seen diachronically also. This means that a more anthropological approach is called for: there should be 'no a priori distinction' between facts which qualify as 'religious' and those which are not normally so identified. 'In the search for relationships (between these two kinds of phenomena) hypotheses are to be made, for instance, on the basis of a fundamental consciousness proper to man or to human society as such...' (*ibid.*: 127).

b) 'Classical phenomenology has, in the last analysis, presented an interpretation of religion instead of researching into it' (*ibid.*: 128). In line with this general criticism Waardenburg lists a number of different kinds of reproaches: phenomenology has no methodological attitude except that of *epoché*; it occupies an ambiguous position between other disciplines, without a distinctive stance; it allows presuppositions and norms that have not been adequately and consciously reflected on; it thus sometimes plays an ideological role, by being either anti-theological, or a mirror-theology, or by idealising religion as such.

c) It is often said, therefore, that behind phenomenology 'a particular theological inspiration' can be seen, even though not ostensibly linked with a particular dogma or ideology. In any case it is necessary to remove this ambiguity, and either stand as theologians or 'emancipate themselves from all theological presuppositions' (*ibid.*: 128).

d) In opposing reductionism phenomenology has itself reduced religion to 'purely religious experience or to a purely religious idea'. This is because it has emphasised ideal contexts divorced from the historical process and has not investigated causal relationships in the way proposed above. This lack of behavioural and institutional investigation has been justified on the grounds of the autonomy and irreducibility of religion; the consequence has been 'the isolation of religion from human reality' (*ibid.*: 128).

e) Phenomenology generally has not evinced a sufficient scientific basis, and has been prone to make unproven generalised statements which are not hypotheses that can be either confirmed or disproved by empirical data. There is similarly insufficient discussion with scholars of other disciplines.

f) In general phenomenology has not been reflective enough, but has been increasingly 'a naive enterprise', moving 'outside human communication and into a kind of solipsism'; there is thus 'lack of self-critical foundation' to this approach (130-1).

Waardenburg's suggestion for a 'new-style' phenomenological research focusses on the dimension in religious life which he calls 'intentionality': *intentions* should be 'its object of inquiry' (*ibid.*: 130). Elsewhere (in Honko 1979: 441-57) he likens religious systems to the 'sign-systems' of languages and their cultural significations. The essential question in understanding this religious 'language' is 'how to grasp its meaning or meanings in view of the intended realities' (*ibid.*: 444). To discover such intended meaning it is necessary not only to know what particular words mean in a given religious discourse; we have also to look to the 'conceptual framework' within which such words are used. Meaning relates to intention and thus to the conceptual world shaping the meaning of the words used. Waardenburg returns frequently to this theme of 'intentionality' as the basic issue in understanding religious life and its symbolism. It is this dimension that enables insight into the 'subject' of religious life, though through the analysis of 'sign-systems' or 'communication-systems' we can arrive at an understanding of its 'objective sense' also. It is like a process of 'decoding' codes of meaning as contained in symbols that make up the 'cores of meaning' in different traditions, feeding 'significance and meaning to the life of the community or the individual concerned' (*ibid.*: 447).

Waardenburg goes on to point to the 'typical radiation effect' of core-symbols in a tradition: from these central points new meaning patterns are perceived that incorporate the whole of life and cosmic reality. In the quest for understanding these meaning-systems, we are dependent upon the ways in which *participants* express the meanings they perceive. This process is essentially 'of a hermeneutical nature'; for there is the problem of how the meaning perceived in their symbol-system by participants of one age and context can be understood by a person in another context. Yet, the 'implied intentions' of religious systems essentially relate to human existence. The starting-point of religious life is that 'man meets reality and ... confronts problems which are given with his environment and with his own nature' (*ibid*.: 450). Religion, thus, 'should be studied as a self-expression of human existence in different cultures, societies and circumstances. The structure and meaning of human expressions, including the religious ones, are related to the very core of human existence, its intentionality'. And yet, in 'religious signification, the signified referent is beyond empirical facticity', for it 'functions as a source of meaning', and cannot be objectively verified (*ibid*.: 451). Thus, Waardenburg's 'new-style' phenomenological approach shows a move from the earlier 'search for timeless essences to a search for meanings inside time' (1978: 87). Religious 'intentions' are assumed to be set in a human context; the more 'holistic approach' (King) is welcome.

2. *An Analytical Phenomenology*: Among the criticisms levelled against classical forms of phenomenology of religion we noted the following: there has not been sufficient critical reflection of methodological assumptions, the acceptance of the concrete historicity of religious traditions, and therefore the historical critical dimension, is suspect, and there tends to be disguised theology, or perhaps anti-theology. Ninian Smart's modified account of the phenomenological task (1973a: 1973b; 1985) provides methodological reflection in the form of sustained critical analysis, which explicitly distinguishes 'Religion' from the task of 'Theology' ('Expression') and that is firmly committed to the particular historical forms religious traditions have taken, as well as to the distinct conceptual systems that emerge. Yet the overall concern is to evoke the inner life and intentions in the course of identifying typical inner structures in the diversity of traditions.

Smart's 'critical reflection' makes it necessary for him to point out (1973b), as others have done, that a number of scholars in religions, including phenomenologists, have fallen into the trap of taking a particularist 'theological' stance, while claiming to speak about religion generally. Otto and Wach, for example, attempted to universalise the experience of the Numinous, that experience of the Transcendent which Otto described as both fascinating and yet aweful. When, however, we investigate religious traditions in their manifest states and types, we find that many do *not* have such a numinous being as their sacred Focus. Thus the aim to give a phenomenological description of what constitutes the essence of religious experience rather describes a particular theological commitment. Wach in fact was strongly critical of the 'historian of religions' who is 'neutral as far as religion is concerned', who has empathy for all others but does not apply this to his own position, and whose chief virtues seem to be scepticism, playful intellectualism, oversophistication and lack of faith (*ibid.*: 59). As Smart counters, this is to confuse methodological neutralism with private neutrality. It would indeed make for all manner of scholarly problems if competence to describe a religious phenomenon were evaluated in terms of the amount of naive faith and existential commitment found underlying it. Smart denies that neutrality is impossible, and does this on closely argued phenomenological grounds.

However, Wach did distinguish between theology and the phenomenological study of religions: 'It is the task of the theologian to investigate, buttress and teach the faith of a religious community to which it is committed . . . it is the task of the comparative student of religion to guide and purify it' (Wach 1958: 9). Smart comments that although Wach is correct in thinking that the comparative study of religion makes or ought to make a difference to Christian theology, it does not follow that this is its central task. It is 'wrong to look upon the study of religion simply as the handmaiden of theology. In fact only by being independent of theology can the study of religion challenge and stimulate theology. Its service to Christian theology then arises because its aims are not theologically defined' (1973b; 65-66).

In spite of his criticism of some aspects of previous phenomenological writing, and although his style of expression is often more that of the logical analysis of recent Anglo-Saxon approaches to the philosophy of religion, Smart's basic concerns are those of a phenomenologist. While clearly no close disciple of Van der Leeuw, he is prepared to begin with Van der Leeuw's seven phenomenological principles. And we find that in his *The Phenomenon of Religion* (1973a) his primary themes are the nature of 'understanding' and of a religious 'phenomenon', the role of 'bracketting', of 'interpolation' and of 'explanation', the 'structures' of religion, typological analysis and the possibility of comparison. We will here look briefly at six concerns (not precisely the above) that emerge from Smart's modified phenomenological position:

a) Phenomenology generally is concerned to uncover and understand in a legitimately coherent and systematic way the phenomena of religion as they are manifest to religious people. Smart accepts this as the primary task of a 'science of religion'. Yet he continually directs our attention beyond the phenomena *qua phenomena* to those Objects which are experienced through such phenomena, yet without discarding the 'phenomenal'. For example, he points out that the term 'phenomenon' can connote 'appearance', suggesting that a religious phenomenon is no more than the religious participant's percep- tions (1973a: 69). The reality of the phenomenon would then be more than 'bracketted'; it would probably be suspected of being *mere* appearance, which we noted could be the case with Geertz' definition. Or there may be an em- phasis on phenomena as 'merely human', when there is in fact always a sense of interplay between the Focus and participant, and an accompanying sense of the transcendent dimension of that Focus. This is similar to the questions raised in the previous chapter regarding Berger and even Van Baaren. Smart makes the further point that the phenomena are often 'manifestly' non-human entities, perhaps animals or 'natural' objects, features of whose non-human existence may be especially significant for their phenomenological reality. The point is that talk of 'phenomena' can mislead into the belittling of sacred character. It is the Focus, or Foci, involved in the phenomena that Smart draws our attention to.

b) Phenomenology has invariably presupposed the *sui generis* and irreducible character of religion; religious phenomena cannot be 'explained away' in terms of some other kind of phenomena, thus making religious life an epi- phenomenon. Here Otto's influence is crucial. Smart basically accepts this pre- supposition, but offers a much more sophisticated discussion of what is in- volved in 'explanation' than is usually the case with defenders of the faith. He gives a variety of reasons (1973a: 37) why it is improper to think of, e.g. socio- logical or psychological explanations of religious phenomena as 'more basic' than religion itself or than its explanations. He sees very limited value in dis- tinguishing between understanding by description and 'understanding by explanation'. This does not take us very far because realistic descriptions invariably 'contain explanations, or at least incipient explanations' (*ibid*.: 57), or 'internal explanations' (*ibid*.: 43-4). He acknowledges that it is possible even for 'external explanations' to be a legitimate way of uncovering the 'mutual dynamic' between religious and these other social/psychological factors which interact dialectically with religion. In this way explanation of religious life that refers to those causal factors not explicitly connected with, say, the sacred Focus, can be very useful in uncovering the functional structuring of religious life and how 'religion and society shape each other' (*ibid*.: 44). In other contexts Smart speaks of the 'aspectual' and 'poly-methodic' nature of the science of religion; the diverse facets of religious life, as the more peculiarly 'religious' phenomena interact with factors usually categorised and investigated by other sciences, make it both legitimate and necessary for such extra-phenomenological sciences to be part of the total investigative task.

c) The phenomenological principle of *epoché* is interpreted in terms of *methodological neutrality*, to which Smart gives great importance as we saw earlier. A phenomenological investigation is to be neutral as regards the ontological status of religious phenomena and statements about them. He points out that the 'Expression' of religion, which he generally identifies with the subject-matter of theology, is not only concerned with *beliefs*. Usually he allows great significance to expressed beliefs, and their cognitive value, as an essential part of the total manifest life of a tradition, and as the appropriate subject for comparative analysis if we are to understand a tradition at every meaning-level. Here, however, he rightly notes that epoché is not merely suspending judgement concerning the question of *truth*. For 'Expression' in religion always includes value and feeling and all the evocative dimensions of a tradition that convey how its participants perceive as well as what they practise. An essential part of all 'bracketted Expression', therefore, is bringing out the 'fine grain', the texture as well as the formal patterns of religious life. 'Phenomenology needs to be evocative as well as descriptive' (*ibid*.: 33). Indeed such evocation is to be an intrinsic part of description; the neutrality called for in a properly phenomenological description 'is not "flat" neutralism . . . an overly external account of a religious practice, mood or commitment can so easily have the effect of destroying any sense of its impact, and thus lose a major aspect of its meaning' (*ibid*.: 34). Thus 'Religion (i.e. the systematic study of religion) incorporates, by bracketting, Expression into its description'; and for such a task neutrality is not only legitimate, it is essential.

d) What Van der Leeuw called the 'interpolation' of phenomena into the experience of the investigator to some extent overlaps with ideas connected with *epoché*. Here, though, Smart argues (*ibid*.: 67-9) that there is not only the need for imaginative *empathy* (as distinct from *sym*-pathy, which would involve a commitment) regarding just how a believer perceives the phenomena in his or her tradition; as we saw above there is also need to evoke empathetically the character of the sacred Focus. In addition there is the need to arrive at understanding of the 'organic structure' within which each phenomenon exists; each is to be empathetically understood in relation to the whole structure of the tradition, so that the total experience of the tradition is 'interpolated' into the phenomenologist's experience, as far as this is possible. And this calls for sensitive 'cross-cultural understanding', involving sensitive comparison too with aspects of other traditions. This comparative procedure helps to 'bring assumptions to the surface' which otherwise would remain hidden (*ibid.*: 71).

e) Despite references, cautiously made, to the 'noumenon' lying behind the phenomenon, Smart clearly does not subscribe unreservedly to the classical phenomenological concept of 'essences'. Yet he sees typological comparison as legitimate and the next necessary stage in the phenomenological process. The discovery of these analogous types within diverse traditions, calling for increasingly sophisticated analysis, does help in understanding each tradition and religion in general. In delineating such phenomenological types, Smart warns against describing merely 'formal' rather than 'material' features. Thus, in identifying 'prayer' as a type, the phenomenologist needs to show how 'the fine grain' of the praying person's activity 'derives from his conception of the Focus of his prayers' (*ibid.*: 77). Again we see Smart's emphasis on evocatively incorporating the features of the sacred Object to which the participant relates. Phenomenology should beware of listing typical categories as so many 'abstracts from formal aspects of varying practices' (*ibid.*: 78).

f) The classical phenomenological category of 'eidetic vision', as intuitive insight by which essences in religion can be grasped, is not part of Smart's approach to the systematic study of religion. In effect it is on this score that Smart is rather sharply critical of Eliade. Yet, the 'empathetic imagination' that Smart sees as so necessary to the task of understanding religious life, each tradition's innate structures, the 'inner logic' of its life, so that we are thus able typologically to compare traditions one with another, does bear resemblance to the 'eidetic vision'. At this point, though, despite his recognition of common 'types', Smart gives considerably more weight (i) to the 'organic web' of each tradition as against 'essences' common to all religion; (ii) to the 'vision' expressed by the interpreters within each tradition, especially to the conceptual dimensions of such 'Expression'; and, similarly, (iii) to the 'logic' of religious structures, discoverable as much by sustained and reflective analysis as by intuitive vision. Smart does, of course, recognise too that interpretation within a tradition will always involve this kind of intuitive vision. Theology is seen as at the heart of things.

Smart in various ways gives similar importance, explicitly or implicitly, to both the theological dimension within religious traditions and to the theological task in relation to the systematic study of religions. (i) A substantial opening part (*ibid.*: 19-23) of his account of phenomenology is taken up with an analysis of the hermeneutical process, especially of key issues in the process by which a tradition's 'Expression' changes in the course of its history. Clearly this is as much a theological issue as it is phenomenological. The 'science of religion' needs to give more attention than in the past to this process of self-interpretation within traditions, as it is crucial in understanding a tradition's 'intention' and the 'meaning' it perceives in its own existence and experience. Hermenuetics is both theological and phenomenological in scope. (ii) Smart also recognises that the self-understanding of a religion, at least a living tradition, is not yet complete. We can expect the process of interpretation to continue. (iii) Then, by giving such prominence to the 'Focus' in the process of systematic understanding, including the 'noumenal' aspect and the interplay between participants and this sacred Focus, Smart ensures a strong theological orientation in his 'science of religion'. This does not mean, of course, that his 'science' is pre-determined by particular theological commitments; his theological neutrality remains throughout. (iv) On the other hand, by recognising the interaction of various dimensions in the religious process (indicated in part by the first six of the dimensions of religion listed in Chapter One, and more explicitly in his emphasis on a 'poly-methodic' or 'aspectual' approach) Smart opens up the way for a more plausible correlation between a phenomenological science of religion and the other 'scientific studies' of religion. But all, in the final analysis, will be dependent upon the total 'Expressive' life of religion.

So, then, Smart sees a systematic Science of Religion as quite feasible, and proposes (1973b) the following criteria for such a 'Science': (a) It is to be an approach that is not determined by any one position from within the field; it does not presuppose a particular theology, but neither is it atheistic. (b) It adopts a 'methodological neutralism in its descriptive and evocative tasks', and though it looks for interpretive theories, it should not build theories into the phenomenological material and descriptions thereof (This point, however, raises questions of what constitutes scientific procedure in relation to data and theory). (c) Description and evocation are to begin from where the participants are and with their experience of the Focus of their tradition. (d) By cross-cultural comparison, there is a process of testing of general theories, in a way that is analogous to scientific experiment. (e) The Science of Religion is necessarily 'aspectual and polymethodic' in making use of any discipline found appropriate to these various aspects of religion. (f) It will incorporate 'dynamic and static typologies' that attempt to illuminate and explain religious phenomena' in general, yet will need to be strictly dependent on 'the particularities of historical traditions'. (g) Finally, Smart also emphasises (1973a: 48) the 'reflexive' character of religious studies, i.e. they affect the development of the subject they study. Already there have been various ways in which religious traditions have been modified by modern religious studies, some traditions more so than others. We can expect that theological 'Expression', especially in its task of reflection upon the meaning of the tradition, will feel most fully the impact of this principle of reflexion upon its functioning.

3. A key link in the principles of a 'science of religion' listed above is the need for 'cross-cultural *comparison*'. For Smart this is to provide a cross-cultural testing process by which to confirm (or disprove) that what has been identified as a typical religious phenomenon is in fact universally so. Comparison thus takes the role of post-understanding verification. No doubt it does; but in Smart's investigative process too it takes a more constructive role than this. Perhaps in his analysis of the constitutive structure of religion – e.g. his dimensional model with its six parts as listed in Chapter One above – Smart has not provided a way to the kind of methodological rigour some comparativists would hope for. Methodologically perhaps providing a more rigorous framework for comparative studies would be Michael Pye's more basic analysis of religion into four aspects (religious action, religious groups, religious states of mind, religious concepts). This is heuristically useful as a way of comprehending the manifest life of religions, on a 'cross-cultural' comparative basis, as such an analysis clearly relates more easily to the most prominent disciplines relating to religious studies. In Pye's 'methodologically sophisticated' analysis (Whaling 1983: 209) the four basic aspects of religion are then further divided into 30 sub-themes, and there are then 11 more modes of comparison, resulting in a complex comparative system designed to ensure that any phenomenological typology is well grounded in the particularities of historical traditions. As Whaling comments (*ibid.*: 270): 'Pye's model opens up innumerable avenues of research into particular comparative topics'.

Concerning the comparative approach, Whaling himself (*ibid.*: 280-2) outlines with considerable perception the prospects for a 'new-style' comparative religion, after having comprehensively surveyed developments in recent decades ('comprehensive' of virtually all developments in the study of religions if we include all of the two volumes he has edited on 'contemporary approaches', especially the outstanding chapter by Ursula King). Properly pursued, the comparative approach is the 'very opposite of normative. The disciplines that feed into it may have their own strong hermeneutical presuppositions but . . . comparative religion is greater than the sum of its parts', and while drawing on these other disciplines, it remains impartial. It is 'not a discipline in the normal sense', yet 'the classifications, comparisons, and models it uses to make sense of the myriads of comparative data fed into it by different disciplines enable it to contribute to a deeper understanding of religious traditions, religious man, and the disciplines concerned' (*ibid.*: 280).

So promisingly constructive is the role of comparative religion, that Whaling believes it will 'take over at least part of the role played in past years by the phenomenology of religion'. In any case the basic concerns of phenomenology, i.e. *epoché* and *Einfühlung* (empathy) in particular, have been accepted in religious studies generally, certainly in comparative religion. But the attempt in phenomenology, through eidetic vision, to identify essential forms, i.e. a typology or morphology, is only *one* way of doing comparative religion. Comparative religion will remain far more diversified than this. Yet it can be, and will be, an 'integral enterprise' which will engender 'mutual understanding' between the constitutive parts or contributing disciplines (*ibid.*: 281). This is how Whaling sees the comparative task:

Limited comparisons of a theme feed into and are modified by general comparisons of the same theme, and these in turn feed into and are modified by structural or typological comparisons that touch upon the theme in question. Likewise, limited comparisons of two religious traditions feed into and are modified by wider comparisons of the two traditions, and these in turn feed into and are modified by general comparisons of all traditions. Furthermore, ... classifications of primal and major religions influence each other; comparisons of particular themes are intertwined with comparisons of other themes; comparisons of themes are intertwined with comparisons of religions; comparisons of spiritualities, ways of being religious, and so on, are linked to comparisons of both themes and traditions. A balance is held between the bias towards similarity found in comparisons that result from implied definitions of 'religion' as a structural element in man, and the bias towards difference found in comparisons that result from implied definitions of 'religion' as religions. Cross-historical comparisons at particular periods lend insights to and borrow ideas from wider models and from similar comparisons at other periods . . . . comparative religion is a web, albeit not a seamless one. It is supportive of, but not subordinate to, the approaches that feed into it . . . .

The intention that the comparative approach, though linked so integrally with other feed-in disciplines, be methodologically rigorous, is abundantly clear. Given Whaling's accompanying concern that it is of crucial importance that the

theological or inner hermeneutical dimension be part of this 'feed-in' comparative programme, that there even be clearer recognition of the inter-dependence
of theology and other 'disciplines' in religious studies, then we do surely have
an approach with considerable promise for both sides of the present divide.

4. *A Dialogical Approach*: In any survey of recent representative scholars in
the field of religious studies, especially when there is concern to see how this
field relates to theology, we are justified in giving a substantial place to the
contribution of *Wilfred Cantwell Smith*. For one thing Smith is a very effective
exponent of what we have called the 'soft' approach, vigorously rejecting what
he sees as a misguided obsession with methodological procedure in religious
studies (in Baird 1975: 1-30; 1976: 138-57). Taking a stance that is deliberately in favour of 'subjectivity' he has been fiercely and eloquently critical of
any study of religion aiming for empirical and detached objectivity. In many
respects, too, his style is more 'theological', expressing in exuberant language
his strongly held commitments concerning the essential character of religious
life, indeed of human life. His writing has, thus, appealed strongly to many
theologians, perhaps more so than any other 'historian of religions'. His vision
of the goal of the 'history of religions' is in many respects also a vision of what
theology can become as he perceives this task. He would, however, disclaim the
role of 'theologian of religion'.

   The various sub-themes that emerge in Smith's exposition of how we are to
come to understand the religious life in an authentic way, and therefore how
we are to study this life, all closely interrelate with his earlier perception of
what religious life essentially is. Though he has modified and clarified his
position on some points, most of what he has written since *The Meaning and
End of Religion* (1962) merely draws out further strands implied in the thesis
then expounded. Smith argues that if we are truly to understand religious
traditions, we should cease to *reify* them in the way that he believes recent
scholarship has done. The very term 'religion' suggests this objectifying attitude
and should therefore be dropped; though no scholar has in fact taken this extreme step, it is surprising how many have modified their language. The point
he intends to make, perhaps somewhat rhetorically, is that religious life is a per-
petually and dynamically changing *process*, integrally part of human history
with its similarly 'processive' character.
   Smith focusses on *cumulative tradition* and *faith* (1962: chaps. 6, 7) as the
two constitutive poles of the historical religious process. The cumulative tradi-

tion comprises the more external, societal dimension of religious life in which participants share, though such sharing too must be seen as a continually changing process. The crucial point of existential and transcendent participation in this process Smith calls 'faith'. This he sees as the essential and constant religious factor in the flux of history; it is not the Transcendent itself, but is rather the human side of the relation to transcendence that characterises religious life. 'Faith differs in form, but not in kind' (1981: 168). Smith recognises that in each religious tradition 'faith' is interpreted differently; but in that faith is that by which the religious person participates in transcendence, he sees it as essentially the same in all cultures. 'God gives us faith, our century our belief' (cf. 1977: 96); that is, the particular culture we share in, by faith, determines the beliefs we hold about transcendence, which Smith frequently refers to as 'God' (though he does acknowledge that this is the particular theistic perception of the Transcendent). It is this generic quality of 'faith' by which people of all kinds of cultures find a link between the mundane and the transcendent; it thus creates the interaction between these two poles of human existence. Faith, then, is a universal characteristic of humanity; it is the fundamental quality of the religious life, though because it represents more adequately that fundamental quality of *human* life in all its dynamism, this term 'faith' can supersede 'religion' as the focal category for religious study. And it is this analysis of what is constitutive of human life that underlies Smith's methodological discussion.

Inevitably, as we noted above, Smith has little patience with overt methodological discussion, though in fact much of his writing involves crucial methodological issues, implicitly if not explicitly. Occasionally this is acknowledged, as when he responds to criticisms of being 'unscientific'. 'There are things in human consciousness waiting to be known . . . some of us are resolved to know them, and have devised methods and procedures and understandings for knowing them and for making them known. It is true that these things are not objects, and cannot be known objectively; but they are real, and can be known accurately, verifiably, humanely' (1981: 65). Smith acknowledges, too, that in relation to the 'cumulative tradition', the other pole of the religious process, 'the tradition at any given moment is observable, is concrete, is objective. It can, therefore, and must, therefore, be studied objectively. This requires the utmost rigour of scholarly exactitude: meticulous care, scrupulous precision and erudite attention to minutiae. All this is needed in order to reconstruct, in the strictest factual accuracy, what the tradition historically was (has been, is)' (*ibid*.: 67).

Such scientifically objective study, however, is 'only the first step', even though an 'inescapable first step'. If there is to be a truly appropriate 'history' of a religious tradition, the *human* dimension must be adequately recognised and given recognition in both the attitude and procedures of the historian. 'For this is *human* history. The tradition came into existence in the first place, and survived, and developed, as an element in the life of human beings; and we have understood it, intellectually, academically, truly, only in so far as we can see human lives in terms of it; can see the significance that the data had for men and women (and children), and the meaning that life had for them because of those data' (*ibid.*: 67). In the final analysis, therefore, the study of religion is not a matter of 'methodological system' (*ibid.*: 76-7). Similarly Smith argues that there is a serious 'fallacy' in 'the contemporary concept of a "discipline", which postulates a particular body of people who esoterically share a certain body of knowledge', and who 'write only for members of their discipline, accept as authoritative criticism the judgement only of . . . the members of their own group' (*ibid.*: 73-4). This, Smith contends, is a travesty of the earlier concept of a *uni*-versity.

In more detail we should take note of the following themes that emerge in Smith's writings:

a) The study of religion is essentially the *study of persons*. If faith is central to religious life, then we should look to personal life as 'the locus of faith'. In response to the frequent criticism of his conceiving of religious life in terms of individuals and their faith, Smith denies that personal life can be equated with 'individual'; an 'individual becomes a person in community' (*ibid.*: 48). The fact is, however, that he does place great emphasis on the individual's existential life in experiencing the community's tradition. Thus, in understanding and interpreting 'faith', though he sees it as in essence unchanging, he argues that even the day to day fluctuations of the individual's experience must be given due weight. He also asserts that there is never communication between one *group* and another, only between individuals in the group.

His main concern, then, is with persons, not with the systems, conceptual and institutional, in which they participate. Thus his interpretation of what a 'temple' properly is involves above all else the study of the existential life of individuals sharing in the life of that temple. This principle can be broadened to include all symbols: the 'meaning' of a symbol can be understood only by taking note of what that symbol means in the life of people. It is impossible to arrive at some general or intrinsic meaning of any symbol; we need to know rather, 'what it has in fact meant, to particular persons or groups at particular times' (*ibid.*: 63). However, Smith does recognise that something of a symbol's meaning can be understood 'objectively' (i.e. as the first stage in a 'history of religions'); more important is also to 'know what it means, has meant, in the lives and consciousness (including the sub-consciousness) of persons' (*ibid.*: 64).

b) If the locus of faith is persons, our goal in the systematic study of religions should be primarily to understand the *inner life of religious traditions*. It is no doubt necessary to look at the diverse ways in which religious traditions manifest themselves externally, and 'more is still to be accomplished in the realm of tangible data' (1959: 35); but these externals are not in themselves finally significant. Smith argues that it has been a 'fundamental error of the social sciences ... to take the observable manifestations of some human concern as though they were the concern itself. The proper study of mankind is by inference'. For, 'the externals of religion — symbols, institutions, doctrines, practices ... are not in themselves religion, which lies rather in the area of what these mean to those involved' (*ibid.*). Here we return to the emphasis on persons: 'The student is making effective progress when he recognises that he has to do not with religious systems basically but with religious persons; or at least with something interior to persons' (*ibid*).

In other places too Smith criticises a rigorous behaviourist approach: 'To understand man, and to understand history, it is necessary to know not only what man does, the behaviourist's little province, but also what he refrains from doing, what he dreams of doing, what he fears to do; what he does with exultation, hesitation, guilt or boredom ... As Dilthey long ago insisted, the behaviour of human beings is to be seen and interpreted as within the context of the consciousness that gives meaning to their lives and to their behaviour' (1981: 64-5).

c) This leads Smith to what he regards as a crucial epistemological principle, not only in the study of religion but in all 'humane science', a theme he outlined in a lecture to the Royal Society of Canada in 1974 (1976: 158-80). By 'humane science' Smith means all knowledge about human life in all its diversity. He does not, he says, speak merely of 'human science, because all science is human, pursued inescapably by human beings'. Smith regards as *disastrous* the adoption of the procedures of *natural science as paradigmatic for all scientific research*, intellectually disastrous as well as humanly so. Any study of the human, he contends, calls for quite distinct attitudes and cannot be objectified without fatal distortion of the reality of their existence. This generally existentialist epistemological stance leads Smith to assert that we must move beyond 'objectivity' as our goal in any study of human life; to objectify in this 'humane' area results merely in 'pseudo-scientific' knowledge (1981: 56-7).

It is presupposed in the West that the only alternative to objectivity is subjectivity. Here Smith proposes a third possibility: *'corporate critical self-consciousness'*. He sees this as a further step in scientific knowledge, as it expands 'from the world of nature, truly to the world of man' (*ibid.*: 59). We will not stay to comment on this anthropocentrism, which in this sense at least still does not move far from a Cartesian dichotomy found strangely, though greatly modified, in much existential thought. Rather we note that Smith defines 'corporate critical self-consciousness' as 'that critical, rational inductive self-consciousness by which a community of persons – constituted ideally by the whole human race – is aware of any given particular human condition or action as it is experienced and understood simultaneously both subjectively (personally, existentially) and objectively (externally, critically, analytically; as one used to say, scientifically)' (*ibid.*: 59). Elsewhere this kind of dialectical knowledge is called 'personal knowledge', and is described in more explicitly dialogical terms. Students of religion are urged to move on first from 'objective' investigation of 'it' to a more personal knowledge of 'they', thus recognising the subjecthood of 'listening and mutuality . . . "we" talk *with* "you"*. The culmination of this process is when "we all" are talking with each other about "us" (1959: 34). Smith acknowledges that this kind of dialogical approach applies primarily to our understanding of living religions; but in principle, he claims, it is equally true of the process involved in understanding any human phenomenon.

d) Smith further affirms that the *verification* principle, so important to scientific procedure, is only maintained in the realm of religious knowledge *when believers themselves are given the opportunity to endorse* descriptions and interpretations of outside investigators. 'No statement about a religion is valid unless it can be acknowledged by that religion's believers' (1959: 42). Obviously there will be a great deal of material relating to the external history of a tradition that need not be so referred to the inner community. Smith here intends primarily 'the faith in men's hearts', i.e. the inner life, 'the meaning that the system has for those of faith'. And in such matters, 'an outsider cannot in the nature of the case go beyond the believer' (*ibid.*).

Smith acknowledges that this proposal, just like the call to a dialogical approach, makes for certain problems. For example, when we think of the changes occuring in the historical process, the believer will often just not recognise any such change as taking place in the sacred tradition. Thus, 'the insider can speak authoritatively only for the present'. But when we are concerned primarily with *meaning*, rather than merely with manifestation, and with moving towards the truth in an ongoing process of interaction, Smith sees dependence on the believer's endorsement as a 'creative principle; for it provides experimental control that can lead a student dynamically towards the truth' (*ibid.*: 43). And while no outsider can refute the believer on what constitutes the truth of his religion, i.e. faith's participation in the Transcendent, it may be possible for 'the outside scholar to break new ground in stating the meaning of faith in, say, modern terms more successfully than a believer' (*ibid.*). In the interpretation of meaning, in other words, the scholar is not bound *exclusively* to the way in which the believer expounds it, though his assent will then be needed, as always. The scholar's task 'is that of constructing an exposition that will do justice to the Western academic tradition, by growing directly out of the objective evidence and by being rationally coherent both within itself and with all other knowledge, and at the same time will do justice to the faith in men's hearts by commending their assent once it is formulated' (*ibid.*: 44).

Smith, then, does attempt to provide room within his synthesis of the subjective and the objective for a scientifically acceptable systematic study of religion. Various questions, however, become inevitable. Huston Smith (1981: 306-10) (actually another scholar on the 'soft' side of the methodological spectrum), for example, points out that Smith 'makes things easy' for his own argument by using 'objective knowledge' in a somewhat extreme epistemological sense. It usually just means 'public knowledge', knowledge that all can examine, which is precisely what he expects of 'humane knowledge', i.e. it will not be esoterically limited to an academic elite. And in any case every scholar has to accept the inevitability of striving for 'objective knowledge' in the more rigorous sense, even when this concerns human consciousness. For every act of reflection on human consciousness on my part in a sense makes it the 'object' of my consciousness. However one may attempt to incorporate and do justice to the subjectivity of others, the human intellectual condition makes some kind of objectifying attitude inevitable — as Smith (W.C.) himself recognises. The crucial question, of course, is just how is this objectified knowledge brought into proper synthesis with human subjectivity. Has Smith pointed the way towards a more satisfactory manner in which we can allow these two epistemological poles to interact?

e) An important task of the professional student of religion, contends Smith, is to *participate in the growing interaction between world cultures and religious traditions* and even to *further activate* this process. Smith contends that in the present situation of growing dialogue and mutuality, the comparative religionist should not remain aloof and detached. There are various ways in which the scholar with competency in more than one tradition can take part in this dialogical situation: (i) He can participate in the dialogue as a representative of his own tradition, not by presenting either a detached view, or an exclusive kind of personal commitment. For the value and purpose of inter-religious dialogue is both learning more fully to apprehend one's own faith and, simultaneously, 'to appreciate the quality and even the ultimate validity (in the eyes of God) of others' (1954: 49). (ii) He can also serve as a 'mediator or interpreter between representatives of diverse traditions or at least as a kind of broker helping them to interpret themselves to each other . . . How better could one's competence in this discipline be tested?' (*ibid.*: 51). (iii) As an observer of the dialogue that in any case is going on, the comparative religionist 'on the sidelines' will probably be called on 'to provide the theory for those practically involved', and thus to facilitate communication. For '*it is the business of comparative religion to construct statements about religion that are intelligible to at least two traditions simultaneously*', and this task is 'intellectually important and historically urgent' (*ibid.*: 52). Here Smith outlined a thesis that he developed in greater detail in his *Towards a World Theology*: we are now in an age of growing cross-cultural interaction and inter-religious mutuality. 'Even a face-to-face dialogue gives way to a side-by-side conversation', where scholars of different faiths no longer confront each other but collaborate in jointly confronting the universe. The practitioner of comparative religion is to be 'a participant in the multi-form religious history of the only community there is, humanity. *Comparative religion may become the disciplined self-consciousness of man's variegated and developing religious life*' (*ibid.*: 55).

In his *Towards a World Theology*, however, Smith in various ways builds on and goes beyond his earlier position. He begins (1981: 3) with 'the vision . . . of the unity or coherence of humankind's religious history', a unity that he regards as an empirically observable fact as well as being a theological conviction. For he sees himself as a historian first and only then a theologian, though the fact that his view of the historical process is described in such explicitly 'theological' terms is here significant. Each tradition's life, if dynamically conceived, is but *'a strand in the religious history of the world'* (*ibid.*: 44) and it is of the commonality that each tradition will be increasingly aware. There is a 'world-process of religious convergence' that is of greater contextual significance than our diverse community traditions. He again affirms that 'ultimately the only community there is... is the community, world-wide and history-long, of humankind' (*ibid.*: 44).

Langdon Gilkey (1981: 298-306), from the standpoint of a philosophical theologian, finds a problem in Smith's understanding of the entire historical process as *Heilsgeschichte*, as the locus of revelation. That this raises a the-ological question is clear: what is the role of 'special revelation'? It is also a question for the history of religions in that the distinctive vision of reality, the focal point shaping each tradition, seems to be less significant than those traditions themselves want to assert. On the other hand it needs to be pointed out that Smith's faith-motif suggests a very specific theological presupposition; in many respects it is a Christian, perhaps even a Protestant Christian pre-understanding of what religion should be. This is partly confirmed when he speaks so often of the focus of 'faith' as 'God'. Gilkey puts the same query in a different way by suggesting that Smith sees the History of Religions as Theology, as having 'redemptive efficacy'. And yet, Smith's emphasis on the inter-connectedness of religious histories, which he sees as making necessary a new synthesis in inter-cultural theological reflection, is surely not *merely* a vision springing out of theological hope; it also reflects — in his exposition writ rather more large and more vividly than usual — empirical realities. There are, of course, other empirical realities that point in the opposite direction; there are also strong fissiperous forces at work driving religious traditions apart. In any case, the trans-cultural shaping of theological reflection is a genuinely religious phenomenon (whatever other phenomena there may be) providing legitimate material for the historian of religions as much as for theologians of various faiths.

f) Despite the strong theological thrust in Smith's writings, certain aspects of his stance suggest an essentially anthropological approach. (Again, Gilkey criticises him for his 'anthropocentrism'). Smith certainly wishes to emphasise, and frequently, that *religion is a human enterprise*, though he would include within this humanness religion's 'transcendent' dimension. Thus, often, trans-cendence is taken as characteristic of humanness, as much as that which characterises the sacred Object of the faith of humans. To be human is always to be involved in the historical fact of interaction between what is mundane and what is transcendent (Smith 1981: 42). The historian of religions, thus, is the historian of mankind in his profound self-awareness (*ibid.*: 49-50). Smith asserts that religion, and participation in transcendence, should not be seen as a strange addendum to human existence. People are not first human, then religious: religious and transcendence-oriented existence is truly human existence (though Smith says he is not claiming that all humans are inherently religious (*ibid..* 53) and that it remains to be seen whether a fully secular existence is possible to humans). His predominant concern, then, is with 'faith' as a universal condition of being human, rather than with the nature of the 'focus' of faith. This seems to be the reason for Smith's radical distinction between 'faith' and 'belief'. Faith is a universal generic quality; belief represents the various ways in which religious traditions have conceptualised in particular the focus of their faith. Smith's basic anthropological stance to some extent weakens interest in the latter.

g) Along with his almost idealist view of the status of 'faith' and the unity of humankind, Smith also asserts that religious studies must recognise the *complex particularity of religious life* in the historical process. *Both dimensions,* it is affirmed, are to be taken with equal seriousness. The history of religion, and all history, is 'intrinsically the locus of both the mundane and the transcendent, unbifurcated' (1981: 3). He is well aware of the 'bewildering' diversity of the world's religious traditions. 'The more I study, the more variegated I find the religious scene to be. I have no reason to urge a thesis of unity among the "religions of the world"' (*ibid.*: 4). There is, he points out, not even unity in any one religion. The unity he affirms, then, is that of historical interconnectedness, and the increased sharing in a 'common history'. There is a complex interaction between four major factors within each tradition: (i) the cumulative religious tradition; (ii) the participant's particular personality; (iii) the particular environment, historical and geographical; (iv) the transcendent reality to which the tradition points and in relation to which it lives. Religious life, therefore, is very complex participation in the historical process, and the ways in which this process changes are uncountable and very subtle. 'Human history, including its religious history, is an intricate and delicate web of human relations' (*ibid.*: 42). It is in the quality of a person's participation (in company with fellow-members) in the transcendent power (identified as 'God') 'that gives their life its religious significance' (*ibid*).

h) Finally, we might note again that Smith does see the possibility of an out-sider acquiring *authentic understanding* of the life of a religion, providing the emphasis is not on investigating a 'religion' in its external manifestations, but on coming to see the world through the eyes of those sharing its inner faith. For it is 'faith' that comprises the core-point, and it is the complex human inter-connectedness that is the most significant 'context' for study. Familiaris-ing oneself with the tradition's doctrines, scriptures, art, practices, history, languages, and so on, may enhance our ability to see with the other's eyes. 'Yet that is only a first step . . . The faith of Buddhists does not lie in the Buddhist tradition; it lies in the human heart; it is what the tradition means to people . . .' (*ibid.*: 47).

As we anticipated at the beginning of the previous chapter, the move from methodologically 'hard' to 'soft' approaches has not been a smooth progression (or 'regression', depending on one's point of view). We cannot but admire the tenacity with which Wilfred Cantwell Smith has continued to affirm aspects of religious life which must surely be reckoned with: the unobjectifiable character of much of the personal dimension in all religious histories in their everchanging historical dynamism, and the corollary of this, the dialogical nature of the-ological interpretation within a tradition as it necessarily interacts with its context and with other traditions, are two of the constitutive factors in the process of understanding religious life. However, obsession with 'persons' (rather than with that to which those persons seek to orient their life, and the structured dimensions within which these persons live out their religious life) can serve, ironically, to obscure other aspects of religious life which are precisely those often neglected by investigators with an obsession with objective scientific rigour, an approach that *can* lead them to look no further than historical processes, social conditioning, culturally functional symbol-systems, and so on. The *meanings*, at diverse levels, of all this, as well as the persons for whom there are meanings and the process by which these meanings are transmitted, are also of paramount importance for a more complete understanding of religious life. In the next chapter, therefore, we look critically at attempts to develop an *integrated* science of religion, i.e. integrated in some way with systematic theological interpretation.

10

An Integral Science of Religion (and Theology)?

For well over a century there has been the intention to develop a 'science of religion', which will not only be a comparative account of diverse types of religious traditions, but in some sense will provide a systematic and thus integrated perspective of the diversity of religious life. It is clear that the various specialised scientific approaches to the study of religion have substantially enriched our knowledge of many different dimensions of religious life. For example, in historical studies in the classical texts; but equally important is the increased understanding about the interaction of religious traditions and other causal factors in the historical process. Sociology and anthropology have brought out this interactive dimension very clearly, even if we might have reservations about some of the theoretical interpretations that have come to be built into such research. And psychology has uncovered depths of the human consciousness and the dynamics of symbolic imagery within the full range of human experiencing that so clearly impinge upon our understanding of the religious life.

Despite these and many other specialist advances, or possibly just because of them, there is today still great *methodological uncertainty*, even confusing contradiction about how religious studies are to proceed. There is 'little or no methodological cohesiveness despite almost a century of discussion and debate' (Wiebe 1981: 47). In particular, there is uncertainty about the possibility of a systematic 'science of religion'. Can we still even envisage such a 'science'? Is it the case that the very nature of the subject precludes the constraints of such a 'discipline'? We can, of course, optimistically still anticipate greater concensus regarding general methodological approach, despite the prolonged growing pains we have seen so far. It is probably misleading and rather fruitless to try to analyse this term 'science', largely because opinion in the English-speaking world on what properly constitutes a 'science' is too divided. Theory of science and scientific epistemological procedure is, however, changing; the older empiricism is no longer quite so widely accepted in British and English-speaking scientific and philosophical circles (cf. Whaling 1983: 379-90). Perhaps there will yet be a time when 'science' simply means systematic knowledge.

One of the problems in the field of religious studies in arriving even at such 'systematic knowledge' is the necessarily wide range of phenomena involved. That there is no definitional concensus is no surprise, though this is not a defence for the blinkered attitude found too often in attempted definitions, i.e. where one or other phenomenal or concomitant aspect of religious life is selected as definitive. It is just this inclusiveness of religious phenomena that often behavioural scientists may use in defence of their varied approaches: to be manageably scientific any study of religion has to be from one or other limited perspective. Does this, however, necessarily mean that our understanding of religions can only be from these limited perspectival investigation? Is some more inclusive, yet still systematic and 'scientific', approach to religious phenomena not possible?

Wiebe has argued (1981) that just in so far as the scientific study of religious phenomena necessarily involves various disciplinary approaches, it cannot qualify as a single 'science of religion'. And no such autonomy or a single methodological discipline is possible, for there is no way in which religious studies can be systematically pursued independently of the social sciences. Wiebe does, however, allow that a distinct critical approach, which can even be 'scientific' in its general stance, is possible. In effect this is a type of philosophy of religion, a critical over-view as it were which does not assume the 'cognitive superiority' of either the social scientist or of the uncritical participant. Interestingly, Wiebe gives considerable weight to the cognitive claims, the theologies and the systematisers, within religious traditions in this critical systematic approach. He even quotes Heiler's dictum, seemingly with approval, that 'any study of religion is in the last analysis theology'. At the same time he cannot allow the 'theological assumption' that any intuitively based 'science of religion' can be over and above the social sciences. Properly perceived, the theological task too is to have an in-built critical stance, rather like the philosophical analysis of religion. Thus we can avoid both the reductionism implicit in taking the social sciences as cognitively superior, and the uncritical assumption that 'the believer is (cognitively) always right', which is a first principle of phenomenologists such as Kristensen and of the dialogical approach of Wilfred Cantwell Smith. No 'science of religion' is possible on such a basis. We are left, then, according to Wiebe, with a more generally framed 'critical religious studies'.

There are, however, a number of scholars in religions who take a much more positive view of the possibility of a systematic 'science of religion'. We have already seen, for example, Ninian Smart's confidence that such a science can develop. He recognises, however, that there are ambiguities which make it a 'soft', even a 'chaotic' science which cannot be reduced to one neatly rigorous method. Yet there can still be an overall, systematic theoretical framework.

We now look at a number of representative positions, each distinct, but expressing a common concern for a more integrated approach to understanding religious traditions; in some cases this involves a clear theological stance, either explicit or implicit, or incorporating theologies into the integral perspective.

1. Some representatives of the *phenomenological* approach, with their commitment both to eidetic vision as the only appropriate mode of understanding religion and to finding common essences in religions, took a further step: to the truly perceiving religious scholar all religious phenomena can be apprehended within a unitive vision, and thus can yield an inclusive insight into ultimate reality. The way in which many Eastern religionists, such as S. Radhakrishnan, would understand the study of religion would also be along these lines. Quite early in the life of the International Association for the History of Religions (cf. Sharpe 1975: 271-85) we find both Eliade and Smith, though from different standpoints, expressing this same concern for a more integral perspective on religious studies. Eliade urged historians of religion to be more aware of and more committed to a 'creative hermeneutic' (1969: 1-3, 61-71). He saw the discipline as the 'New Humanism', with the explicit task of improving the 'hermeneutics of religious data', and thus consciously and systematically contributing to the task of interpreting to the world the meaning and potency of religious realities; their's is a task of cultural and religious renewal, so creatively interpreting religious traditions as to take them into a period of new global awareness of the religious level of life. The increasingly de-sacralised condition of the modern western world calls for its redirection away from its obsession with the profane and back to sacred reality. Even historians of religion have been swept along with the tide, so devoting themselves to historical materials and empirical data that they have neglected, partly through 'spiritual timidity' in face of current positivist values, the vital task of *interpreting the sacred meaning of their data*. The *science* of religion, then, is this integral hermeneutical task; merely informing about facts is not enough: 'In the end, the creative hermeneutic *changes* man; it is more than instruction, it is also a spiritual technique susceptible of modifying the quality of existence itself' (1969: 62). Thus the science of religion is to 'contribute to the elaboration of a universal type of culture'. Just like every other religious liberative

technique, this new science is to 'deliver man from his chains . . . in order to open him to the world of the spirit' and to 'render him *culturally creative*'. This is the 'crucially important' goal of the science of religion (*ibid.*: 67).

Joseph Kitagawa, who followed Wach and Eliade at Chicago, also sees the need for an 'integral understanding', for 'telescoping the long and complex historical development of men's religions' (1968: 200). He acknowledges that 'this is probably the most controversial aspect of our discipline'. Such an integral perspective is 'caught between theology and the social sciences', thus lying 'between normative (theological) and a descriptive (social science) stance'. For Kitagawa, however, the unifying task seems to be continuous with the work of the historian of religion and the social scientists. It is they who must 'carry the awful burden of articulating' this vision, through theoretical interpretation based on their empirical sciences. Perhaps Eliade too would not argue with this point. But we must still be clear what is being said: the student in religion, whether we call it a 'new science of religion' or not, without reference to grounding in any one particular tradition, but rather in a wide range of traditions, is to be the source of a new visionary interpretation of reality and its meaning. What is called for in effect is a new vision that is inclusively religious and therefore transcendent to particular religions or particular theologies. It is thus a new theology or philosophy, such as has always been the case when attempts have been made – sometimes eminently successful of course – to move beyond any particular historical grounding to an inclusive (metaphysical) interpretation based on a more integral perception of reality.

In that Eliade's writing has had considerable impact upon quite a wide range of readers with general cultural interest, including a number of theologians (though his influence on the history of religions' field professionally, or methodologically, has been surprisingly limited), it will be useful to look at Guilford Dudley's (1977) account of his work – a generally approving account – in more detail. Dudley makes very clear his disapproval of those studies in religion, of which there are many, that have not been concerned with any integral hermeneutical outlook in their work, especially when these studies are based on a naive empiricist belief in the 'procedure of observation, inductive reasoning, and empirical verification'. There is irony, he comments, in the fact that *religionists* of all people have been so committed to this kind of positivistic empirical method (in order to gain respectability for their discipline) at a time when their epistemological model has been 'devastatingly criticised by both philosophers and scientists' (*ibid.*: 121-2). Basing his argument on methodological theory put forward in relation to scientific knowledge by Imre

Lakatos, Dudley contends that a viable methodological procedure in religious studies requires setting up some 'core theory' around which to build a 'protective belt' that will, as it were, take up any blows inflicted by contradictory empirical evidence (*ibid.*: 125). The 'core theory' can then be modified and adjusted without necessarily nullifying that original perception of the nature of religion (*ibid.*: 127-9).

Eliade, claims Dudley, has provided one such viable, outstandingly fruitful and necessarily inclusive theory of what constitutes religion. In this way he defends Eliade's 'comprehensive system for explaining all religious behaviour and thought' (*ibid.*: 158). Dudley concedes that Eliade is often not consistent, does not always give examples carefully, and clearly sets out with theoretical assumptions about what religion is, in particular with an 'archaic ontology' drawn from the Indian yogic tradition, and this acts almost paradigmatically for his perception of authentic religious life. Yet, he still argues that Eliade's is one of the most appropriate methodological styles to have emerged in religious studies — especially because of its integral hermeneutic vision.

In this chapter we are not so much concerned with the variety of methodological questions involved in a detailed analysis of Eliade's work or Dudley's defence of it. We note merely the premiss of both that only a comprehensively interpretive theory of religion is sufficient or appropriate in view of the integral character of religion itself. The methodological notion of an explanatory core-theory, itself fairly impregnable, by being very flexible, with more vulnerable but protective subsidiary hypotheses supporting and defending the central theory, fits neatly into this underlying assumption. Others, such as Ursula King (in Whaling 1983: 11) have also pointed out the need for commensurability of method and subject-matter in any science. The science of religion also has to evolve a methodological approach that is appropriate to 'the multidimensional realities found in the institutions, expressions, and experience of religion' (*ibid.*: 136). This is undeniable: but if the central explicating theory cannot itself be touched by investigative testing — only peripheral supporting motifs being changed by such a process — it is doubtful how this can function as a systematic interpretive basis for any 'science of religion'. And has Eliade's theoretical framework in fact proved fruitful in advancing religious studies generally (as Dudley argues it is potentially able to do), for all the importance of many of his insights?

2. A somewhat earlier scholar concerned for an integral understanding of religion was *Friedrich Heiler*, whose position has been called a 'history of

religions theology' (Rudolph). Again, his thought is of special interest in that it has shaped the perception of religion of some theologians, including Bernard Lonergan. Heiler (Waardenburg 1973: 474-8) describes religion as constituted by concentric circles: an outer crust of 'outer manifestations', and two further enclosing belts first of doctrines, and with special reference to 'reverence and surrender, love, and faith'; then, at the true heart of all religion, the transcendent divine reality, 'the intended object' of religious phenomena. The focal point of this is *Deus absconditus*, or the hidden dimension of God, around which is *Deus revelatus*, or the revealed dimension of God, comprised of 'holiness, truth, and love'. These concentric circles are further divided into three segments, so that the component elements of each circle relate integrally to the corresponding segment in other circles, leading into the reality of God at the centre. Heiler sees this as an expression of the *analogia entis*, in which 'the created being corresponds to the non-created divine being' (Waardenburg *op. cit.* 477).

It is to this essential core, the reality of the divine being, that the student of religion is to penetrate if there is to be authentic understanding. Methodologically, therefore, in a true science of religion, the student 'treats the religion of mankind as a whole, and views the lower and higher forms of religion together. Every single manifestation is traced from its most primitive to its most spiritual' (*ibid.*: 475). It will be rather obvious that such an integrated 'science of religion' has found favour with very few scholars also committed to the 'history of religions', especially those giving more weight to their distinct histories. While there is some truth in the criticism (by King in Whaling 1973: 91) that Heiler's model 'has been constructed on the premises of Christian theology' in many ways it is no more typically Christian than a number of other 'theological' accounts of religion, and would in fact fit reasonably well into various other theistic systems.

Like Eliade, Heiler believed that the proper study of religion would have very practical benefit and would lead to the 'Unity of Religion' (as seen by his address to the IAHR Congress in Tokyo 1958, and in an article entitled 'The History of Religions as a Preparation for the Cooperation of Religions'; in Eliade and Kitagawa 1959: 132-60). Such a concern is, of course, somewhat different from the point at issue in this chapter: can there be an integral science of, and perception of, religion? Can the essence of all religions thus be systematically apprehended? Naturally, when the goal of religious unity is seen as essential to the task of a science of religion, the transcendent unity of all religious phenomena will also most likely be presupposed, as with both Eliade and Heiler.

Of a piece with this view of the transcendent unity of religions is Heiler's emphasis upon certain *religious* qualities in a student of religion. There must be a basic respect for all religions, even the same sense of *wonder* that is 'the beginning of all philosophy'. There must also be personal religious *experience*: 'One cannot be engaged in ethics without a moral sense, in the history of art without any artistic experience . . . in the study of religion without any religious feeling; in the broadest sense of the word *similia similibus cognoscuntur* (Like knows like). In order to understand religion, the scholar has to bring love with him'. Thirdly, it is necessary to take seriously the religious 'claim to *truth* . . . Religion is about a final reality . . . God, revelation, eternal life are realities to religious man. Any study of religion is in the last analysis, theology, to the extent that it does not concern itself with psychological and historical phenomena only, but also with the experience of transcendent realities'. Heiler then tries to clarify further his view of a science of religion as ultimately 'theology' 'This taking seriously a religious view of reality is, to a certain extent, a faith, but not a faith in the sense of a fixed or confessional dogma . . . but of a universal faith, a faith transcendental in mankind' (Waardenburg 1973: 473-4).

It seems difficult to argue about some of these qualities: for a science of religion to do justice to the 'transcendent realities' within religious traditions does surely call for peculiar qualities of scholarly sensitivity. That such a scholar must actually be a religious person is less easy to defend, though the seeming assumption of some 'hard' empiricists that personal religious faith is a positive handicap overlooks the benefits of an intuitional level of perceiving the inner life of a religious tradition, a way of perceiving that may well have been finely attuned through personal religious experience. No doubt the scholar less enamoured of such intuitional 'understanding' would counter this by pointing out that a highly developed personal religious life is likely to ensure very strong prejudices and presuppositions concerning what religion is, and therefore determines the way traditions other than one's own are perceived and interpreted. If, however, a musical analogy is any help, it can be pointed out that a western person making a study of Indian music is likely to be better equipped for such a task if there is already a sound knowledge and appreciation (i.e. 'experience') of styles and structures of western music; the ear will probably be that much more ready to become attuned to a very different cultural form, even if in the process of 'transposition' from one musical form to another a different conceptual explanatory framework will need to be developed. In authentic understanding of a religious tradition, however, the *empathy* that is needed is not to be identified with some particular religious experience.

In all these theories of an integral science, and their assumption of and search for the one Transcendent that is to be disclosed in all religions to the sensitive, discerning student, there is in effect a *'theology beyond theology'*. Heiler's systematic structuring of religious life is typical of a theistic system. Thus we find that 'in the final analysis' it is not only a theological sensitivity that is called for, but a *particular theological framework* that is to provide the basis for the study of all religions and theologies. The 'faith' which Heiler admits to be part of this approach is more of a 'confessional dogma' than he recognises. The 'universal faith' emerges by making one particular type of religion, even if a quite catholic form of theism, normative for all faith; and his unitive Transcendent is just not inclusive enough for the full range of religious types.

3. A considerably more sophisticated approach to an 'integral science of religion', which 'combines systematic and critical reflection with a penetrating analysis of methodological principles' (King, in Whaling 1983: 142), has recently been proposed by Georg Schmid. His early argument (1979: 9-10) that a science of religion 'generally becomes necessary at the point where one's own traditional religion becomes a problem and calls for scientific clarification', is a dubious point. While it is true that in recent religious history there has been a decline of naivity in matters of faith, it hardly seems the case that perceiving one's own tradition as problematic is a reason for 'scientific clarification'. So many other kinds of response would seem equally possible and indeed have taken place. Schmid (*ibid*.: 174) criticises Heiler for being 'timeless-unhistorical'. In a way rather similar to Heiler, however, Schmid identifies three levels of religious life: (i) Religious data, empirically observable and thus subject to direct scientific research and interpretation; (ii) religious experience, which is never directly observable, yet is also not entirely beyond the reach, by inference, of an empirical approach; (iii) then the ultimate level of religious life is 'the reality of religion', that which is its trans-empirical 'intention' (here we see a generally Kantian epistemological framework). Schmid differentiates between the 'religious reality' and the 'reality of religion'. The former is the scientifically researchable phenomena of religious traditions, along with the 'whole manifold of religious life and experience which expresses itself or conceals itself in religious data; sacrifice, prayer, meditation, thanksgiving, worship, search, petition, celebration, experience, remembrance, realisation, belief, hope, imitation, astonishment, rebellion, enthusiasm, confession, teaching and obedient action' (*ibid*.: 11). As distinct from this 'religious

reality', the 'reality of religion' means '*what is intended in all this life and experience*, the whence and whereto of all the searching, hoping, believing and worshipping'. Only the former 'is the immediate object of the science of religion'; and this science can be pursued systematically, i.e. on the basis of such critical reflection, and with deliberate and rigorous methodological procedures, taking into account modern as well as classical manifestations of religious life, and indeed even of 'secular' manifestations that are outside all institutional religious life.

On the other hand Schmid gives crucial importance to the 'reality of religion' (i.e. to the reality lying beyond all phenomenal expression of religion) in authentic understanding of 'religious reality' (i.e. investigable manifestations). For the '*meaning* of religious data opens itself only in the relationship of religious life to the reality of religion', i.e. there is true understanding only insofar as we look at the outward manifestations of any religious act or expression in its relationship to the intentioned reality lying behind such religious forms. The *intention*, in other words, is essential in understanding any religious life (*ibid*.: 93-4). The 'togetherness' of description, comprehension and understanding is crucial to a truly integral science of religion.

Indeed, even at the descriptive level, if we are to attain 'pure description' of all that is 'given' in religious phenomena, there has to be an uncovering of those elements to which our descriptive sciences often remain blind (*ibid*.: 69-72). Though Schmid rather overstates his case, he points to a serious limitation often to be seen in scientific approaches to religion, perhaps even a distorting constraint: 'Modern science of religion allows as the only valid object of its interest something which is completely secondary to religion' (*ibid*.: 33). Here, as in some other aspects of his position, though certainly not in his concern for greater methodological clarity, precision and efficacy, Schmid is rather close to W.C. Smith. Not only in the emphasis on religious life as essentially that which *persons* experience, but his interpretation of ritual acts, myths and symbols, is also very close to Smith's, though the object and objectivity of (the 'reality' of) these phenomena is more significant for Schmid: 'The center of interest in myth is, for one who experiences the life of the myth, the superb reality which expresses itself in the myth, which makes itself present and audible in the believer. The importance and center of the symbol is not the bare facticity of the sign but the reality in which the symbol shares and which it signals' (*ibid*.: 34).

Then, too, 'explaining' such phenomena on the basis of any *one* dimension of the relational life of religion will necessarily be misinterpretation. Indeed, to 'understand' adequately not only are the interrelationships of data within religion to be taken fully into account; such relations are to be understood 'according to their own intention' (*ibid*.: 94), i.e. as realised implicitly in the lived experience of religion.

It is perhaps to be expected also that Schmid sees a more intrinsic relationship between theology and the science of religion than is usually acknowledged. Science of religion, he affirms, has necessarily 'seen itself constantly accompanied, implemented, placed in question and challenged by theology' (*ibid*.: 158). In any case, theology must be taken as data of foremost significance for the science of religion. Moreover, Schmid, like Pannenberg (to whom he strangely makes no reference) contends that just as science of religion reflects on religion as a whole, theology (here, *Christian* theology) is the science of the religion of Christianity insofar as theology is properly systematic and scientific. There is, however, a 'pseudo-scientific theology' which is speculative, propagandist and ideological (*ibid*.: 160-1). None of this type of theological articulation is properly reflective scientific theology; indeed, it is not truly theology at all, it would seem, according to Schmid. For true theology is in the end to relate reflectively and systematically to the 'reality in religion', just as the science of religion relates to the reality of religion as a whole. The two share a common goal: an 'encompassing perception of their respective subject-matters' (*ibid*.: 162). 'Integral science of religion and integral theology not only have a common subject matter, but also seek a most encompassing and thorough description, comprehension and understanding of this common subject matter'. Any present contradiction and tension result from the inability of the two to 'do justice to their common interests' (*ibid*.: 163). Both sciences can be and are often 'heretical'. However, insofar as they are concerned for their proper common goal, they are dependent on each other (*ibid*.: 165).

It has to be acknowledged that Schmid's analysis of the methodological issues with which he is concerned, is done with great conceptual sophistication as well as phenomenological insight. It is clear, too, that a number of the concerns central to the preceding chapters of this book are in accord with Schmid's. The differences, however, are equally significant:

a) To claim that true science of religion and true systematic theology share an identical goal, is very different from saying that there will be increased interdependence when each discipline is true to its task. Not to distinguish distinct goals in each case is surely to do a disservice to both.

b) While it may be true that a science of religion must be concerned with all religions, Schmid's continual reference in the singular to 'the whole of religion' as that which a science of religion is to understand, and understand in its wholeness, would seem not to take seriously the need to maintain a dialectic of what Schmid calls the 'specific' and the 'integral' interests (*ibid*.: 27f.). Indeed, despite the methodological sophistication, there is a clear tendency not to give sufficient weight to the 'integral' nature of *each* specific religious tradition, especially as expressed in its theological self-understanding and in its diachronic history.

c) The definition/description of religion poses problems: 'Religion is the reality of a person. It is all that refers the personhood of a person not only to what is real but to reality . . . Religion is the attempt to find the way beyond the individual thing to the whole. It is the infinitely manifold, continual referal and referring of man to the ground, goal, meaning and middle of all that is real. Religion is his attempt to correspond to this reality' (*ibid*.: 150-1). Of the many comments that could be made about such a position I confine myself to the following: (i) Referring to the varied types of sacred Foci of all religions in their distinctive particularity as 'the reality of religion' in the singular is a transcendentally and ontologically loaded stance in more ways than one. For example, to assume and even to make explicit, that there is *one* transcendent reality lying behind the many religions is to testify to faith, and of a particular kind; to speak of it as the *reality* is equally so. In other words the particular is universalised; there is a theology-beyond-theologies. (ii) Religion is here universalised in another sense: it is made to include *all* authentic or 'real' human existence, which methodologically so widens the scope of the subject-matter as to be almost meaningless. (iii) Seeing a movement from the 'individual thing to the whole' is similarly taking up a particular ontological position. Some other 'theologies' might want to stress the need to move back again continually to the 'individual thing' as equally part of the movement to reality. (iv) The emphasis on *persons* (as in W.C. Smith) in the context of some kinds of objectifying approach might be justified. To what extent can we ground all understanding of either a single tradition or more universal types of religious life on persons, or identify religion with 'the reality of *a* person'? To what extent, methodologically, can we limit understanding of a religion (apart from religion in its totality) to the testimony of persons, when clearly so much historical material is not of this kind? What does it really mean, for example, to say that 'the whole of religion discloses its meaning to one who lives it'? (*ibid*.: 64).

d) The impression is given in places, is presumably the assumption underlying the virtual identity of science of religion and theology, that 'the whole of reality' can be disclosed through any one religion. For example, in relation to the Bhagavad Gītā it is said (modifying Radhakrishnan's claim that it represents religion 'in its universality') that it can lead to 'the understanding of... the reality of religion' (*ibid.*: 147). One may well, on the basis of a particular theological stance, affirm this; but can such a faith-claim be part of methodological assumption for a 'science of religion'?

e) The virtual identifying of the goals of theology and science of religion seems mistaken, even if there is some similarity of goal especially in the case of certain kinds of systematic theology, and even if we might happen to believe as Christians that much more theology should be closely convergent with the science of religion. My own analysis of the theological process, phenomenologically perceived, would give far more weight to the particularity of grounding in the concerned central vision, i.e. the 'reality' as perceived by a particular tradition. That this calls for continual critical interaction with contextual life, including the visionary life of others, is another matter.

f) To assume, based on Kantian epistemology (as Kaufman, cf. Chapter 11), that neither theologies or scientific studies of religion are in immediate relationship with the 'reality of religion' can be taken in two ways. If it means that, for example, God is no more 'known' to theologians than to those engaged in the science of religion, then there is good reason for representatives of the concerned theology to protest. If it merely means that the one ultimate Reality lying beyond all religious traditions is not known directly to either theologians or scientists of religion, then we have to agree, though in a modified way: we might say that those who, like Schmid, do speak of this one 'reality of religion' are able to speak thus out of *theological* conviction rather than as a consequence of being scholars in the 'science of religion'.

4. Moving on to the more explicitly theological side of the spectrum of integrative methodological perspectives, we find H.R. Schlette and W. Pannenberg as the most articulate exponents of a theology of history of religions. Of others who have attempted to integrate theology and science of religion in a more correlational sense we shall take note of Charles Davis and George Rupp by way of example.

  C. Davis (1981, which shows further development of an earlier article along similar lines in 1974) picks up Schmid's point that the very emergence of a science of religion is a symptom of the experience of one's tradition as problematic. He argues that 'the modern science of religion rests upon a change of religious consciousness, that is, upon a shift in religious faith' (*ibid*.: 13). He contends that the attempt by many students of religion to keep personal religious faith distinct from the neutral study of religious phenomena, and to be unconcerned about questions of truth and value in relation to these phenomena, is 'hermeneutical and philosophical naiveté'. He is equally clear that theology cannot keep scientific studies in religions merely as auxiliary disciplines, or as a tool to its own purposes, allowing such approaches the tame and 'limited function of gathering and ordering the data' of world religions. For one thing it is unrealistic to imagine that religious studies will or can function in this neutral way. All students in religions have their presuppositions, their values, their commitments.

For the theologian the central problem is 'how to avoid cognitive relativism without falling into ethnocentrism' (*ibid*.: 14). Davis then outlines ways in which distinct attempts to resolve the dilemma have been made by the transcendentalist theologies of Karl Rahner and Bernard Lonergan; he finds that the attempt in both remains 'essentially Kantian, in so far as it follows Kant's procedure of going behind knowledge to its conditions of possibility and establishing those conditions as universal'. For this reason, every form of the transcendentalist move 'is vulnerable to Hegel's criticism of Kant's epistemology, namely that Kant has to presuppose the knowledge he is claiming to ground' (*ibid*.: 15-16). While Lonergan's stance is less obviously Kantian than Rahner's, for Lonergan 'the ultimate basis of our knowing is not necessity but contingent fact, and the fact is established, not prior to our engagement in knowing, but simultaneously with it' (*ibid*.: 16). Yet even Lonergan's assumption of an 'invariant dynamic structure of the (religious) subject' involves a 'cognitional theory', as expressed through a particular culture, historically conditioned. This transcendent method too, then, 'cannot serve as an invariant basis for cross-cultural communication'.

Davis sees a possible alternative in 'dialectical criticism' (not merely Hegelian) where any 'universal' is not presumed, but *lies ahead* in the process of investigation and interpretation. 'We begin where we are, within the particularity of our own tradition . . . We do not claim universality for it, but a reflective critique allows us to uncover the limits of that particularity . . . The universal can never be abstracted from the particular, because our conception and formulation of the universal elements are inevitably particular. Dialectic is, therefore, a continuous movement between the particular and the universal', through the critical uncovering of the meaning of particular traditions, we are

able to 'discern the universality of the meaning, value or truth embodied in it ...
perhaps helped by other traditions' (*ibid*.: 17).

Theology, then, 'begins with the particular and moves towards the universal'.
But 'the science of religion begins with the universal as embodied in a variety
of particulars and moves towards a better grasp of these particulars' (*ibid*.: 17).
This process involves three levels of reflection on religious experience: original,
scientific (theoretical) and critical. The first is bound up with religious life, for
'there is no religious life without religious reflection' on the meaning of such
life-experience. And this is the creative source of all religious reflection. Then
there is 'scientific' or systematic and theoretical reflection resulting in more
precise and technical formulations of original meaning, a systematic process
which employs a variety of methods. Critical reflection both responds to contextual challenges, and thus fulfils its 'foundational task', recognising that there
is both authentic and inauthentic elements in the tradition's life that need
corrective reflection..

Both theological reflection within a particular tradition and the science of
religion with its more universal, broad-based perspective, must engage in all
three levels of reflection. 'Original reflection' is part of the science of religion;
and theology needs to, and increasingly does, 'pass over' into other traditions
and thence back again to its own life-grounding. 'In doing so the theologian
is joining in the experience that lies at the origin of the modern science of
religion'. For the science of religion equally involves 'a shift in religious experience' to a systematic focus on the 'universal qualities' of the life of religions.
'Hence the science of religion is constantly converging to the different particular
theologies, such as a Christian theology, Muslim theology and so on, in an
effort not to lose the concrete substance in its pursuit of the universal'
(*ibid*.: 19).

At the theoretical level too science of religion and theology 'increasingly
coincide'. For, 'the transformation of original reflection into systematic
reflection, with its use of an explicit methodology and a technical vocabulary,
raises questions that cannot be handled within the closed context of a particular theology'. Then, on the other hand, 'it has also become clear that the
theoretical techniques developed by the science of religion in the West' have
their cultural assumptions and probably need modifying if they are to be
transposed to other cultural forms. Thus, 'an integral science of religion ...
must learn from the principles enshrined in the particular theologies, if it aims
at a true universality. In a sense there is a theological moment, that is a religious
and cultural particularity, in every version of the science of religion' (*ibid*.: 19).

We can recognise Davis' systematic reflection on these two disciplines, with their convergence and their need for further interaction, as of seminal importance. The crucial question, however, is clearly that of what kind of 'universality' is here looked for in the science of religion. Indeed, because the discussion of the principles of a science of religion is developed at such a theoretical level, without reference at all to actual 'universal' types, with critical and systematic reflection on how these types converge in actual traditions, it is not always possible to say precisely what Davis is intending. There also remains the usual problems of just how the different levels of 'reflection' are to be integrated, e.g. again how do behavioural studies relate to the ultimate science? But perhaps on this issue we can, as Davis does, only call in the aid of a 'critical dialectic'.

5. *John Hick*, a philosopher of religion working within a framework of clear theological commitment, albeit critical theological commitment, has frequently written of the need for a more inclusive theological attitude. A 'Copernican revolution' is needed in theological attitudes, which would be exemplified in the change from a Christo-centric to a Theo-centric perspective; for Hick sees the exclusive revelatory and soteriological claims traditionally made for the unique person and work of Christ as the major obstacle to positive Christian acceptance of religious pluralism. Hick has not worked out very explicitly how the two disciplines, theology and science of religion, interrelate, nor is his discussion theoretically as sophisticated as that of Davis for instance; but he does at least try to ground his proposals in what he sees as key themes in other religious traditions.

Hick has often expressed (e.g. 1973) general agreement with W.C. Smith's understanding of the religious process and in a recent essay (in Whaling 1984) in which the first part is an appreciation of Smith's work, he goes on to outline the following path by which Christians can 'move to an acceptance of religious pluralism'. World faiths, Hick contends, 'embody different perceptions and concepts of, and correspondingly different responses to the Real . . . and within each of them the transformation of human existence from self-centredness to Reality-centredness is manifestly taking place . . . Thus the great religious traditions are to be regarded as alternative soteriological "ways" along wich men and women can find salvation/liberation/enlightenment/fulfilment' (*ibid.*: 156). Hick recognises the problem (posed, e.g. by N. Smart) of assuming some privileged vantage-point from which to view the variety of religious paths and see them as parts of an ultimate Whole. This is a problem implicit in the

ancient Indian parable of the six blind men who feel various parts of an
elephant, and identify them as a tree, wall, rope, etc. On what basis can anyone
claim that while all religious traditions are partial, there is a unitive Reality
lying behind them? Hick replies that the claim for partial reality by each tradition is a hypothesis made on the grounds of the religious experience of many
humans, within their varied traditions, of 'a limitlessly great transcendent
Reality' (*ibid.*: 156-7). Assuming this as a genuine experience in one's own
tradition, we then have 'to take account of the fact that there are other great
streams of religious experience which take different forms . . .'. It is, of course,
possible to respond to this pluralism with an exclusive faith: only *our* faith
is truly in touch with reality. Or we can be inclusivist: all other realities are
somehow included in our own experience of reality, so that one's own faith
retains its normativity – perhaps in the form of saying that 'contact with
the Transcendent . . . occurs in its purest and most salvifically effective form
within one's own tradition'. As there is little empirical evidence for such claims,
we need to go beyond this kind of inclusivism 'to a pluralism which recognises
a variety of human contexts within which salvation/liberation takes place'
(*ibid.*: 158).

In attempting to respond to the kind of questions this stance evokes, Hick
moves boldly into the field of comparative religion. *First* – 'Each of the great
religious traditions affirms that as well as the social and natural world of our
ordinary human experience there is a limitlessly greater and higher Reality
beyond' (*ibid.*: 159). In this Ultimate is our final good; yet it is beyond 'our
earthly speech and thought'. Thus we need to leave aside our particular divine
names and speak of it as the 'Ultimate Reality'. This transcendental way also
involves the distinction between the infinite Real in itself and as experienced
and conceived on the finite level. Thus 'in Hindu thought' there is *nirguṇa* and
saguṇa Brahman, with similar distinction in Taoism and Mahāyāna Buddhism.
Secondly, we need to note the similar Kantian affirmation that has so influenced
recent epistemological thinking in numerous sciences: 'Our environment is not
reflected in our consciousness in a simple and straightforward way, just as it is,
independently of our perceiving it'. Rather, our senses select but a minute and
relevant part. Thus, 'its character as an environment within which we can learn
to behave appropriately can be called its meaning for us' (*ibid.*: 160). And
this all-important dimension of meaning functions at various levels in our
experience, up to 'the ultimate meaning' and integral perceptions of religion –
each of which will be 'in specific forms'. Hence our pluralist situation.

Two major types or 'dominant religious concepts' emerge: God, the Real as personal, and an Absolute, the Real as non-personal; and these 'dominate the entire range of the forms of religious experience' (*ibid.*: 161). Both are experiences only in specific religious forms and concrete situations of human history. The Real, as personal is named differently in each concrete tradition, each personal deity (e.g. Jahweh and Śiva) lives within 'different worlds of faith, partly creating and partly created by the features of different human cultures' (*ibid.*: 162). From the pluralist point of view, they are not rival 'claimants to be the one and only God, but rather two different concrete historical *personae* in terms of which the ultimate divine Reality is present and responded to by different large historical communities'. Similarly, the Absolute is 'schematized in actual religious experience to form the range of divine *impersonae* – Brahman, the Dharma, the Tao, Nirvana, Sunyata, and so on'. Although each is perceived as direct experience of the Ultimate, the pluralistic evidence implies that 'they are formed by different religious conceptualities which developed in interaction with different spiritual disciplines and methods of mediation' (*ibid.*: 163). In all these interpreted experiences 'the Real is experienced, not *an sich*, but in terms of the various non-personal images and concepts that have been generated at the interface between the Real and different patterns of human consciousness' (*ibid.*: 163). Hick then goes on to draw out the implications of this 'pluralist' perspective for the theological interpreters of each tradition.

Numerous kinds of response could be made to Hick's thesis. There is a commendable attempt to avoid an idealist disregard of the distinctive experiences of historical traditions (not found so clearly in some of Hick's earlier writings). Theoretically the particulars of each distinct tradition are given due weight. However, we have to ask if the personal-impersonal schema (though identifying two significant types) is not too simplistic an analysis of types of sacred Foci to serve as the basis for an inclusive theory of how each tradition, and its theologians, are to interact with other traditions. Is there an adequately grounded and reflective 'science of religion' underlying this theory? For example, is it not cutting away the historical ground for each tradition's feet to ask that they forget the particular names of their God (names so potent in manifesting the sacred transcendence) and in future speak only of 'the ultimate Reality'? As a very unrealistic demand it is also unhistorical. Then, the nirguna/ saguna distinction is assumed as typical of all Hindu thought, when in fact it is but one strand; many perceive God-with-qualities as the ultimate reality. And in impersonal systems, it is said, the Real is not experienced as such. As Hick himself implies, this would not be acceptable to many of those traditions.

Again, then, we must ask whether the implied integration of theology and science of religion is not based on assumptions about the nature of religion that have somehow taken an intuitive leap distinct from the investigations of the various sciences of religions; the historical grounding is not firm enough.

6. In an essay (a refined restatement of some of the points developed in *Beyond Existentialism and Zen*, 1979) in the same publication as that of Hick's above, *George Rupp* (who also begins with an appreciation of themes worked out by W.C. Smith on the nature and study of the religious life, particularly his concept of 'corporate critical self-consciousness') attempts more explicitly than Hick to point to the necessary convergence of theology and the history of religions. Such is the growing common ground between them, Rupp assumes, that any sharp distinction is now untenable. This development has implications for both, especially when we realise how recent is the clear differentiation between them. The notion that there should be a 'separate scholarly guild' of those intended to provide 'objective' information about religious traditions is an 'innovation of the Enlightenment' (*ibid.*: 170). Yet, we should also recognise how 'enormously productive' this separation has been for the history of religions both in the rich range of material information that has come from it, and in cross-cultural understanding. The distinction between theology and the scientific study of religions in fact cannot now be removed; but their interrelations do need to be reconsidered. We have to move 'beyond the mutual stereotypes that have become both inaccurate and unproductive' (*ibid.*: 171). The history of religion has been far too self-consciously concerned to *contrast* itself with the theological discipline. Theologians 'are suspect insofar as they combine the historical description of data with concern for the normative commitments of a particular religious community. In its sharpest form the contrast is, in short, between objective and value-free study on the one hand and ideologically determined apologetics on the other' (*ibid.*: 171). There is irony in the appeal of academics to this value-free stance, not only in view of the concern of students to ask very normative questions; the study of religion by its intrinsic nature 'should aspire to become a model of responsible attention to normative questions', questions that receive little attention in modern secular universities. There is also irony in the 'uncritical stance' towards the values of those committed to investigating religious traditions, when it is seen as improper to consider even the possibility of the truth of the religions being studied. Yet this 'disinterest in the normative claims of others is not altogether unlike the position of theologians' in the modern university climate (*ibid.*: 172).

Students in religion should be able to move on 'to participate self-consciously and self-critically in two or more traditions as parts of a more inclusive whole'. If this also moves on to re-examination of one's own tradition, the study will be 'fully cross-cultural'. For the theologian too, the task of representing one's own tradition will be increasingly bound up with understanding other traditions, as there is a growing sense of 'an increasingly shared history'. This situation 'poses a fundamental challenge to the whole enterprise of theology' (*ibid.*: 173).

Thus, while there is convergence, there is a clear distinction between the situations facing those two disciplines, The theologian's special task is 'to represent the tradition of a particular community so as to interpret and in turn also to shape the experience of its members, as there is growing self-conscious participation in the religious life of humanity as a whole' (*ibid.*: 173). While the tradition's images, ideas, rituals, etc. in their particularity 'decisively shape the experience that the theologian interprets', theologians today necessarily 'participate in multiple traditions even when they affirm their own community as fundamental to their particular identity'. In the task even of formulating 'the universalistic intention of theology and its analogues in non-theistic traditions' there is already 'a comparative dimension' (*ibid.*: 174). Although there was awareness of other traditions in the past, there is today greater recognition of the changes that have taken place within traditions, and thus of the 'systematic parallels in the development of historically only remotely related traditions' (*ibid.*: 174). While there may be still strong resistance to the implications of these developments, any appeal to dogmatic and other self-evident authority becomes 'relativised'. We cannot escape this 'comparative dimension' nor the awareness of the diversities within our own traditions.

Rupp then argues that religious traditions have in fact always 'made their claims on the basis of their illumining and influencing contemporary experience', rather than merely to 'some self-evident authority' (*ibid.*: 175). It is 'lived experience' that religions have been in interaction with, and this dimension of religious life is sharpened by 'the increased awareness of change within and parallels between communities. As a result, the question of criteria for adjudicating the relative adequacy of such claims becomes an inseparable issue for theology and its counterparts in non-theistic traditions' (*ibid.*: 176). Such criteria must focus attention on both descriptive and normative adequacy. Rupp goes on: 'Standards of descriptive adequacy thus seek to measure the extent and the depth to which the symbolic resources of a tradition have the capacity to incorporate into that frame of reference any and every datum of experience . . . a capacity which in turn requires the vitality to accommodate new insights not anticipated in the tradition itself' (*ibid*.: 177). Yet such 'descriptive adequacy' is incomplete 'apart from its normative dimension'. Thus questions regarding 'the hierarchy of values presupposed in religious positions', especially ultimate goals, are of crucial import in understanding and assessing those positions. When the latter is 'deliverance to a realm or an existence sharply distinguished from life in space and time', clearly an uneasy kind of interaction between 'lived experience' and the tradition's life results.

Nor will there be 'easy agreement' in the interaction of diverse traditions. Yet the continuing 'appropriation' of dimensions of life in other traditions is inevitable. There is to be 'a constructive process which requires critical engagement with the commitments of a particular community and comparative assessment of alternative positions in multiple traditions' (*ibid*.: 178). Rupp sees this process as 'both a crucial dimension of the comparative history of religion and a critically important resource for religious communities (and their theologians) worldwide' (*ibid*.: 180). The result will be continuing mutual correction, perhaps drawing out 'submerged tendencies', perhaps introducing changes of emphasis, though recognising that there are limits to 'the elasticity and adaptability of religious traditions' (*ibid*.: 179).

Although Rupp's style is quite distinct from that of Pannenberg whose position we discuss next, there does seem to be considerable indebtedness to Pannenberg's thought. As similar questions arise by way of response to both, we will leave a critique of Rupp for the moment.

7. By far the most thorough and to that extent significant theological attempt to present an integrated science of theology and religious studies is the 'theology of the history of religions' of *Wolfhart Pannenberg*, especially as elaborated in his *Theology and the Philosophy of Science* (1976). We can only pick up selected aspects of his thought here. In developing his theological method, Pannenberg begins from the assumption that its essential *object, theos,* provides the centre and unity of theological discourse. Theology begins and is shaped by this unity of vision provided by its central object. While there is clearly some convergence here with the position of Barth and others, Pannenberg is quite critical of Barth's procedure. And for Pannenberg, unlike Barth, to begin with a sense of God as *problematic* seems very appropriate to the mystery of his being that theology presupposes. God's otherness precludes any cognitive complacency; here is a fitting object for systematic, critical enquiry. God can be, for the theologian, no mere 'established fact' (as in Vedanta). We must,

moreover, presuppose the 'co-given' character of God, if theology is to be truly scientific: 'The reality of God is *co-given* to experience in other objects . . . is therefore accessible to theological reflection not directly but only indirectly' (1976: 301). One of the implications of this is that theology cannot be limited to a 'science of Christianity', not merely because this would preclude so much human experience that is equally valid ground for theological reflection, but because theology's proper object, God, cannot be identified with any particular empirical phenomenon such as Christianity. 'Theology can do justice to Christianity only if it is not a science of Christianity but a science of God. As a science of God its subject-matter is reality as a whole, even though as yet uncompleted whole of the semantic network of experience' (*ibid.*: 265). (At one point here we see some convergence with Barth's thought: theology is about God and his revelation, it is not the science of the Christian religion).

Pannenberg, however, does accept that there is direct religious experience of God, a sense of an immediate encounter with the reality of God. Human life in this way stands 'in constant relationship to the fundamental mystery of life, which transcends any immediate situation' (*ibid.*: 301). Yet, religious experience even of this immediate kind acquires 'intersubjective validity' only when it becomes 'relevant to men's understanding of the world and of themselves'; any experience of religious immediacy must be communicated in mediate terms significant of meaning to others. Theology has thus always to seek to communicate intersubjectively and 'must direct attention to this indirect way in which the divine reality is co-given', and co-given in *all* objects, though there can only be *anticipations* of a totality of meaning and of reality. '*The reality of God is always present only in subjective anticipations of the totality of reality, in models of the totality of meaning presupposed in all particular experience. These models, however, are historic, which means that they are subject to confirmation or refutation by subsequent experience*' (*ibid.*: 310).

Such a theological basis makes it possible, even inevitable, for Pannenberg then to incorporate all religions, and their varieties of experience, into his world-view. He notes that earlier Christian theologians were unable to draw out this intrinsic logic of a faith grounded in a particular history; when the knowledge of God is always in conjunction with 'experience of the world', we should be led to see essentially the historical nature of that divine self-revelation (*ibid.*: 311). Pannenberg then takes the next crucial step by pointing out that it is in *religious* experience, historically conditioned, that people have come to discover meaning for the totality of their life and cosmic life. He also makes the converse point: 'Wherever an understanding of reality as a whole is articulated' we may regard this as a 'religious' perspective. Thus, 'religions and their history are to be regarded as the locus of specific perceptions of particular self-revelations of the divine reality in human experience' (*ibid.*: 313). No longer can we distinguish between supernatural gospel and merely natural revelation. And this, Pannenberg contends, is the intrinsic logic of Christian faith in the revelation of God in Christ.

There are, in religions, many experiences anticipating a totality of meaning, yet each 'is always in some way or other connected with the historical religions . . . Theology as a science of God is therefore possible only as a science of religion, and not of the science of religion in general but of the historic religions' (*ibid.*: 314). This basis for theology provides the clue of what each distinct theology is: '*Christian* theology, on this view, would be the study of the *Christian* religion, the science of Christianity'. However, 'the investigation of religions, and therefore of Christianity, has a theological character only when it examines religions to see to what extent their traditions provide evidence for the self-communication of a divine reality' (*ibid.*: 315). Other approaches to religions are possible — psychological, sociological, even phenomenological — which compare and classify 'the manifestations of religious experience'. But none of these is the theology of religions which 'looks at the specifically religious intention in religions'.

Then, on the basis of just such a history-oriented view of revelation, a theological investigation of religions will also include a *testing* process: the investigation 'would examine how far the conception of reality as a whole expressed in the religious tradition in fact takes account of all the currently accessible aspects of reality and is therefore able to identify the God described and worshipped in the religion as the all-determining reality' (*ibid.*: 315). In this way Pannenberg applies an empirical criterion to religious experience: 'The traditional claims of a religion may therefore be regarded as hypotheses to be tested by the full range of currently accessible experience. They are to be judged by their ability to integrate the complexity of modern experience into the religion' (*ibid.*: 315). This criterion is then slightly modified: there is to be examination of 'the different ways in which religions have been able to take account of the experience of reality to which their adherents have been exposed and the ability of the different traditions to cope with the experiential situation of mankind today' (*ibid.*: 316).

Pannenberg concludes by affirming his belief that theology is able on this basis to classify religions according to levels of 'anticipatory grasp of reality'.

Theology will 'then be able to meet these questions with hypotheses which will take account of the different statuses of the religions, of the superiority of the current state of one religion's tradition over that of others' (*ibid.*). He sees this testing of religions for their 'power to illuminate reality' as 'no more than the systematic and conscious performance of what actually happens in the history of every religious tradition when the gods of a religion proved themselves in the sight of the members of the religious group to be capable of mighty acts or not' (*ibid.*: 364).

And Pannenberg regards this systematic theological procedure outlined above, which includes comparative theology, as the only discipline by which to make the most significant theme of religion, i.e. 'the communication of divine reality', the object of truly scientific investigation. Any other scientific approach can only be an 'auxilary discipline of a genuine science of religion' (*ibid.*: 365). He asserts that while this approach will necessarily be *critical,* in the sense of examining the relative reality of traditions, it 'does not produce an interpretation of religions on the basis of a previous religious position. It is therefore distinct from the attempts of a *dogmatic* theology of religions which have been made in the recent past particularly by Catholic theologians', Rahner for example. While Schlette is applauded for testing the reality of religions 'by the standard of their own understanding of the divine reality', he is criticised for still trying 'to fit religion into an existing Christian framework' and for still keeping the science of religion (seen as having a neutral attitude towards the question of truth) distinct from a theology of religions; Schlette sees the latter as a 'specialist area of theologico-dogmatic systematics' (*ibid.*).

Pannenberg, on the other hand, denies that his own approach is 'anything like an *interpretatio christiana* of non-Christian religions assumed in advance in accordance with an existing position'. He specifically rejects Gensichen's criticism that his view of the history of religion is 'based on premises specific to Christian theology' (*ibid.*: 366). The fact is, however, that Pannenberg's premises regarding the 'divine reality', regarding its necessarily self-revealing character, its revelation through historical situations, the significance and validity of contemporary empirical or existential experience, just do not fit the understanding of reality found in some religious traditions in the same way they do others, including of course the Christian faith. With criteria so clearly weighted in favour of theistic and 'historical' traditions, it is hardly then possible to argue that we must judge religions only by the standard of their own self-understanding. We have to ask a similar question of Rupp's position outlined above: when there are such normative presuppositions in the criteria for 'adequacy', does this not place certain religions immediately at a disadvantage? And who is to select from the vast range of 'contemporary human experience of the world' those existential situations – many of which are mutually contradictory – by which to provide criteria of adequacy in evaluating religions?

It is symptomatic that Pannenberg already presumes the advantage of Judeo-Christian historical faith as having been able to adjust and reinterpret itself in the face of continuing changes in history, while 'mythical' religions, based on some past golden age, have been washed away, unable to cope with such changes. He writes thus mainly of Mediterranean religions, no doubt that historically speaking did prove unable to survive in any institutional form. But was it necessarily their inability to adapt that was the main cause of their disappearance? There is little evidence that all myth-bound religious traditions of India, for example, are being fatally weakened by the changes of modern history. The evidence, for example, of substantial numbers of westerners turning to such myth-bound faiths for any sense of meaning and reality would surely point in the other direction. And the apologists of these religions would claim that it is 'dogmatic' and revelation-bound faiths that are less flexible and that will prove unable to survive.

This is just one indication of an inadequate grounding in the history of religions in Pannenberg's theological approach (as in the case of others reviewed above) for all its considerable appeal at many points. It is certainly an outstanding theological attempt to struggle systematically with the fact of other faiths, and to analyse the implicit structures of the theological process. Pannenberg clearly wishes to see, eventually – and his whole perspective is based on faith in an anticipatory process, in the course of which there is need for numerous temporary compromises – a single discipline, a theology of the science of religion. And this is a very appealing vision. He does allow within this unified systematic scheme considerable room on the one hand for continuation of distinct theologies, and on the other hand for the continuation of various scientific studies in religions. However, these latter are to function merely as 'auxiliary disciplines', providing necessary data to the theology of science of religion. Likewise, each religion's theology is to function at a subordinate level in the integral theological task. Pannenberg's 'critical theology of the history of religions', is not *merely* a Christian theological interpretation of religions and their theologies; but neither is it a synthesis in which all can interact on equal terms. The 'critical' perspective is clearly not an impartial one on the basis of which mutual correction can take place.

By way of conclusion we might concede that it is necessary:

a) to develop what might be called a 'theological science of religion' in some ways analogous to other approaches to religious studies (such as the sociological science of religion, etc.). In other words this would be a comparative theology, not grounded in any particular theology, but concerned to draw out common theological patterns from varied sources, as well as to clarify certain distinctive types. This, however, is not primary theology.

b) We should expect that various theologies, grounded primarily in one or other religious tradition, will more systematically incorporate symbolic imagery, conceptual material, ethical and other practical material into their theological reflcection, material appropriated from other traditions.

c) Yet, to attempt a thorough synthesis of these two basic approaches into one 'theology of history of religions' or a 'theology beyond theologies', as *the* way of theologising does not seem historically realistic or theologically viable. Much closer convergence is possible, but in the end it needs to be either a theology that appropriates history of religions material, or history of religions that takes theology more seriously. When a 'theology beyond theologies' does emerge, we have what is either another newly emergent theology (a theology *among* theologies) or a metaphysical system which is so historically and religiously 'ungrounded' as not to be 'theology' at all. (A third possibility is that it is a form of comparative theology, i.e. a science of religion, as mentioned above).

It is thus difficult to envisage the systematic science of religion and the systematic theological process of any religious tradition as converging to the extent of becoming virtually identical. That far more interaction and mutual dependence is called for than has so far been recognised either by theologians or 'religionists' has to be conceded. But the methodological confusion arising from the two becoming an integral science would be as problematic as the methodological inadequacy when theologies and religions (or sciences of religions) are polarised. The task of moving towards greater integration of the various sciences (including perhaps the 'theological science of religion') and towards developing an inclusive *comparative science of religion* is imperative; but it is a highly complex task to be engaged in with great systematic vision and with rigorous attention to historical and empirical data. It is the movement from the latter to an integral interpretation (and back again) that is, however, methodologically crucial to each of the sciences of religion, as well as to theology.

11

The Contribution of Religion
to the Theological Task

1. In a period of human history, such as the present century, characterised by rapid and seemingly radical changes both in the outer and inner structuring of human existence — i.e. socio-cultural consciousness as well as socio-political institutions — there are peculiar challenges posed for religious traditions and especially for their meaning-interpreters, their theologians. In particular there is the question of an appropriate response, or responses, to be made to the emerging sense of a global human consciousness. Talk of a 'global consciousness' may sound too metaphysically interpretive, reflecting the perceptions only of an elite few; for contemporary history also makes it clear that separatist tendencies of various kinds — ethnic, linguistic, cultural/religious, economic, political — are increasing too. Yet we can certainly speak of a new human awareness, especially among the increasingly urbanised peoples of the world, of the *plurality of cultural traditions and religious world-views*. Diverse religious traditions, with their distinct views of reality, and their distinct life-values, have been increasingly brought into inter-penetrative social situations. This new situation elicits varied responses. For some, such pluralism is wholly threatening and must be resisted; for others (probably less in number, but a highly significant response nevertheless) the pluralism provides a liberating sense of inclusive human consciousness bringing what they feel even to be a newly inclusive religious experience. To speak of a radical 'Copernican revolution' (Hick 1973; cf. Lipner 1977) having taken place at the level of religious consciousness may be over-stating the case. Indeed, it could be argued that the contemporary situation of cultural interaction does not in *essence* change the conceptual task in any tradition, but that it has merely provided traditions with more easily available resources for their task of interpreting visionary meaning in response to changing human contexts. Perhaps there will also be a newly perceived urgency in this task. There is now the possibility of deeper levels of conceptual interaction between vision and context, which makes the task of visionary interpretation all the more challenging and unavoidable.

As we noted above, it is clear that the theologian of any tradition *can* respond to the close proximity of other religious traditions in any of a number of different ways. Frequently there will be reflection merely on the bare fact that other faiths do exist. Much Christian 'theology of religions' over the years has functioned at this level − recognising that the Christian faith is not the only world religion, and usually arguing that there must be ultimately either conquest of (even if 'conquest' at the conceptual level only) or coexistence with these other world-faiths. Then even when the need for interaction of faiths at a dialogical level has theoretically been proposed, it is very rare to find Christian theologians (indeed, theologians of any faith) who have either responded at a professionally competent level to the findings of scholars in the field of religions, or who have personally struggled to acquaint themselves with original texts and other resources from traditions which might be seen as of special significance for reflection within their own tradition. In other words, few theologians have struggled sufficiently to become competently informed in more than one tradition. Perhaps there is a justified diffidence; how can there be meaningful or even fair response to a religious system of which so much less is known in comparison to the extensive and rigorous grounding expected in one's own tradition in order to be accepted as an interpreter? It would have been good if all theologians and philosophers of religion had been at least as cautious as this before commenting on other religions; comparative comment and evaluation has so often been based on inadequate understanding. Yet this proper need for caution merely accentuates the need for greater commitment to, more adequate exposure to and study of religious traditions to which some kind of theological response is so inevitable. And, of course, in recent years there are greatly increased opportunities for more thorough and more authentic understanding, both through the publications of scriptures and writings on the life and faith of all the great world religions, as well as through more personal acquaintance.

As an aside we might note the unfortunately increasing pressure on scholars in all fields, as well as in various branches of religious and theological studies, to specialise strictly in their one discipline; few are able to give time and energy to attaining even minimal competence in other areas of knowledge outside this narrow field. Yet only thus can they incorporate resources from other appropriate fields. Surely there is some other alternative than to be either a theological dilettante in religions, superficially skimming here and there, or to remain a reputable specialist in one narrow field of study. Indeed, in many branches of learning as well as in the area of religions/theology, there is increased need for inter-disciplinary and comparative approaches as a means to enriching human understanding and to making it more relational and integrated. The theologian of a tradition, then, seeking to respond appropriately to other faiths, needs to acquire at least a sufficiently authentic understanding of those traditions to ensure genuine reflective interaction between the visionary centre of the one and the visionary centre of others as expressed in their varied phenomena. The systematic theologian will no doubt have special concern to understand and respond appropriately to the systematised *conceptual* resources of the other faith(s); but the conceptual systems alone cannot be the only point of interaction, or the interaction will remain merely at a level of cerebral comparison with little appropriation of resources that can lead to a revisioning within the tradition. There is the need, therefore, to respond to and reflect upon the deeper imagery, grounded in which the theologians of the other faiths have built up their conceptual systems. We might, for example, think of such primal imagery as light, water, earth, tree, body, wheel and such basic symbolism that will generally be found in common in numerous traditions; in Chapter Three we noted how such interactive reflection can take place at the level of theological art. By reflecting on what roles these images have in other faiths, and how they are responded to and interpreted in the conceptual systems, we might expect that ways will open up to appropriate aspects of such imagery into one's own modes of interpretation. Despite difficulties in finding the key to Raimundo Panikkar's hermeneutical (or historical) stance, it is clear that much of his writing is of this creatively interpenetrative kind; more theologically accessible is the response to Islam in the work of Kenneth Cragg. It is at this level of theological reflection that authentic, appropriating interpenetration can take place. And it is only with this inter-faith reflective level of theologising that we can avoid either ungrounded theosophical syncretism, or merely constructing another 'theology of religions', in which the thought, faith and life of the other tradition is interpreted solely in terms of one's own doctrinal perspective.

But does not every theologian's 'response to and appropriation of' possible resources in other traditions necessarily have this pre-shaped, pre-determined approach if a theologian is to remain faithful to his/her tradition's central vision? How else can there be the perception of coherent meaning, or an integrated theological perspective? The answer is that while every theologian's perspective *is* shaped by a faith-commitment and this does provide an integrated grounding from which to systematise consistently — and this will involve the selecting and interpreting of appropriate material in the re-visioning process — the other tradition can also come to function at that visionary level in the theologian's consciousness, enhancing, filling out, providing new directions for the tradition's own central perceptions. And there is also the possibility — confirmed by the evidence of studies in other religions by some theologians in the past — that the theologian's understanding and exposition of the other tradition may be accepted by representatives of that other tradition as an authentic contribution to interpretation of their faith. No doubt in turn the particular shaping and interpreting done by the 'other' theologian will provide new insight and give new direction to the tradition he/she thus interprets; and so the interpenetration proceeds.

There seems little doubt that it is *not fear of incompetence* in another tradition that has prevented theologians from this kind of mutual appropriation as part of their contextual interaction, but fear of debilitating *relativism* or of inauthentic *syncretism*. There is in general far less diffidence about responding to those contemporary dimensions of human experience *other* than religious. The quip by Monsignor Ronald Knox that 'Comparative Religions makes one comparatively religious' still expresses a fairly general theological attitude. Even within the history of Comparative Religions itself we can see how scholars from the Christian tradition were ill at ease with the thought of their religion being merely 'comparative'. One of the reasons for the loss of favour of the term itself (i.e. 'Comparative Religion') was the tendency in earlier forms of the discipline to try to establish, within the framework of evolutionary theory, that gradual revelation has taken place from primitive forms up to the fullest revelation of the divine; and Christian exponents of this revelationary ladder saw its culminating step in their own religion. Similar is the idea that Christianity is the 'fulfilment' of all other religions, or that it is the 'Crown of Hinduism', as Farquhar for example, put it (Sharpe 1975: 151-4).

Every religious tradition has, in fact, to come to terms with its necessarily 'relative' status, even though it will invariably also have the conviction of being in touch with *absolute* reality, as we noted in Chapter Two. This need to come to terms with the relative character of one's religious tradition *may* be hastened by the findings of Comparative Religions, but should be seen as due to more basic factors in the religious life and especially in the theological process. In the first place it is precisely the *transcendent* character of the revelatory vision at the centre of the tradition that will typically lead to the recognition that the full reality of this vision lies still beyond what has been expressed. Thus there is a dialectic of the absolute and relative *intrinsic* to religious life and expression, explicitly so in many traditions. Further, the intrinsic need for the meaning of the transcendent vision to be interpreted in interaction with ever-changing circumstances of historical contexts implies necessarily a sense of the relative character of the tradition, as it unfolds in human history.

Ernst Troeltsch was one of the first Christian theologians to struggle with the question of how we can have an absolute commitment to the truth of our tradition's vision and at the same time recognise the fact of its *historical relativity*. Earlier attempts (in *The Absoluteness of Christianity*, 1972 edit.) to develop a theology of history had led him to conclude (Cf. *The Place of Christianity Among the World Religions*, in Hick and Hebblethwaite, 1980; 11-31) that while there are a number of faiths naively claiming absolute validity, Christianity has the most valid claim to this, for Christian theology is intrinsically more universal. This means, 'we simply leave aside the question of the measure of validity possessed by the other religions' (*op. cit.* 22). Further study of the actual character of the other great faiths — itself a significant cause for change in theory — convinced Troeltsch 'more and more that their naive claims to absolute validity are also genuinely such' (*ibid.*: 23). We need, though, 'to recognise that they are expressions of the religious consciousness corresponding to certain definite types of culture' (*ibid.*: 27). There is a continuing process of religious development, therefore, and each can contribute to the other while in this stage between divine Source and perfect Goal. Yet Troeltsch contended firmly that merely by acknowledging the *historicity* of our particular sense of what is the truth we need not weaken the conviction that it is fully true, nor need we weaken our commitment to it as the truth. There will still be a creative rivalry, 'but it must be a rivalry for the attainment of interior purity and clearness of vision' (*ibid.*: 31).

To return to the specific context of a *plurality* of religious traditions: rather than see the necessarily relative status of one's tradition as something to be deplored, or ignored, or in some way resisted, each religion, or each theology which is concerned with the communication of the meaning of its central perception of reality should be able to welcome the existence of other religious traditions, and therefore welcome the contribution of religious studies, as necessary to *its own self-understanding*, and to the effectiveness of its *self-communication*. For theology cannot function reflectively and contextually in an isolated state of independence from other religious traditions and ignorant of the findings of religious studies. Theology, then, is dependent upon religious studies for greater understanding of other traditions, understanding of the manifold dimensions of their life. However serious a theologian of one tradition may be in his/her intention to understand other faiths, especially those faiths that in various ways impinge upon his or her own tradition, appropriation of the fruits of specialist study is the only possible way by which such wider understanding becomes possible. This is, of course, not only the case for theologians, but for historians of religions and others too. The sociologist of religion cannot normally be expected to be an expert in religious texts: the scholar in Indian philosophical systems or in Islamic history may not be able to do *original* anthropological work in the tribal traditions, though in both these fields knowledge of primal and folk traditions contribute a great deal, and, as was argued earlier, in all fields more *integrated* knowledge of religious and cultural life is desirable. With no great Herculean effort it is *possible* for those who are specialist in particular areas to become acquainted with the major findings of scholars in other areas.

Similarly, it is possible for the *theologian* to attain at least sufficient understanding of *some* other traditions to be able to respond theologically. Diverse levels of understanding are present in each tradition; authentic 'theological' understanding, therefore, is not a matter of knowledge of every textual, historical and cultic detail of a tradition, but some *insight*, grounded in at least adequate acquaintance with the tradition as a whole, insight into the key perceptions of reality that give integration to the concerned tradition. We may add that the theologian of another tradition will naturally have particular interest in the conceptual interpretations of the central imagery of the other faith. Thus this 'theological' understanding will need to be somewhat different from the primal intuitive apprehension of a believer or participant, whose conceptual knowledge may in fact be minimal. The theologian will also need, of course, more than an intuitive vision even in the case of his or her own faith, if there is to be interpretation and communication of meaning. But there should be informed ability to respond to the other faith's imagery and theology at the same conceptual level — even if not with precisely the same inner authenticity and commitment — as there is reflection on the imagery of his/her own tradition.

2. So far we have still not probed deeply enough the issue of why this interfaith appropriation is necessary at all to theology's *functioning as theology*. In the *first* place it is of special significance that theology is typically grounded in a *religious* tradition. The political ideologies, the humanist philosophies, and scientific world-views of our time are all 'symbol-systems' too, and are therefore important constituents in the poly-symbolic context within which each theologian now seeks to interpret his or her tradition; but those symbol-

systems which explicitly point to a sacred and transcendent Focus, with an accompanying fertile matrix of meaning, and with all manner of phenomena analogous to those in one's own tradition, surely call for theological reflection and interaction in a distinctive, more expectant way? It is those focal points of sacral resonance, in inter-religious situations, where the theologian sees evidence of experience of transcendence strangely analogous to his own, that should provoke his anticipation more than any other kinds of common human experience. The fact is, though, that this kind of expectancy has *not* been part of the theological attitude within a majority of religious traditions, and perhaps within the western Christian theological tradition in particular, until quite recently. In this matter, therefore, while we need not see inter-religious dialogue and a 'creative hermeneutic' as the primary task of 'religionists', we can expect that they will help in pointing theologians to the sensitivity and understanding they need in order to be more competent and effective theologians.

Then, *secondly*, when a theologian is able to respond to and reflect upon the central imagery and perceptual world of another tradition, or other traditions, it may well be possible to gain *clearer visionary perception* within one's own tradition; the perception will be enhanced (rather than changed into some other type of vision) when the greater clarity is in ways implicitly appropriate to the central vision of one's own tradition, so that the new dimensions of understanding this affords merely serve to create sensitivity and fuller appreciation of the same visionary matrix. Numerous religionists with a theological interest, such as Van der Leeuw, Wach and W.C. Smith, have spoken of the 'fuller vision', or the 'new understanding of their own faith', that has resulted from the study of other religions. It is not difficult to see, for example, that for a generation of Christians that by and large has lost on the one hand the sense of the glorious attributes of the God of large portions of their own scriptures, exposure to Islamic faith is a salutary experience. Or, where Christian spirituality appears to have lost an all-integrating sense of God-consciousness, a 'fuller vision' of what the New Testament can mean by such texts as 'Christ in me' may well be recaptured by exposure to types of Indian religious experience. Needless to say this is not all a one-way movement, as is made clear for example by the influence of Christian faith on Indian religious perceptions in the past 150 years from the Brahmo Samaj onwards, and by the influence of Islamic attitudes earlier, especially the Sufi movement on some sections of Hinduism.

Thirdly, exposure to other faiths can help towards a more clear understanding of the *distinctive* features of one's own faith, as well as clearer insight into its innate structures — how doctrines, symbols, ethics, and other aspects of the tradition all relate to each other. The fervent devotee of the adorable otherness of God, when confronted with a religion committed primarily to inner enlightenment and inner purification, as in non-dualist Vedanta, or the Buddhism of the Elders, or Jainism, will probably see with a new and perhaps exhilarating clarity the distinctive features of his or her own faith. Or a religious system in which the individual works out his own destiny solely by his own efforts, as in those Indian systems in which the doctrine of karma is given absolute priority, will be more clearly aware of what it is he believes in when seen in juxtaposition to a system in which transcendent divine grace is taken to be the only ultimate means for any personal destiny to be satisfactorily realised.

This kind of juxtaposed contrast, however, is not the only way exposure increases self-understanding. When properly pursued the comparative method greatly increases sensitivity to what is happening in every aspect of one's religious life. Reflective analysis is as much part of theology as is the immediacy that accompanies the theologian's basic commitment. It is when the theologian looks again at central phenomena in the religious life in which his/her theology is to be grounded, having explored in some depth the inner functioning of another faith, that theological analysis of one's own faith becomes more aware of its inner dynamics, thus more *religiously* informed. Theology then *can be* both more sensitive to the interaction of the tradition's constituent symbols and doctrinal forms, and for this reason more conceptually precise, more authentically grounded in the life of the tradition.

The *doctrine of grace* in different religious contexts can serve by way of illustration: a theologian whose tradition provides a particular setting for this doctrine can gain insight into its intrinsic character by looking at the same kind of doctrine expounded in a quite different setting. It might be thought, for example, that the doctrine of *karma* (which strictly speaking makes the individual's actions determine his destiny, there being no identifiable origin to the action-consequence process) could relate to a doctrine of divine grace only by way of contrast. In some Hindu theistic systems, however, both doctrines are accepted and interact with each other — even if one or the other has to take on a priority role. In the Indian religious system as a whole *karma* is considerably more prevalent than grace. Yet, in the theistic 'synthesis', at least in some forms of it, divine grace determines the role taken by and the meaning given to the doctrine of *karma*, rather than the reverse. It is the gracious qualities of God that prevail over the causal chain. This kind of investigation into the ways in which divine grace operates — and in particular how it first cooperates with and then dominates doctrines that would apparently neutralise it — such investigation must surely give the theologian of a grace-grounded system valuable insight into the innate character of a concept to which the tradition is committed. The extent to which this new understanding might change style of theological expression is the question I take up in the following points.

Fourthly, increased understanding of other faiths can help to ensure that *theologians do justice to the range of conceptual dimensions implicit in their own faith.* Theology may be the conceptual articulation of a core-vision, but there are no guarantees that the tradition's theologians will be able fully to explicate the originating vision; all manner of socio-cultural contingencies operate here. One tradition, deservedly or not, may throw up far more capable theologians than another tradition. There may, of course, be some kind of correspondence between types of religious core-visions and the conceptual competence of theologians, but this does not seem confirmed by the evidence.

Moreover, the hermeneutical process is delicately complex, so that at any stage in a system's development a new emphasis, quite a legitimate change of outlook perhaps, can suddenly alter the course of that development and in so doing obscure some other authentic facet of the tradition. Or perhaps a doctrinal issue latent in the vision may lie unrecognised and unexpressed until some much later stage in the hermeneutical process. In other words, it is quite possible for theologians to miss the point of their tradition's vision, or at least to miss important secondary points. In this case it is certainly possible for exposure to another tradition to be the means by which the obscured dimension might be discovered and brought to light.

In principle, then, this theological appropriation is not a matter of disloyalty to tradition, or of spurious syncretism, for the theologian can expect to remain committed to the primal religious vision of the heritage. Doubtless there is always the possibility of reading meaning *into* one's tradition and texts rather than drawing out implicit meanings that have been stimulated by cross-cultural contact. Anyone can in theory read into one's religion what has actually been taken from another source altogether and then claim legitimation for it on the basis of some peripheral aspect of the tradition, perhaps an obscure proof-text. In one sense it could be argued that all theological development results from exposure to and interaction with conceptual sources *other* than the tradition and its core-vision in itself. In spite of Karl Barth, the creative periods in the history of Christian theology seem to prove this point. But the borrowed conceptual insights can only contribute authentically to the tradition, or persist within that tradition as acceptable forms of expression for the community as a whole, if those insights are conceptually coherent with the core-faith originating the whole theologising process. However, conceptual coherence still allows room for a broad range of influence by, and even borrowing from, other traditions.

Fifthly, greater understanding of other religious traditions will show, in spite of the need to note each one's integrity, that there is both *convergence of religious practices*, and some practices by which the liturgical, practical and ethical life of one's tradition *could be enriched*. Precisely which practices are appropriable and how this is to be done is a matter for the concerned 'theologians'. At the ethical level we may note how the Southern Baptist preacher, Martin Luther King, found aspects of the Hindu Mahatma Gandhi's 'passive resistance' eminently appropriate for the civil rights campaign of which he was a leader. *Satyagraha* involved some very peculiarly Hindu concepts of what 'truth' is and how it is to be 'grasped', the doctrine of 'non-injury to life', and so on. These, in turn, had been appropriated by Hinduism from the Jaina (perhaps also Buddhist) tradition. In the process of appropriation they do, of course, become modified in their conceptual undergirding; but that makes them no less appropriable.

As a religious meditative discipline we might take the practice of *Yoga* again by way of illustration. Today, both East and West, yogic exercises are not only practiced for explicitly religious reasons, but also as a means to physical and mental health. This 'secular' extension of what was in origin a more specifically 'religious' and cultic activity may well be quite legitimate and beneficial. Even within the religious milieu of earlier India, yoga was an important discipline in a remarkably wide range of traditions as we have seen. In atheistic Jainism and Sāmkhya, various forms of Buddhism, non-dualist Vedānta, as well as in various vigorously theistic sects, yoga was practiced as the means by which the seeker after release (variously conceived) either achieved the first stage of his pilgrimage, or even by which it was completed. Yoga was, in other words, strangely adaptable to a variety of religious goals.

Yoga was never simply 'the means by which the soul is yoked to God', as is the usual modern theological interpetation. Even so, there seems to be sufficient justification for the attempt of a few pastoral theologians in the Christian faith to incorporate the yogic discipline into their tradition (e.g. Déchanet 1974; De Mello 1978). The loss for many of a regular personal discipline, of the practice of contemplation, of spiritual techniques accompanying a commitment to self-denial – these and other features of contemporary Christianity suggest that the imaginative use of yoga may be precisely what is needed to recover aspects of the tradition now somewhat obscured.

Sixthly, exposure to and understanding of other religious systems can help in the theological task of *coherently articulating and communicating faith*. Whatever need there may be for formulating some kind of analogical relationship between the 'religious' world (and its vocabulary) and the 'non-sacral' world, there seems little justification for the attempt of some theologians to take non-sacral experience as the primary source for their theological concepts and the only communicable form of the expression of these concepts. To argue even for the inherent lack of cognitive meaning in religious terms looks rather like a clear declaration of intent to commit theological suicide. If the aim is to eliminate all theologising, that is another, though equally misguided, matter.

If theologians could learn to explore the rich conceptual mines of other religious systems they would frequently discover unexpected seams of valuable theological material often quite unprospected and untapped outside the traditions concerned. But to expect that the conceptual systems of other faiths, whether ancient or modern, will provide ready-made solutions to present-day theological problems, Christian or otherwise, would be a ridiculously superficial hope. That they may provide important clues and valuable insights into ways of thinking and speaking about transcendent perceptions of reality, clues and insights that are viable in other religious systems, given the appropriate conditions, is not precluded merely because they emerged in other and distinct religious contexts. The inner coherence of each system does not necessarily rule out the kind of conceptual convergence that I have been assuming (but cf. Baillie 1928; Kraemer 1938, 1956). Our fear of crude syncretism should not be allowed to inhibit completely our attempts at conceptual exploration.

It is in the classical Indian theological systems in particular that we find the most sustained and sophisticated discussion of many of the questions disturbing theologians today, even if the issues are often put in rather different form. When it is the *coherence* of theology that is at stake, the central issues all revolve around the problem of religious epistemology, in particular how can we know and speak about that which is transcendent to the empirical world at which level we normally cognise and converse. Of what kind is our knowledge of 'God'? The sheer energy with which Indian theologians engaged in discussion of such epistemological issues, and the unexpected range of positions they defended and opposed, apart from the impressive force of their ability to argue a position coherently, is as much in support of the suggestion that theologians of all faiths would profit by exposure to these discussions as is the fact of their peculiarly *religious* perceptiveness.

Undeniably, theology is able to lose its way, in the sense of taking an interpretive turn that conceptually, and maybe in the way it works out its *ethical* stance, is aberrative; of this some of the fringe developments in the history of Christian theologies is surely sufficient proof. It is this loss of essential grounding and central faith that so many Christian theologians become apprehensive about when it is suggested that theology must interact positively with the faiths of others. In reality, for all the sharp polemics against alien faiths in various (but not all) periods of the Jewish/Christian past, with new missionary converts often having been led to take an exaggerated alienating stance in relation to their cultural environment, at the level even of primal perception there has often been a process of appropriation, though perhaps unconscious. We find such appropriation even in what was seemingly such an exclusive cult as ancient Israel's Yahwehism, enabling this cult to be more cosmically inclusive for example (cf. Ficker 1983). Clearly in the development of Christian faith and doctrine from the first century onwards there is a similar process of appropriation that brought about far richer articulation of the meaning of the Christ as Saviour of the World than would have been possible if the Christian community had remained an exclusively messianic cult.

3. Then, there is another level of theological reflection at which there can be beneficial appropriation of the fruits of religious studies. For theology to understand more clearly its theological role, its placing within the structures of a religious tradition, or the dynamics of the theological process, the *comparative perspective* in particular can contribute much; placing theology *typologically* can help in understanding what theology is to be if it is to fulfil its role as a typical religious phenomenon. The comparative perspective thus can act in a normative way, providing a corrective role, even if this will need to be largely a matter of self-correction.

While there is little difficulty in finding some examples of theological self-correction that is at least in part a result of the impact of religious studies in this century, in general this has been far less than we might have expected or hoped for. The recent emphasis in Christian theology on the 'analogical imagination' (Tracy 1981) as both the mode and locus of theological endeavour, is no doubt to some extent the result of wider studies in religions. There is among theologians of this kind a post-liberal concern to be grounded in and adequately to respond to the mythic/symbolic matrix of their tradition. Tracy's continual reference to this grounding as the 'classical text' is unfortunately limiting, and presumably reflects his concern to take sufficient account of the hermeneutical thought of Gadamer and Riceour, for whom it invariably seems to be the written text that is the other creative pole with which 'context' is to interact.

We could also, no doubt, identify a number of theologians whose position has been influenced perhaps by the transcendentalist interpretation of religion by F. Heiler, or by the personalist dialogical approach of W.C. Smith, or by some of the central emphases in the archetypal morphological interpretation of M. Eliade. In general, however, strangely and ironically, theological attitudes in the past 40 years or so have not been influenced so much by phenomenological and post-phenomenological understanding(s) of the religious life, but rather by the theories and findings of the behavioural sciences and by associated philosophies, sometimes surprisingly taken as normative*.While at an earlier stage it was chiefly psychological theory that dominated theology, more recently it is anthropology and sociology, especially as found in the service of radical ideology. In much liberationist-related theology, for example, it is specifically Marxist theory that is presumed, possibly in modified form, as the starting-point from which to reflect on the significance of the Christian faith. In this case again it is not studies in religion (i.e. social/anthropological) that

---

*For example, George Lindbeck, in a highly acclaimed account of the nature of doctrine (Lindbeck 1984) rejects either a cognitive (propositional) or an experiential-expressive approach, as well as a combination of these approaches, and finds the conceptual categories provided by a 'cultural-linguistic' perspective as the only convincing way of understanding the function of doctrine within a tradition, as each tradition is challenged by today's ecumenical and pluralistic cultural situation. He distinguishes the function of doctrine rather sharply from theology in general (perhaps rather too sharply), and argues that doctrine should be taken as having merely a 'regulative' force in relation to the faith found plausible by a community in a given cultural context. While there is much to agree with in Lindbeck's account of the structure of religious sytems, the integral link between the faith that shapes plausible patterns of doctrine and the focal vision embodied in the doctrinal dimension of the ecclesial grounding of a religious system does not seem to have been given the key role it surely must have.

have prompted the awareness that the societal dimension is extraordinarily potent in shaping theological commitments; it is rather the powerful impact of Marxist theory, which tends to devalue the cultural-religious dimension in relation to socio-economic realities. With this view of the theological task we would not expect that fuller understanding of religious phenomena will be a way to 'self-correction' in theology, for religion itself is seen usually as a corrupting factor, as part of the oppressive structures. Thus gospel/faith and tradition/religion are set over against each other; to this extent liberation theology and the Barthian position are at one. And yet, further studies in religious/social structures *can* surely perform a 'corrective' role. For, given a less inflexible ideological stance, it might be possible through further anthropological research to see the inalienable religion cultural dimension of being truly human, and the potential for social transcendence and even transformation in the mythic-ritual process. Given this theoretical framework, there would obviously be a correspondingly different role seen also for the theologian in elucidating the liberating meaning of the central vision perceived at the heart of this process. For the ethical force of the liberation motif as such, indeed the force of Marxist analysis of liberation needs, can hardly be ignored by any theologian today.

Thus, as a result of religious studies from the side of the behavioural sciences as well as a typological classifying of theology, i.e. as a typical kind of phenomenon within religous traditions (being 'type-cast' as it were), it is certainly possible to set out general *criteria* by which at least to assess how typical a given theological stance is. It would even seem feasible thus to *evaluate* whether such a system is actually functioning as theology or not, though a number of Christian theologians would no doubt argue that this reduces the distinctive task of Christian theology to a general common (phenomenological) denominator. In the final analysis of course the effectiveness of a theology in providing life-enabling and liberating meaning to a community in particular historical circumstances will not depend upon typological soundness; but in terms of a tradition's continuing plausibility in the future, it is surely necessary for theologians to take more serious note of the ways in which in many kinds of traditions and periods of history, meaning-interpreters have functioned within those traditions.

4. In the light, generally, of the typifying features listed at the end of chapter three, we shall now have a look at the 'theological method' of Gordon Kaufman, who has made an outstandingly sophisticated and in many ways stimulating

analysis of the theological task. As his writing is so closely argued it is not easy to summarise briefly. It is clear that Kaufman defines 'theology' in a much more narrow sense than the stance taken in this book which assumes that it can include all meaning-interpretation within a religious tradition. His 'theology' is very definitely *systematic* theology, it is critical and 'reconstructive' theology, and what is assumed is that 'theology' pertains primarily to Christianity. Yet Kaufman is one of those theologians wishing to interact positively with the scientific study of religions, seeing the need for dialectical interrelationship, with neither being subsumed under the other (1972: 17-37).

Kaufman begins his *Essay on Theological Method* (1975) by affirming a radically theo-centric approach to the theological task. It is essentially reflection on the concept 'God' that gives theology its 'distinctive character'. The focus for reflection, however, is the conceptual problem in relation to God: 'God' is intrinsically problematic, and can only be a *concept* as far as the theologian's task is concerned. His theo-centrism, therefore, is of a perhaps exaggeratedly remote or detached kind; the 'distancing' from the primal vision is very deliberate and is seen in fact as proper to the theological task. Thus theological reflection is sharply distinguished from any forms of direct expression of 'devotion to the symbols of faith'. It is rather 'the attempt to understand those symbols and the way they function in human life'. Theology aims 'to criticise and reinterpret (the symbols of faith) . . . and finally . . . to reconstruct them, sometimes radically'. Kaufman recognised that all this critical reflection must arise 'out of response to religious symbols and their meaning, but . . . is a *deliberate human activity* directed towards criticising and reconstructing . . .' (*ibid.*: ix-xi).

Kaufman rejects both scriptural revelation and religious experience as the essential basis for the theological task. As against the position of Barth and similar systematic theologians, reflection on God is not primarily the exegesis or interpretation of authoritative documents in the tradition. He is critical of acceptance of the givenness of the classical text in hermeneutical thought as, for example, taken over by David Tracy in his 'analogical imagination' (1982). The theological task is not to be based on what is already definitively given. Nor is it to be seen as the interpretation of faith for those already within that 'theological circle'. There can be no presupposing of some self-evident divine revelation. Indeed, what is transmitted as 'revelation' is itself part of the problem that the theologian must attempt to resolve. For every statement in transmitted faith has 'been created and developed in and through human processes of reflection on life . . .' (Kaufman, *op. cit.*: 2). Although there are particular traditions of meaning and 'special communities of interpretation', Kaufman contends that this is 'obviously not the place where theological reflection actually begins' (*ibid*.: 3).

The overlap of secular and theological language is given considerable significance: 'The entire vocabulary of the church . . . consists of ordinary words from the everyday language of people . . . their meaning, thus, is tied to the life of the culture as a whole and can be grasped only in connection with that broad cultural base and experience' (*ibid*.: 3). Kaufman goes on to acknowledge that the meaning of theological words has also been affected by the life of the church, but these technical meanings of a tradition's words is not the starting point for theology. Special religious meanings can only be 'parasitic upon' ordinary meanings; theology, therefore, has 'public, not private or parochial, foundation' (*ibid*.: 8). In this way it is no more esoteric or exclusive than the discipline of any other 'community'.

Kaufman mentions two ways in which ordinary words do become special in theology. Theology 'attends to certain key terms' ('holy', 'divine', 'sacred', 'transcendent') as they especially related to the ultimate key-word, 'God', which is the 'central and most problematic theological term' (*ibid*.: 9). And theology is not merely concerned with *understanding* such words, but with 'reflection upon them, criticism and interpretation of them, and deliberate extension, refinement or reconstruction of their meaning and use'. In this way theology is basically 'metaphysical' in character, for it is concerned with 'formal analysis and clarification of an understanding of reality', and some 'ultimate point of reference'. But it is a 'metaphysics with a special commitment and orientation, namely to grasping that ultimate point of reference specifically as *God* and thus setting out a picture of reality and the world which focusses in God' (*ibid*.: 15).

Along with this insistence upon the theo-centric nature of the theological task, Kaufman also gives extreme emphasis to the humanness of theology: 'Theology is and always has been a human work: it is founded upon and interprets human historical events and experiences; it utilises humanly created and shaped terms and concepts; it is carried on by human processes of meditation, reflection, ratiocination, speaking, writing, and reading' (*ibid*.: 3). Whatever may be their faith in the present activity of God, theologians cannot begin with any assumption that God is involved in their work.

This fits in with his assertion that theology cannot be seen as 'the articulation and interpretation of experience' (*ibid*.: 4). There is, Kaufman affirms, no possibility of uncovering, phenomenologically, some 'pre-theological basis of theology'. He explicitly rejects the position of Schleiermacher, L. Gilkey and R.R. Niebuhr, who take religious experience to be the ground of theology. An initial problem in this position, for Kaufman, is that there is little concensus about what constitutes primary religious experiences; nor can he accept the idea of primary individual experience, then individual reflection, followed by communication of its meaning to others, as an account of the experience-expression process. He points rather to the primacy of language in the cultural theological process, the key factor shaping experience. There is no such thing as raw pre-linguistic experience of 'transcendence'; each such experience is 'shaped, delimited and informed by the linguistic symbols . . .' Without this symbolic, meaning-shaping language to 'guide our consciousness', experiences of transcendence 'would not be available to us at all' (*ibid.*: 5). Thus all cultural/religious symbols 'carry nuances of meaning derived from their various uses in the language . . . ' All religious experiences, therefore, are 'highly complex modes of consciousness which would be of a very different sort were they formed and informed by different linguistic symbols' (*ibid.*: 6). In this way Kaufman sees *language* as a more primary grounding for theology than religious experience.

From this Kaufman infers that 'historical study' is the only way to understand, even at the theological level, the meanings of religious language, and thus of the religious experiences found in the theologian's tradition. For theology, in its critical reflection on the concept 'God', is to be constructed on the basis of those 'complexes of images and conceptual structures' that have become part of human consciousness (and not only the consciousness of a particular religious community) largely through language and its cultural functioning. Kaufman does, however, recognise the particularity of such a cultural/linguistic process and suggests, with a strange ignoring of other 'theological' cultures, that this explains why theology is 'especially characteristic of Western Christian history' (*ibid.*: 7). Presumably it is because 'theology' is defined in his rather idiosyncratic Kantian/conceptualist way that he sees no analogous process in other cultures, in spite of his avowed intention elsewhere to interact dialectically with scientific and phenomenological studies in religions.

The distinctive features of any such analogous process, and its specific linking with the language of a culture, does of course need to be emphasised. Religious experience, as we saw earlier, is in any particular case at least in interaction with, even if its meaning is not wholly 'determined by', the images and the linguistic and conceptual categories available in the tradition of the 'experiencer'. Even if, as Kaufman admits, theology cannot proceed independently of experience, the latter is not a primary shaping factor in the process as he sees it. The 'raw pre-conceptual, pre-linguistic ground of religious experience is simply not available to us for direct exploration, description or interpretation, and therefore cannot provide us with a starting point for theological work' (*ibid.*: 7).

Kaufman then bases his 'devaluation' of experience, and thus his understanding of 'theological method', on a radically Kantian epistemological argument: theology is essentially the imaginative *construction of concepts about 'God'*, i.e. is a 'second-order activity' not related to God as objective reality, because it is epistemologically just *not possible to perceive, or to know God directly*. 'God' is of necessity always a concept, the creation of the human conceptual act; 'God' can never be directly experienced, in the same way that 'world' is a concept that can never be directly experienced as such: no one actually perceives the 'world' in its totality. To attempt to describe 'God' as though he existed objectively and independently is to fatally 'reify' God, according to Kaufman. Here he approves Kant's dictum that 'God' is the mind's most profound and highest creation, and thus cannot be an object of experience or perception. 'God' is that mental concept 'by means of which it brings unity and significance into all dimensions of life' (*ibid.*: 24). But to regard 'God' as 'some kind of describable or knowable object over against us is at once a degradation of God and a serious category error'. The reality of 'God' cannot be thought of 'on the model of the objectivity of perceivable things' (*ibid.*: 27). And for this reason theology can no longer think of its task as presenting a picture of how things really (and objectively) are. 'Rather, theology must conceive its work as more like building a house: using materials given in experience, it is in fact *constructing a world* the fundamental design of which is *not found in the materials themselves*' (*ibid.*: 28, latter italics mine). There can be no objective correspondence between our imaginatively constructed picture of 'God' and his reality. There is no 'percept' that corresponds to our concept. We know 'God' only by inference. We need, therefore, continually to reshape the construct 'God' so that it can be a more effective instrument for bringing order into life (*ibid.*: 28).

There is, then, a pragmatic test by which we can evaluate the success of this theological construction, and here too Kaufman is very close to a Kantian position. Does our imaginative interpretation of 'God' contribute to the beneficial ordering of human life and to a more meaningful perception of the universe? For it is the work of 'myth-makers' and theologians to bring about 'the ordering of experience in such a way as to make it possible to see meaning in it, to see what place human life has within the whole of reality, and thus to see what we can do, how we should act' (*ibid.*: 28). Theology has, thus, a 'meaning-bestowing function' in western culture (*ibid.*: cf. 31-4). While 'myth-making' and 'thology' here seem to be virtually equated, at least in function, elsewhere (1972: 41-71) Kaufman attempts to delineate a 'transcendence without myth', as Bultmann and various other theologians have done, though not on the basis of the Heideggerian existentialism Bultmann assumed as his theological model.

In addition to a pragmatic test for theology, Kaufman proposes that another way of ruling out arbitrary 'imaginative construction' is to provide a theological method that will 'discern and formulate explicit criteria and procedures for theological construction' (*op. cit.*: 36); in the past theologies have been far too 'arbitrary and idiosyncratic, influenced by fundamentally irrelevant or disastrously misleading psychological and cultural conditions ...' Theology, though unable to objectify its focal subject-matter, must somehow 'attain greater objectivity' (*ibid.*: 36). This is the 'second-order' level of theologising that we need, moving beyond first-order theology, which originated in the 'myth-making activities of primal men and women . . . (when) the gods were taken to be real and active', and when religious expression was lacking the critical, reflective approach we need today (*ibid.*: 37-8). We now need to be aware of other possible theological options, examining them comparatively and analysing their significance for human life. For this, however, it becomes important to find adequate criteria for evaluation, and then for rejection or acceptance.

An even greater need for development in theological procedures is to move on to *third-order theology*, which will go beyond that largely analytic and descriptive task to the reconstructive one of attempting deliberately 'to formulate theological conceptions and to create theological symbols . . . to which thoughtful contemporary men and women can give themselves' (*ibid.*: 38-9). This ultimate task, however, does not mean giving up the 'second-order' detached analysis and reflection.

A further issue of some importance in Kaufman's thought is the interrelation of 'God' and 'world' (*ibid.*: 45-6). For example, cosmological conceptualising is seen as the necessary ground and presupposition of reflective theology. The 'God'-concept is taken as emerging in response to the 'world'-concept and radically relativizes it, preventing the 'world' from becoming absolute or final. For 'God' is seen as the free and independent ground of the 'world' or of the whole. This calls for a double move by the imagination: the creation of an integrated whole, on the basis of diverse experiences, and then of the 'God' who is conceived as lying behind that constructed whole, and without which the 'God'-concept would not arise. Thus there is an 'interpenetration' of 'God' and 'world', though 'materially the concept of God is logically prior to that of world, because of the way in which the world is conceived as decisively affected by the thought of God as its creator or ground' (*ibid*.: 46).

This 'interpenetration' suggests a constructive process with three steps: it begins with experience of the 'world', and returns to such experience, but 'in between are major constructive acts of the imagination, the generation of notions of the world and God' (*ibid*.: 46).

In general, then, Gordon Kaufman has provided us with a sustained and seminal attempt to analyse the methodological task of the theologian. He focusses clearly on what he sees as the central issue, reflection on the meaning of the concept of God. That this focal object always has to be conceptually distanced as the 'God-problem' is obviously not typical of generations of those who believed equally that they were engaged in the theological task. In other words, Kaufman's intellectualism, intrinsic to his basic Kantian stance no doubt, is in reality one peculiar, modern type of 'theology'; he unnecessarily limits the range of theology. More directly expressive forms of theology need not thus be implicitly dismissed as not properly engaged in the theological task. In fact, Kaufman gives such normativity to the perceived needs of secularised, intellectually oriented, western 'thoughtful contemporary men and women', that there is not only a somewhat culture-bound attitude towards what constitutes theology; there is also the suspicion that he is primarily an apologist, defending the very possibility and legitimacy of theology as a respectable intellectual discipline in the context of a religiously tone-deaf society, a society that has also taken Kant with ultimate seriousness as interpreter of the human epistemological condition. Kaufman is explicit that theology is not 'parochial', by which he must mean not intended for the community of faith, and thus not grounded in faith; it is 'public', for the raw materials of theology are openly available to the secular world as much as to the community of faith.

That there is a process of dynamic interaction between the language, symbol-systems, the life-interpreting process in peculiarly 'religious' experience and the secular world of those with seemingly no religious commitment is undeniable; indeed it is a crucially important aspect to be recognised in the theological process and its necessarily analogical dimension. Kaufman, however, does not seem to allow sufficient weight to the peculiarly sacral or religious dimension of the process. Even 'God' does not seem to be taken with any great seriousness as the sacred Object of the experience and tradition of communities of faith. Thus, while occasionally allowing room for seeing the theologian as 'myth-maker', he also attempts to delineate a transcendence that is 'without myth'. '. . . God-language is not necessarily hopelessly mythological and old-fashioned' (1972: 69). The symbolic dimension of human existence is very prominent, but not the peculiar role of symbolism within communities in which certain symbols and clusters of symbols take a key role by communicating, or by being interpreted as communicating, crucial perceptions of reality that relate to and are grounded in the cultic life of that community, rather than being generally symbolic for the human cultural process as a whole. (In introducing the 2nd edition of the 'Essay', there is some recognition of this). There seems, in other words, to be insufficient attention to the particularities of religious communities and their traditions, especially to their cultic and liturgical life. More attention to theology as 'ecclesial reflection' (Farley 1972) is needed.

It is significant that Kaufman is so dismissively critical of David Tracy's 'correlational' theology of the 'analogical imagination': Tracy gives a central place to the hermeneutical process seen as the interpreting of the meaning of a 'classical text' in response to the serious critical problems posed by faith's secular context. To Kaufman this is an unconvincing 'conservative' position; there is a 'fidelity to classical expressions of the Christian scriptures' that is far too uncritically accepting of their givenness. There must be 'a much deeper and more profoundly dialectical interpenetration of these two theological modes into each other (i.e. the community's tradition and the modern critical attitude), each affecting and decisively transforming the other'. Much of Kaufman's critique of Tracy's use of the term 'classic' is highly illuminating; 1982: 398-400). The question is, has Kaufman himself given room for this kind of deep 'dialectical interpenetration'? He acknowledges that there are 'particular traditions of meaning' and 'special communities of interpretation', but he asserts strongly that 'obviously' these are 'not the place where theological reflection actually begins'. True, it will no doubt be in the process of 'dialectical interpenetration' with other worlds of meaning that we find the sparking point for critical reflection, or for reflection that calls for fresh forms of articulating the received 'meaning'. Indeed, there will be no 'meaning' until the tradition is reflected upon in a way that provides life-significance, conveys a convincing perception of reality, within whatever happens to be the converging context in which earlier 'meaning' begins to lose plausibility.

Yet, throughout the interpenetrative process, unless there is a continuing sense of some integrating primal vision of the transcendent Focus, it is difficult to account for any continuity of meaning along with resurgence of freshly visioned meaning. And that matrix of primal vision is necessarily embodied in the community tradition, perhaps especially embodied in some 'classical text' (though on this point we have already conceded that the concept might be unnecessarily limiting). We can also add that while one of Tracy's central concerns is to respond to the fact of religious and cultural pluralism, Kaufman gives an impression more of a mono-cultural context for the theological task, despite occasional references to cultural worlds other than the Christian.

Similarly in Kaufman's discussion of whether or not theology is to be grounded on experience, meaning *religious* experience or experience of the *transcendent*, there is insufficient weight given to the *interaction* of experience and the process of theological reflection. Again, in places such an interaction is acknowledged, as we have seen; but religious experience, whether mystical or of any other kind, in general is played down. It certainly cannot be taken, Kaufman argues, as the fundamental ground of theological articulation. Much greater weight is given to our apparently compelling *modern experience of the world understood in a non-sacral, non-religious sense*; certainly the highly conceptualised 'world' of our rationalist technological age looms very large in Kaufman's perception of what theology is. But on what grounds, for example, do we have to accept Kant's conviction that there can be no direct perception of God, that it is epistemologically impossible to know God directly? Obviously, it all depends on what you mean by 'know'. However, rather than attempt any kind of analysis of possible ways of knowing God 'directly', what needs to be stressed is that religious people in many different kinds of tradition have explicitly believed that they do have direct perception of their sacred Focus, and that they are able to reflect on this perception. To deny the reality of this categorically, or to say that at least the theologian must not ground his reflection on such perceptions, does seem to place impossible constraints upon the theological task in many religious traditions. What we can admit with Kaufman is that as soon as we are involved in the task of 'reflection', which theology will necessarily involve, even *critical* reflection, as received interpretations of God become problematic, there will always be some degree of distancing from the level of primal visioning. But, the interacting reflection on primal vision, and on the tradition's interpretations of this, will surely aim continually for a more authentic grounding in such primal perception. That this primal perception is invariably and typically processed in conjunction with all manner of other shaping factors does not negate its epistemological primacy; that there is a '*mediated* immediacy', to use a phrase of John Baillie's, has been the conviction of a number of religiously sensitive and contextually reflective theologians (cf. Chapter Three above).

Nor does this imply that our knowledge of God is necessarily *inferential* as Kaufman asserts. Again, the interpenetrative character of the epistemological process needs to be taken more seriously. The religious person's, or a religious community's, integrating vision of that which gives ultimate meaning to their world will rarely be accepted by them as a mere inference based on a series of factors that are other than the Focus of their faith. They will invariably be convinced of the self-authenticating quality of their vision. Why should the theologian within that tradition, or in some way concerned to reflect upon central features of that tradition, begin with the assumption that the sacred Focus of faith is in reality an object of inference? Why take for granted that the process of reflection on that Focus of faith necessarily removes the theologian from epistemological interaction with primal perception, even if 'distancing' *is* involved as part of the process? Are we to assume perhaps that theological knowledge cannot be religious knowledge? And is it not a denial of either the possibility of any kind of peculiar *religious* knowledge, or the availability of the peculiar perceptions of the theologian's tradition to the theologian, if we say that the only way to come to understand the meaning of the symbols, especially the linguistic symbols, of that tradition is through 'historical study'? No seriously reflective theologian can doubt the value of rigorous research into the historical process by which the meanings of our symbol-systems have changed through the ages; or that empirical study of contemporary meanings is also of value. But to assume that this is *primarily* how the theologian will come to understand the meaning of the sacred Focus of the tradition and what forms possible reinterpretation should take, is strangely limiting of the task of conceptual reconstruction.

Finally, we might note Kaufman's conviction that in the final analysis there is to be a pragmatic and thoroughly anthropocentric test for the reality and truth of the reconstructed 'God'-concept. 'If the idea of God helps to sustain our action and ourselves as agents, helps to further harmonize and

develop man, enhancing his moral sensitivity . . . then it is right to allow that
belief to shape one's policies of action . . . it is right . . . to believe in God' (19
72: 108-9). He hastens to add in this particular essay that 'God' is not *'merely*
imaginery', for there is a 'real referent', even if the 'real referent' cannot be
identified with the 'available God'. Often it seems to be Kaufman's main
concern to ensure that the theological task stands peculiarly above the 'religious' life of prayer, worship and meditation rather as the noumenal stands
above the phenomenal. Or is the reverse the case: Kaufman intends to preserve
the proper *transcendence* of God, and for this reason any talk about this
transcendent being must be at the lower level of concepts and critical reflection on ideas about the reality beyond, as to some extent understood by
such transcendentalists as the non-dualist Vedantin, Śankara? This hardly
seems to be the case. Perhaps, rather, too much 'transcendence' is given to the
theological task of conceptual reconstruction, in spite of the repeated emphasis
that theology is a thoroughly *human* endeavour, based on humanly communicated raw materials, and with humanly oriented goals. Even so, Kaufman
stirs reflection on what a theologian should be doing in ways that few contemporary western theologians have been able to.

Conclusion

Distinct Yet Interdependent Approaches

The basic contention underlying the preceding chapters has been straight-forward, even if this has drawn in quite a number of subsidiary themes. It has been intended to show that in spite of certain distinctive aims and modes of functioning making it necessary to *distinguish* the theological task within a religious tradition from other forms of systematic investigation found in 'religious studies', there are also significant and substantial areas of *inter-dependence* between these two basic approaches. Theologies, or the ways in which religions express the meaning of their inner life, will remain distinct because the primary grounding for their meaning-formulation is necessarily, though not exclusively, that of a distinctive vision of reality as embodied in a particular religious tradition. And while visionary interpretation will take place (especially in a world in which the impact of cross-cultural exchange is increasingly a felt reality) in interaction with a more inclusive human context, its meaning-articulation will nevertheless be shaped primarily by its inner matrix of myth/symbol/cult.

Each theology needs to recognise, therefore:

1. That its primary gounding is a specifically *religious* grounding, which means that it should welcome any potentially instructive insight into the richly varied dimensions of religious life, the inner structuring of religion, and the diverse causal factors to be found in the functioning of religion, such as the sciences of religion are able to provide.

2. Theologies also need to recognise that in the task of interpreting the multi-layered meaning of their peculiar visionary matrix there are potentially appropriable resources in other religious traditions, if interpretation is to make the most inclusively communicable and liberating impact. In other words, both the sciences of religion and the traditions themselves *can* provide illuminating input for theologians, input which *can* actually enhance the task of vision-interpretation.

3. Theologies should also recognise that in this process of reflection on and interpretation of the tradition's core vision, and thus in the articulation of diverse levels of meaning, there still remains the task of drawing out the integral character of the visionary matrix by way of an inner theological coherence (however dialectically and perhaps paradoxically expressed). Thus there is the task of establishing priorities and ultimate life-goals; and in this task too, comparative studies *can* bring clarity of insight.

In what sense, then, is science of religion 'dependent' on theology, or rather, on the theologies of those religions?

1. Any form of scientific investigation of religion needs to recognise (if it is seriously committed to the investigation of *religion*) that each theology (if functioning authentically as *theology*) articulates a tradition's meaning, is a conceptual expression of that tradition's inner matrix of myth/symbol/cult; theology is thus implicitly and importantly part of religion's life and is crucial to any attempt to understand religion. That some theologies are less integrally expressive of the authentic inner life of the concerned religion is another matter, a matter indeed about which the critical evaluation of a phenomenological science may well be valid. In any case, in seeking systematically to investigate and understand a religion's life, theological expression of all kinds provides crucial data for whatever scientific frame of reference is adopted. Any study of religion intending to be empirically 'descriptive' must incorporate prominently the self-understanding of each tradition as embodied in its varied forms of theological expression.

2. In particular, scientific investigation must incorporate, as evocatively as possible, the integrating sacred Focus which participants in religious traditions see as of crucial significance. Some scholars would want to restrict such attempts at evocative description of the sacred dimension of religion merely to phenomenological (and theological) studies. It is, however, difficult to see how, for example, a sociology of religion is sociologically descriptive of *religion* when there is little or no regard for that dimension of their existence *as a religious* community to which participants would point as *the* integrating factor. Even if they point to both the 'focus' and its 'integrating' potency in very different ways, the phenomenological identity will probably be recognisable.

That no scientific perspective on religion can be restricted solely to categories and concepts derived from within religious traditions must be taken for granted. The 'explanation' of a sociology of religion will necessarily be a sociological interpretation; but no interpretation can claim to be an interpretation of *religion* unless the distinctively religious dimension is incorporated as a significant factor. Implicitly to deny such a religious dimension by working within, for example, a restrictingly positivist frame of interpretation is hardly 'interpretation' at all.

3. We can go a step further and suggest that in the ultimate analysis scientific accounts of religious life, being necessarily interpretive of meaning, function in some ways analogous to theological interpretations. Though there are obvious differences too – in aim and in the process involved – there is in common the attempt to provide an account of the meaning of what may be seen as some 'hidden' reality of the concerned tradition(s). In the case of a scientific account, the 'meaning' is given from the perspective of a particular discipline, or within its interpretive framework. We cannot of course push this analogy too far; but we should note that whether the scientific investigator intends it or not, his/ her interpretation has its own impact upon the theological process. For, in its interaction with contextual life, theology will no doubt at some point be sensitive to the interpretation of the concerned science, either by seeing its potential for compatibility and thus for 'plausibility', or by way of reactive rejection.

4. While closer 'analogy' will be between the phenomenological approach and the theological, or between the comparative science of religion (especially if comparative *theological* science of religion) and theology, or between some types of philosophy of religion and theology, in all these cases a crucial difference remains. Each 'science of religion' (or philosophy of religion), perhaps especially the comparative or phenomenological science of religion, is concerned to investigate and interpret the meaning of as many and as diverse traditions as possible. It is only from such an equally inclusive perspective and thus on the basis of multi-religious typological patterns of meaning that a science of religion can be built up. However much a theology may wish to and be able to enhance and extend its self-interpretation by opening itself to the imagery and to perspectives of other religious traditions, in the end its grounding will necessarily be in one central vision; this will be its *primary* integrative and interpretive matrix of meaning. A science of religion, even if concerned mainly with theological expression, cannot be grounded primarily in such particularity. The

inclusiveness possible to many theologies, an inclusiveness which we may well hope will be increasingly realised in further inter-religious exchange, is of a rather different order. Theology and Religion must be recognised as thoroughly interdependent, but their distinctive procedures cannot be overlooked.

Bibliography

Almond, P.C.
1982   *Mystical Experience and Religious Doctrine. An Investigation of the Study of Mysticism in World Religions.* Berlin: Mouton.
Ayyangar, S.S.
1981   *Tiruvaymoli English Glossary* (2 vols.). Bombay: Ananthacharya Indological Research Institute.
Baal, J. van.
1971   *Symbols for Communication. Religion in Anthropological Theory.* Assen: Van Gorcum.
Baaren, T.P. van and Drijvers, H.J.W. eds.
1973   *Religion, Culture and Methodology.* The Hague: Mouton.
Baillie, J.
1939   *Our Knowledge of God.* London: Oxford University Press.
Baird, R.D.
1971   *Category Formation and the History of Religions.* The Hague: Mouton.
– ed.
1975   *Methodological Issues in Religious Studies.* Chico: New Horizons Press.
Banton, M. ed.
1966   *Anthropological Approaches to the Study of Religions.* London: Tavistock.
Barth, K.
1936   *Church Dogmatics*, Vol. I, pt. 1. Edinburgh: T. and T. Clarke.
Bary, W.T. de
1972   *The Buddhist Tradition in India, China and Japan.* New York: Random.
Bastow, D.
1980   'Metaphysical Knowledge in the Yoga-Sutra', *Scottish Journal of Religious Studies* 1: 101-18.
Beattie, J.
1964   *Other Cultures. Aims, Methods and Achievements in Social Anthropology.* London: Cohen and West.
Bellah, R.N.
1970   *Beyond Belief.* New York: Harper and Row.
Berger, P.L.
1969a   *The Social Reality of Religion.* London: Faber and Faber.
–

1969b   *A Rumor of Angels, Modern Society and the Rediscovery of the Supernatural.* New York: Doubleday.
–

1979   *The Heretical Imperative, Contemporary Possibilities of Religious Affirmation.* New York: Anchor/Doubleday.

– and T. Luckmann
   1966   The Social Construction of Reality. A Treatise in the Sociology of Knowledge.
          New York: Doubleday
Bharati, A.
   1965   The Tantric Tradition. London: Rider.
Bhatt, S.R.
   1975   Studies in Rāmānuja Vedānta. Delhi: Heritage.
Bhattacharya, A.
   1936   Studies in Post-Śankara Dialectics. Calcutta
Bhattacharyya, G.
   1961   Studies in Nyāya-Vaiśeṣika Theism. Calcutta: Sanskrit College.
Bhattacharya, N.N.
   1982   The History of Tantric Religion. Delhi: Manohar.
Buitenen, J.A.B. van, ed. and trans.
   1956   Rāmānuja's Vedārtha-Saṃgraha. Poona: Deccan College.
Buren, P. van
   1963   The Secular Meaning of the Gospel. London: SCM.
Campbell, J.
   1959, 1962, 1964, 1968   The Masks of God. New York: Viking.
Carman, J.B.
   1974   The Theology of Rāmānuja, An Essay in Inter-religious Understanding. New
          Haven: Yale University Press.
Cragg, K.
   1956   The Call of the Minaret. New York: Oxford.

   1976   The Wisdom of the Sufis. London: Sheldon.

   1986   'Fundamentals and Initiatives in Islamic Hermeneutics', Bangalore Theological
          Forum, 18: 97-106.
Dasgupta, S.N.
   1975   A History of Indian Philosophy. Delhi: Motilal Banarsidass
Davis, C.
   1974   'The Reconvergence of Theology and Religious Studies', Sciences Religieuses
          4: 205-21.

   1981   'Theology and Religious Studies', Scottish Journal of Religious Studies 2:11-20.
Dechanet, J.-M.
   1974   Yoga and God. London: Search.
Dudley III, G.
   1977   Religion on Trial. Mircea Eliade and His Critics. Philadelphia: Temple Uni-
          versity Press.
Duraisingh, Christopher
   1979-80 'Indian Hyphenated Christians and Theological Reflection', Religion and
           Society, 26: 95-101; 27: 81-101.

   1984   'Ninian Smart's "The Dynamics of Religious and Political Change": An Indian

Response', *Bangalore Theological Forum*, 16: 169-78.

Eliade, M.
1961   *Images and Symbols. Studies in Religious Symbolism.* New York: Sheed and Ward.

–
1969   *The Quest: History and Meaning in Religion.* Chicago University Press.
– and Kitagawa, J.M. eds.
1959   *The History of Religions. Essays in Methodology.* Chicago University Press.
– and Tracy, D. eds.
1980   *What is Religion? An Enquiry for Christian Theology* (= Concilium 136). New York: Seabury.

Farley, E.
1982   *Ecclesial Reflection. An Anatomy of Theological Method.* Philadelphia: Fortress.

Ferré, F.
1961   *Language, Logic and God.* New York: Harper.

–
1962   *Exploring the Logic of Faith.* New York: Association Press.

Ficker, R.
1983   'Uniqueness and Interdependence. Israelite Religion and its Religious Environment', *Bangalore Theological Forum*, 15: 87-127.

Gadamer, H.-G.
1979   *Truth and Method.* London: Sheed and Ward.

Geertz, C.
1973   *The Interpretation of Cultures.* New York: Harper.

Gensichen, H.-W.
1970   'Tendenzen der Religionswissenschaft', in Simers, H. and Reuter, H.-R., eds. *Theologie als Wissenschaft in der Gesellschaft*, 28-40.

Gilkey, L.
1969   *Naming the Whirlwind. The Renewal of God-Language.* Indianapolis: Bobs-Merril.

–
1981   'A Theological Voyage with Wilfred Cantwell Smith', *Religious Studies Review*, 7: 298-306.

Goldziher, I.
1981   *Introduction to Islamic Law and Theology.* New Jersey: Princeton University Press.

Gombrich, R.F.
1971   *Precept and Practice. Traditional Buddhism in the Rural Highlands of Ceylon.* London: Oxford University Press.

Hardy, F.
1979   'The Philosopher as Poet, A Study of Vedāntadeśika's *Dehalīśa-Stuti*', *Journal of Indian Philosophy*, 7: 277-325.

–
1983   *Viraha-Bhakti. The Early History of Kṛṣṇa Devotion in South India.* Delhi: Oxford.

Harris, M.
    1968   *The Rise of Anthropological Theory*. New York.
Harvey, V.A.
    1966   *The Historian and the Believer*. Philadelphia: Westminster.
Heelas, P.
    1978   'Some Problems with Religious Studies', *Religion*, 8. 1-14.
Helfer, J. ed.
    1968   *On Method in History of Religions* (*History and Theory* 8). Wesleyan University.
Hick, J.F.
    1973   *God and the Universe of Faiths*. London: Macmillan.
    –
    1974   *Faith and Knowledge* (2nd ed.). London: Collins.
    –, ed.
    1974   *Truth and Dialogue. The Relationship between World Religions*. London: Sheldon.
    – and Hebblethwaite, B., eds.
    1980   *Christianity and Other Religions*. Glasgow: Collins.
Honko, L. ed.
    1979   *Science of Religion. Studies in Methodology*. The Hague: Mouton.
Iyangar, M.B.N., trans.
    1966   *Tattva Traya of Pillai Lokacharya*. Madras: M.C. Krishnan.
Jaini, P.S.
    1979   *The Jaina Path of Purification*. Delhi: Motilal Banarsidass.
Kaufman, G.D.
    1972   *God the Problem*. Cambridge: Harvard University Press.
    –
    1975   *An Essay in Theological Method*. Missoula: Scholars Press.
    –
    1981   *The Theological Imagination: Constructing the Concept of God*. Philadelphia: Westminster.
    –
    1982   'Conceptualizing Diversity Theologically', *Journal of Religion*, 62: 392-40.
Kingsbury, F. and Phillips, G.E.
    1921   *Hymns of the Tamil Saivite Saints*. London: Oxford University Press.
Katz, S., ed.
    1978   *Mysticism and Philosophical Analysis*. London: Sheldon.
Kitagawa, J.M.
    1968   'The Making of a Historian of Religions', *Journal of Academy of Religion*, 36: 191-201.
Kraemer, H.
    1938   *The Christian Message in a Non-Christian World*. London: Edinburgh House.
    –
    1956   *Religion and the Christian Faith*. London: Lutterworth.

Kristensen, W. B.
1960   *The Meaning of Religion. Lectures in the Phenomenology of Religion*. The Hague: Mouton.
Kuhn, T.S.
1970   *The Structure of Scientific Revolutions*. 2nd ed. Chicago University Press.
Lannoy, R.
1971   *The Speaking Tree. A Study of Indian Culture and Society*. London: Oxford University Press.
Leeuw, G. van der
1963   *Religion in Essence and Manifestation* (1st published in German 1933) New York: Harper.
Lindbeck, G.A.
1984   *The Nature of Doctrine*. Philadelphia: Westminster.
Ling, T.
1979   *Buddha, Marx and God*. (2nd ed.) London: Macmillan.
Lipner, J.J.
1977   'Does Copernicus Help? Reflections for a Christian Theology of Religions', *Religious Studies*, 13: 243-58.

–

1984   'The World as God's Body. In Pursuit of Dialogue with Rāmānuja', *Religious Studies*, 20: 145-161.

–

1986   *The Face of Truth. A Study of Meaning and Metaphysics in the Vedantic Theology of Rāmānuja*. London: Macmillan.
Lonergen, B.J.F.
1970   *Method in Theology*. London: Darton, Longman and Todd.
Lott, E.J.
1976   *God and the Universe in the Vedantic Theology of Rāmānuja*. Madras: Rāmānuja Research Society.

–

1979   'Finite Self and Supreme Being. Vedantic Types of Analogical Method', *Bangalore Theological Forum*, 11: 2-35.

–

1980   *Vedantic Approaches to God*. London: Macmillan.

–

1980   'Rāmānuja's Śarīra-Śarīrī-Bhāva. A Conceptual Analysis', in *Studies in Rāmānuja*. Madras: Rāmānuja Vedanta Centre, 21-40.

–

1981   'The Conceptual Dimensions of Bhakti in the Vaiṣṇava Tradition', *Scottish Journal of Religious Studies* 2: 97-114.

–

1985   'The Science of Religion in an Indian Theological Context', *Bangalore Theological Forum* 17: 1-18.

–

1986   'Evaluating Vedantic Types of Transcendence', *Rāmānuja Vāṇī* 9: 51-62.

Macquarrie, J.
1966   *Principles of Christian Theology*. London: SCM.
Malinowski, B.
1974   *Magic, Science and Religion*. London: Souvenir.
McLeod, W.H.
1976   *Guru Nanak and the Sikh Religion*. Delhi: Oxford University Press.
Mello, A. de
1978   *Sadhana: A Way to God*. Anand: Gujarat Sahitya Prakash.
Moore, P.G.
1973   'Recent Studies in Mysticism', *Religion* 3: 146-56.

–
1978   'Mystical Experience, Mystical Doctrine, Mystical Technique', in S. Katz, ed.,
       Mysticism and Philosophical Analysis. London: Sheldon, 101-31.
Nandimath, S.C.
1979   *A Handbook of Virasaivism*. Delhi: Motilal Banarsidass.
Nicholls, W.
1969   *The Pelican Guide to Modern Theology*. London: Penguin.
O' Flaherty, W.D., ed.
1979   *The Critical Study of Sacred Texts*. Berkeley: Lancaster-Miller.
Otto, R.
1923   *The Idea of the Holy*. London: Oxford University Press.

–
1932   *Mysticism East and West*. New York: Macmillan.
Oxtoby, W., ed.
1976   *Religious Diversity. Essays by W.C. Smith*. New York: Harper and Row.
Panikkar, R.
1978   *Myth, Faith and Hermeneutics*. New York: Paulist.
Parrinder, G.
1970   *Avatar and Incarnation*. London: Faber and Faber.
Pannenberg, W.
1970   *Basic Questions in Theology*, Vol. I. London: SCM.

–
1976   *Theology and the Philosophy of Science*. London: Darton, Longman and
       Todd.
Penner, H.H. and Yonan, E.A.
1972   'Is a Science of Religion Possible?', *Journal of Religion*, 52: 107-33.
Pettazzoni, R.
1954   *Essays on the History of Religions*. Leiden: Brill.
Pummer, R.
1972   '*Religionswissenschaft* or Religiology?', *Numen*, 19: 91-127.

–
1975   'Recent Publications on the Methodology of the Science of Religion', *Numen*,
       22: 161-82.
Pye, M.
1972   *Comparative Religion. An Introduction Through Source Material*. Newton
       Abbot: David and Charles.

Radhakrishnan, S.
   1929   *Indian Philosophy*, 2 vols. London: Allen and Unwin.

— 1940   *Eastern Religions and Western Thought*. Delhi: Oxford University Press.

   1953   *The Principal Upanishads*. London: Allen and Unwin.
Raghavan, V.S., ed.
   1974   *Visishtadvaita Philosophy and Religion*. Madras: Rāmānuja Research Society.
Rahman, F.
   1974   *Islam*. London: Weidenfeld and Nicolson.

— 1980   *Major Themes of the Quran*. Minneapolis: Bibliotheca Islamica.
Ramanujan, A.K.
   1973   *Speaking of Śiva*. London: Penguin.
Raschke, C.
   1979   *The Alchemy of the Word. Language and the End of Theology*. American
           Academy of Religion Studies in Religion, 20.
Richards, G.
   1980   'Towards a Theology of Religions', *Journal of Theological Studies*, 31: 44-66.
Robertson, R., ed.
   1969   *Sociology of Religion, Selected Readings*. London: Penguin.
Rudolph, K.
   1962   *Die Religionsgeschichte an der Leipsiger Universität und die Entwicklung der
           Religionswissenschaft*. Berlin: Akademie-Verlag.

— 1981   'Basic Positions of *Religionswissenschaft*' , *Religion*, 11: 97-107.
Rupp, G.
   1979   *Beyond Existentialism and Zen. Religion in a Pluralistic World*. New York:
           Oxford Univeristy Press.
Sahi, J.
   1986   *Stepping Stones. Reflections on the Theology of Indian Christian Culture*.
           Bangalore: Asian Trading Corporation.
Sahlins, M.D.
   1968   'Culture and Environment. The Study of Cultural Ecology', in Manners, R.A.
           and Kaplan, D., eds. *Theory in Anthropology*. Chicago.
Sampatkumaran, M.R., trans.
   1969   *The Gītā-Bhāshya of Rāmānuja*. Madras: Educational Review.
Santoni, R.E., ed.
   1968   *Religious Language and the Problem of Religious Knowledge*. Bloomington:
           Indiana University Press.
Schimmel, A.
   1975   *Mystical Dimensions of Islam*. Chapel Hill: University of North Carolina.
Schlette, H.R.
   1966   *Towards a Theology of Religions*. London:
Schmid, G.
   1979   *Principles of Integral Science of Religion*. The Hague: Mouton.

Schrader, F.C.
1973   *Introduction to the Pañcharātra and the Ahirbudhnyā Samhitā.*2nd Ed. Madras: Adyar.
Sharpe, E.J.
1975   *Comparative Religion. A History.* London: Duckworth.
Shinn, L.D.
1977   *Two Sacred Worlds. Experience and Structure in World Religions.* Nashville: Abingdon.
Singh, T. et al.
1960   *Selections from the Sacred Writings of the Sikhs.* New York: Macmillan.
Sircar, M.
1927   *Comparative Studies in Vedantism.* Madras.
Skorupski, J.
1976   *Symbol and Theory.* Cambridge University Press.
Smart, N.
196   'The Interpretation of Mystical Experience', *Religious Studies,* 2: 75-87.
–
1968   *The Yogi and the Devotee. The Interplay of Upanishads and Catholic Theology.* London: Allen and Unwin.
–
1969   *The Religious Experience of Mankind.* London: Collins.
–
1973a   *The Phenomenon of Religion.* London: Macmillan.
–
1973b   *The Science of Religion and the Sociology of Knowledge.* Princeton: Princeton University Press.
–
1984   'The Dynamics of Religious and Political Change. Illustrations from South Asia', *Bangalore Theological Forum,* 16: 79-96.
Smith, Huston
1981   'Faith and its Study. What Wilfred Smith's Against and For', *Religious Studies Review,* 7: 306-10.
Smith, H. Daniel
1969   *Vaiṣṇava Iconography.* Madras: Pañcarātra Pariśodhana Parishad.
Smith, W.C.
1978   *The Meaning and End of Religion.* London: SPCK (1st published 1962).
–
1967   *Questions of Religious Truth.* New York: Scribner.
–
1976   *Religious Diversity* (ed. W. Oxtoby). New York: Harper and Row.
–
1977   *Belief and History.* Charlotteville: University of Virginia Press.
–
1979   *Faith and Belief.* Princeton: Princeton University Press.
–
1981   *Towards a World Theology.* London: Macmillan.

Spiro, M.
  1966   'Religion: Problems of Definition and Explanation', in M. Banton, ed. *Anthropological Approaches to the Study of Religion*. London: Tavistock.

  1979   'Symbolism and Functionalism in the Anthropological Study of Religion', in L. Honko, ed. 322-339.

Staal, F.
  1975   *Exploring Mysticism*. London: Penguin.

Streng, F.
  1970   'The Objective Study of Religion and the Unique Quality of Religiousness', *Religious Studies*, 6: 209-19.

Suzuki, D.T.
  1927   *Essays in Zen Buddhism*. London: Luzac.

  1955   *Studies in Zen*. New York: Philosophical Library.

  1957   *Mysticism: Christian and Buddhist*. New York: Harper.

Tabib, G.S.
  1975   *Selections from the Holy Granth*. Delhi: Vikas.

Tilak, B.G.
  1935   *Bhagavad-Gītā Rahasya*. Poona; Tilak.

Tillich, P.
  1953   *Systematic Theology*, Vol. I. London: Nisbet.

Torrance, T.
  1969   *Theological Science*. London: Oxford University Press.

Toulmin, S., Hepburn, R. W., and Macintyre, A.
  1970   *Metaphysical Beliefs* (2nd ed.). London: SCM.

Tracy, D.
  1981   *The Analogical Imagination. Christian Theology and the Culture of Pluralism*. London: SCM.

Tucci, G.
  1980   *The Religions of Tibet*. Bombay: Allied.

Vincent, J.J.
  1968   *Secular Christ*. London: Lutterworth.

Waardenburg, J.
  1973   *Classical Approaches to the Study of Religion. Aims, Methods, and Theories of Research*. Vol. I. *Introduction and Anthology*. The Hague: Mouton.

  1978   *Reflections on the Study of Religion*. The Hague: Mouton.

  1979   'The Language of Religion, and the Study of Religion as Sign Systems', in L. Honko, 441-57.

Wach, J.
  1958   *The Comparative Study of Religions*, ed. with an introduction by J.M. Kitagawa. New York: Columbia University Press.

Wainwright, G.
1980   *Doxology: The Praise of God in Worship,Doctrine and Life*. London: Epworth.
Walpola, S.R.
1978   *What the Buddha Taught* (1st published 1959). London: Fraser.
Watt, W.M.
1962   *Islamic Philosophy and Theology*. Islamic Surveys 1. Edinburgh University.

1979   *What is Islam?* (2nd ed.). London: Longmans.
Werblowsky, R.J.Z.
1960   'Marburg – and After?', *Numen*, 7 : 215-20.
Whaling, F., ed.
1983, 1985   *Contemporary Approaches to the Study of Religion*. Vol. I, *The Humanities*; Vol. II, *The Social Sciences*. Berlin: Mouton.

1984   *The World's Religious Traditions. Current Perspectives in Religious Studies.* Essays in Honour of W.C. Smith. Edinburgh: T. & T. Clarke.
Wiebe, D.
1975   'Explanation and the Scientific Study of Religion', *Religion*, 5.

1979   'The Role of "Belief" in the Study of Religion. A Response to W.C. Smith', *Numen*, 26: 234-49.

1981   *Religion and Truth. Towards an Alternative Paradigm for the Study of Religion.* The Hague: Mouton.

1983   'Theory in the Study of Religion', *Religion*, 13: 283-309.
Woods, R., ed.
1981   *Understanding Mysticism*. London: Athlone.
Zaehner, R.C.
1957   *Mysticism Sacred and Profane*. Oxford: Clarendon.

1958   *At Sundry Times. An Essay in the Comparison of Religions*. London: Faber and Faber.

1960   *Hindu and Muslim Mysticism*. London: Athlone Press.

1969   *The Bhagavad Gītā*. London: Oxford University Press.

Index

Vision, Tradition, Interpretation

Buren, P. van, 72

Calvin, J., 73
Campbell, J., 21
Canaan(ite), 22, 128
Capra, F., 163
Carman, J.B., 54, 74, 79, 143, 145, 149
Cartesian, 123
Catholic(ism), 8, 69, 78, 119, 133, 225
China, 120
Christ, 27, 70, 71, 127, 129, 132, 240
Chāndōgya Upanishad, 134
Christian, Christian theology *passim*
Cobb, J., 8
Cole, O., 81
Comparative Religions, 1-4, 180, 185,
   190-2, 198, 232, 255
Constantine, 60
Corinth, 60
Cragg, K., 55, 66, 231

Darśana, 20, 23, 41, 82, 91, 122, 144
Darwin, C., 39
Dasgupta, S.N., 53, 94
Davis, C., 9, 214-7
Dayanand Saraswati, 64
De Bary, W., 44-5, 67
Dechanet, J.-M., 239
De Mello, A., 239
De Smet, R.V., 111
Dharma, 25-6, 28, 31, 32, 45, 53, 64, 72,
   85, 93, 99, 100, 103, 113, 118, 219
Dharma-śāstras, 27
Dialectic, 79-80, 91, 109, 112, 124
Dialogical approach, 5, 8-9, 192-201
Didache, 84
Dīksha, 19
Dilthey, W., 181, 195
Dīn, 27, 85
Divya-deśa, 144
Doctrine, doctrinal *passim*
Dudley, G., 4, 13, 155, 206-7
Duhkha, 44
Dumont, L., 20
Duraisingh, C., 128
Durkheim, E., 40, 162-3, 166

Dynamic process, 31-2, 198-201 and
   passim

Easter, 127
Eckhardt, Meister, 133
Eidetic vision, 180-1, 188
Ekklesia, 24
Eliade, M., 9, 21, 33, 37, 73, 123-5, 130,
   162, 188, 205-7, 241
Entelecheia, 181
Epoché, 180-2, 187, 191
Ethical dimension of religion, 26-8 and
   passim
Evangelist, 68

Farley, E., 89, 249
Farquhar, J., 232
Ferré, F., 176
Ficker, R., 240
Four Great Truths, 117
Franciscans, 60
Frazer, J.G., 40

Gadamer, H.-G., 83, 160, 241
Gandhi, M.K., 238
Geertz, C., 33, 165-6, 186
Gennep, A. van, 17
Gensichen, H.-W., 1, 9, 225
Gilkey, L., 199, 245
Gombrich, R.F., 97
Granth Sahib, 81
Greek(s), 22, 120
Guru, 23, 25-6, 50-1, 68, 74, 80-1

Hadith, 31
Hajj, 32
Hardy, F., 75-7
Harris, M., 18, 27
Harvey, V.A., 4, 161
Hebblethwaite, B. 233
Heelas, P., 165
Helfer, J., 123
Heidegger, M., 179, 247
Hegelian, 8, 175, 179, 181, 215
Hepburn, R., 75
Hero-stones, 68